Dear West Customer:

West Academic Publishing has changed the look of its American Casebook Series®.

In keeping with our efforts to promote sustainability, we have replaced our former covers with book covers that are more environmentally friendly. Our casebooks will now be covered in a 100% renewable natural fiber. In addition, we have migrated to an ink supplier that favors vegetable-based materials, such as soy.

Using soy inks and natural fibers to print our textbooks reduces VOC emissions. Moreover, our primary paper supplier is certified by the Forest Stewardship Council, which is testament to our commitment to conservation and responsible business management.

The new cover design has migrated from the long-standing brown cover to a contemporary charcoal fabric cover with silver-stamped lettering and black accents. Please know that inside the cover, our books continue to provide the same trusted content that you've come to expect from West.

We've retained the ample margins that you have told us you appreciate in our texts while moving to a new, larger font, improving readability. We hope that you will find these books a pleasing addition to your bookshelf.

Another visible change is that you will no longer see the brand name Thomson West on our print products. With the recent merger of Thomson and Reuters, I am pleased to announce that books published under the West Academic Publishing imprint will once again display the West brand.

It will likely be several years before all of our casebooks are published with the new cover and interior design. We ask for your patience as the new covers are rolled out on new and revised books knowing that behind both the new and old covers, you will find the finest in legal education materials for teaching and learning.

Thank you for your continued patronage of the West brand, which is both rooted in history and forward looking towards future innovations in legal education. We invite you to be a part of our next evolution.

Best regards,

Louis H. Higgins
Editor in Chief, West Academic Publishing

SPORTS AND THE LAW

EXAMINING THE LEGAL EVOLUTION OF AMERICA'S THREE "MAJOR LEAGUES"

■ ■ ■

By

Peter A. Carfagna

AMERICAN CASEBOOK SERIES®

WEST®

A Thomson Reuters business

Mat #40887437

© 2009 Thomson Reuters
   610 Opperman Drive
   St. Paul, MN 55123
   1–800–313–9378
Printed in the United States of America

ISBN: 978–0–314–90758–5

PREFACE

"Sports and the Law: Examining the Legal Evolution of America's Three 'Major Leagues'" represents the culmination of my many years of "sports law" legal practice (as a partner at Jones Day; Chief Legal Officer at IMG; and now as Senior Counsel at the Calfee Law Firm) and of law school teaching (first at Case Law School and now at my alma mater, Harvard Law School.)

The book synthesizes the major legal precedents that have shaped the evolution of America's three "major leagues"—Major League Baseball (MLB); the National Football League (NFL); and the National Basketball Association (NBA). In so doing, it traces the impact of MLB's "antitrust exemption," in juxtaposition to the "non-statutory labor exemption" that applies to the NFL and NBA. In particular, the legal history of each league's Constitution/By Laws; Collective Bargaining Agreements (and related work stoppages); and its "Uniform Player Contracts" are examined through illustrative "hypothetical" group negotiation and drafting exercises. Initial legal challenges to each of the (now familiar concepts) including "the amateur draft," "free agency," "age eligibility," and the leagues'/players' "intellectual property rights" demonstrate the unpredictable outcomes created by the intrusion of external legal authorities (e.g., courts, arbitrators, etc.) upon the current structure of each league and its related Commissioner's "authority."

The book concludes by recounting the tortured history of "franchise relocation" law, as well as the importance of first obtaining, and then carefully drafting, a "naming rights agreement" for any newly constructed "major league" venue.

Peter A. Carfagna

September 2009

*

ACKNOWLEDGMENT

In publishing this second "sports law" book with West since I began teaching at Harvard Law School after leaving my position as Chief Legal Officer at IMG, I would first like to thank Staci Herr of West who has been unceasingly supportive of my efforts to reduce my Harvard Law School courses to a textbook form that would be useful to other "sports law" instructors and practitioners. Also, as I did in the Acknowledgments in my first West Law textbook, "Representing the Professional Athlete," I would to thank Harvard Law School Professor Emeritus Paul Weiler (under whom I studied at Harvard in 1979, and with whom I have stayed in close touch since then) for his lifetime contributions to the field. To follow in Paul's footsteps at Harvard is humbling indeed, because his teaching "Sports and the Law" from his "magnum opus" textbook at Harvard for nearly 30 years created the "level playing field" from which all sports law professors are now fortunate enough to operate.

Further, I would like to acknowledge and give thanks for the unflagging support provided for my teaching and scholarship by the administration at Harvard Law School, including Deans Elena Kagan and Martha Minow, Interim Dean Howell Jackson, and Vice Dean for Academic Programming, Professor Andrew Kaufman. Without their support, and the indefatigable efforts of my 2008–09 Teaching Assistant, Megha Parekh, who helped me transform my HLS course into this text, the publication of this second book would not have been possible.

Finally, as I did in the Acknowledgments in my first book, I would like to thank my wife Rita, and the rest of my family, for providing me with the never-ending support "back home," that enabled me to travel to Harvard each week to teach the most wonderful students in the world—a luxury that is truly "priceless" in the world of academia to which I am proud to contribute once again with this publication.

*

SUMMARY OF CONTENTS

TABLE OF CONTENTS

*

TABLE OF CASES

References are to pages.

SPORTS AND THE LAW

EXAMINING THE LEGAL EVOLUTION OF AMERICA'S THREE "MAJOR LEAGUES"

*

CHAPTER 1

THE MORAL INTEGRITY OF THE SPORT: THE ROLE OF THE COMMISSIONER AND THE LAW

■ ■ ■

Introduction

Though the building blocks of professional sports are the athletic skills of the players, the mortar holding these blocks together is a nexus of contracts between the players, clubs, and league. In each of the three "major leagues," the constitution and collective bargaining agreement provide foundational support for the structure and governance of the league. These foundational documents state the scope of and the limitations on the authority of the Commissioner, who is entrusted with overseeing the league. Today, Major League Baseball (MLB), the National Football League (NFL), and the National Basketball Association (NBA) each have a Commissioner entrusted with protecting the "best interests" of the game, though the contours of the position vary by league.

Chapter 1 begins with an overview of the Commissioner's current powers in each league, and then examines the exercise of Commissioner's powers—at various points during league history—as applied to gambling, misconduct on the field, drug use, and diversity in sports. As you read the cases below, consider whether or not in a particular situation the case was resolved within the league's internal procedures on in a court of law. When do you think that internal resolution, under the auspices of the Commissioner, is best? What issues ought to be reserved for a court of law? When answering these questions, does it make a difference to you if the Commissioner's decision affects a player or a third party? A contractual or a constitutional right?

I. THE COMMISSIONER'S POWERS

The oldest of the leagues, MLB, was the first to create a Commissioner. The position was created in response to the "Black Sox Scandal" of 1919.[1] Commissioner Kennesaw Mountain Landis was appointed to over-

---

1. For more information on the Black Sox Scandal, you may want to read ELIOT ASINOF, EIGHT MEN OUT: THE BLACK SOX AND THE 1919 WORLD SERIES (2000).

see the league. While Commissioner Landis may have had the powers of a "benevolent but absolute despot [with] all the disciplinary powers of a proverbial *pater familias*,"[2] subsequent MLB Commissioners have seen the office's authority erode as the Major League Baseball Players Association (MLBPA) emerged and gained strength. The current MLB Collective Bargaining Agreement (MLB CBA), which runs from 2007 until 2011, provides the most important limitations on the Commissioner's once plenary powers. Once the Commissioner actually assesses a disciplinary penalty, the standard of review for punishment imposed upon a player for misconduct is "just cause." Players who are disciplined may appeal to an impartial arbitrator or a three-arbitrator panel chaired by an impartial arbitrator. Discipline for on-field conduct may only be appealed if it results in a fine greater than $5,000 or a suspension of more than ten games. Commissioner actions "involving the preservation of the integrity of, or the maintenance of public confidence in, the game of baseball" are exempt from the ordinary grievance procedure, if the Commissioner so desires. Furthermore, the "best interests" power includes not only financial but also moral issues. However, if the Commissioner invokes this power, the MLBPA can reopen the CBA if it finds his decision "unsatisfactory."

By contrast, in the NFL, the Commissioner maintains nearly complete control over the area of player discipline. Under the NFL CBA, if the Commissioner decides to punish a player with a fine, suspension, or both, for "conduct on the playing field" or "conduct detrimental to the integrity of, or public confidence in, the game of professional football," the player's only recourse is an appeal to the Commissioner himself.[3] As for disputes pertaining to terms and conditions of player employment, involving the interpretation of the NFL CBA, the NFL Player Contract, or the NFL Constitution and Bylaws, are resolved under a different procedure before neutral arbitrators.

Finally, in the NBA, the two most significant contractual provisions currently governing the Commissioner's authority are Article 35 of the NBA constitution and Article XXXI of the NBA CBA. Article 35, which lists various offenses and their maximum penalties, is the starting point for the Commissioner's power to address misconduct. Article 35 requires that each team include a clause in its player contracts binding the players

---

2.   Milwaukee Am. Ass'n v. Landis, 49 F.2d 298 (N.D. Ill. 1931).

3.   NFL Collective Bargaining Agreement Art. XI, § 1(a) (2006). The "conduct on the playing field" clause contains an exception for penalties "imposed upon players for unnecessary roughness or unsportsmanlike conduct on the playing field with respect to an opposing player or players [which] shall be determined initially by a person appointed by the Commissioner after consultation concerning the person being appointed with the Executive Director of the NFLPA, as promptly as possible after the event(s) in question. Such person will send written notice of his action to the player, with a copy to the NFLPA. Within ten (10) days following such notification, the player, or the NFLPA with his approval, may appeal in writing to the Commissioner." *Id.* at Art. XI, § 1(b).

to this provision. In general, the Article 35's clauses enable the Commissioner to fine a violator up to a maximum of $50,000 and possibly issue a suspension, depending on the infraction. For example, Article 35(d) broadly enables the Commissioner to fine a player up to $50,000 and/or suspend the player if the Commissioner finds in his opinion that the player's conduct during a game is "against the best interests" of the sport. Conduct that does not conform with "standards of morality or fair play . . . or that is prejudicial or detrimental to the Association" is punishable by a fine not exceeding $50,000, a definite or indefinite suspension, or both. For a player wagering on the outcome of a game, the "decision of the Commissioner shall be final, binding and conclusive and unappealable." With the exception of this gambling clause, Article 35(h) holds that all other Commissioner actions taken pursuant to Article 35 are appealable. Teams will appeal to the Board of Governors, while players are directed to follow the grievance procedures under the NBA CBA.

Article XXXI of the NBA CBA sets out rules governing grievance procedures, as well as the standard of review for the arbitrator to employ. In general, a Grievance Arbitrator reviewing a disciplinary action must resolve "whether there has been just cause for the penalty imposed." If the Commissioner acts concerning "the preservation of the integrity of, or the maintenance of public confidence in, the game of basketball," then the Grievance Arbitrator is directed to apply an "arbitrary and capricious" standard of review to the appeal of a fine and/or suspension having a financial impact greater than $25,000 on a player. Commissioner decisions involving "the preservation of the integrity of, or the maintenance of public confidence in, the game of basketball" resulting in a financial impact of less than $50,000 on a player are similarly only appealable to the Commissioner. Furthermore, a fine or suspension imposed on a player for "conduct on the playing court (regardless of its financial impact on the player)" can only be appealed to the Commissioner.

When evaluating the "commissioner's authority" decisions below, consider the breadth of the Commissioner's power relative to the degree to which the player's alleged offense threatens "public confidence" in the sport. On the other hand, consider the extent to which arbitral scrutiny of a Commissioner's decision under the Collective Bargaining Agreement tends to increase according to the severity of the punishment imposed.[4]

II. GAMBLING

Allegations that players, coaches, referees, and other professional sports personnel are betting on games raise the specter that games are decided not by the players' skills, but rather by the money at stake. *Rose*

---

4. A concise summary of the Commissioner's authority in each of the three leagues to discipline players based on off-field conduct is set forth in Appendix A of the accompanying *v. Giamatti* and *Molinas v. National Basketball Association* involved circumstances in which the Commissioner of the MLB and NBA, respectively, had issued a lifetime ban for gambling.

Though the narrow legal issue in *Rose v. Giamatti* was whether the Cincinnati Reds were a necessary party to the lawsuit, thereby destroying federal jurisdiction based on diversity, the issue of paramount importance was what penalty all-time hits leader Pete Rose would face from Commissioner Bart Giamatti as a result of his betting—while employed as Reds manager—on his team to win. Rose's gambling violated MLB's anti-gambling policy, posted prominently in each MLB locker room.

Commissioner Giamatti hired a lawyer to investigate rumors of Rose's betting. The Commissioner argued that he was empowered to do so under Article I of the Major League Agreement (MLA), which gives the Commissioner the power to investigate and take action against an act that is not in the best interests of the game. Rose argued that as a result of this investigation, the Commissioner could not give Rose a fair hearing because the Commissioner had already prejudged the facts. Though Rose won a 10–day restraining order in state court,[5] he could not prevent Commissioner Giamatti from removing the case to federal court. The Reds were not a necessary party to the suit, and therefore, the requisite diversity for federal jurisdiction existed. More importantly, the Ohio court reasoned that the contract between Rose and the Reds incorporated the MLA, and the Agreement states that Rose is subject to the discipline of the Commissioner, not the Reds.

Ultimately, Rose and Commissioner Giamatti reached a litigation-ending settlement that stipulated (1.) Rose was permanently banned from any employment or association with MLB, (2.) there would be no hearing into Rose's alleged gambling activity, and (3.) Rose's acknowledgment that the Commissioner has the authority to investigate and act in reaction to any matter the Commissioner believes is contrary to the best interests of baseball.[6]

In *Molinas v. National Basketball Association*,[7] Commissioner Maurice Podoloff indefinitely suspended Jack Molinas, a player for the Fort Wayne Pistons, for betting 10 times on the Pistons to win. Molinas's bets—which he voluntarily admitted placing—violated the NBA policy prohibiting players from betting on any games in which they were to play. Five years after his unsuccessful suit against Commissioner Podoloff for the penalty—and after Molinas graduated from law school—Molinas filed an antitrust suit against the NBA, claiming that the punishment illegally and unreasonably restrained Molinas's ability to trade with his services. In rejecting Molinas's antitrust suit, the Court found that the punishment was necessary to enforce the NBA's strict anti-gambling policy and to

---

Teacher's Manual. Sample final exam questions and answers are set forth in Appendix B of the Teacher's Manual.

5. See Rose v. Giamatti, 721 F.Supp. 906 (S.D. Ohio 1989).

6. See Rose v. Giamatti, 721 F.Supp. 906 (S.D. Ohio 1989) and Rose v. Giamatti, 721 F.Supp. 924 (S.D. Ohio 1989).

7. 190 F.Supp. 241 (S.D.N.Y. 1961).

restore public confidence in the game and that Molinas had failed to prove a conspiracy existed.

Compare the legal challenges brought forth by Rose and Molinas. What role does the MLB "antitrust exemption" play in the outcomes of these two cases?

The NFL has had its fair share of player malfeasance as well. When Commissioner Pete Rozelle discovered that two of the league's best players, Paul Hornung of the Green Bay Packers and Alex Karras of the Detroit Lions, had bet on NFL games in contravention of the standard player contract, Commissioner Rozelle indefinitely suspended both players. Unlike Rose and Molinas, Hornung and Karras were reinstated after one season, and Hornung is currently in the Hall of Fame.

Is an indefinite, lifetime suspension, appropriate, or is too severe of a penalty? Should it matter if a player or manager is betting on his own team, or on other teams? What, if any, should be the court or arbitrator standard of review of Commissioner penalties against players and managers who have allegedly been gambling?

III. MISCONDUCT ON THE FIELD

At what point should the law intervene for "misconduct on the field"? How can one evaluate, on a principled basis, when a physical act on the field or court goes beyond that which is tolerable, in the context of a physical game, and transcends into the realm of assault? Compare *Sprewell v. Golden State Warriors*,[8] which stemmed out of an incident during an NBA practice, with the Pacers–Pistons arbitration,[9] which stemmed from a fight between players and extended into the stands, with *McSorley*, which stemmed from an incident during an NHL game.

During practice, Latrell Sprewell choked and threatened to kill coach P.J. Carlesimo, departed the practice facility, and returned to choke and threaten his coach once again. Immediately thereafter, the Golden State Warriors suspended Sprewell. Upon learning of the incident, Commissioner Stern suspended Sprewell for one year, and the Warriors subsequently terminated Sprewell's contract. As explained in Part I, pursuant to NBA rules, any disciplinary decision by a Commissioner that exceeds $25,000 is reviewable by an arbitrator to determine if the punishment is for "just cause." Though the arbitrator found that dual punishments were permissible, upon review, the arbitrator determined that Commissioner Stern's punishment was too severe, and reduced the suspension from 82 to 68 games. Further, the arbitrator determined that the Warrior's termination was void for lack of just cause, because the suspension already made it

---

8. 266 F.3d 979 (9th Cir. 2001).

9. National Basketball Ass'n v. National Basketball Players Ass'n, 2005 WL 22869, at *1 (S.D.N.Y. 2005).

impossible for Sprewell to play. The Ninth Circuit upheld the arbitrator's decision upon appeal.

In November of 2004, in the final minute of a game in Detroit, Ron Artest of the Pacers and Ben Wallace engaged in a brief shoving match. After the players were separated, a spectator threw a beverage that struck Artest. Artest proceeded to charge into the stands, striking blows against several fans. Fellow Pacer Stephen Jackson also entered the stands and fought with spectators, as teammate Anthony Johnson left the bench to confront another fan. Meanwhile, Jermaine O'Neal attempted to enter the stands, was restrained by an arena official who he pushed away, and then struck a fan who had descended onto the basketball court.

Commissioner Stern invoked his "best interests" powers in suspending Artest for the remainder of the season, Jackson for thirty games, Johnson for five games, and O'Neal for twenty-five games. The players and the NBA filed an appeal under the grievance procedure, claiming a lack of "just cause." The NBA argued that the dispute was not arbitrable and that any appeal was solely within the Commissioner's power to review. The NBA objected to the grievance procedure and did not attend the arbitration. At the conclusion of the hearing, the arbitrator upheld the full suspensions of Artest, Jackson, and Johnson, but found insufficient just cause to support Jackson's suspension of twenty-five games and reduced it fifteen games.

Before the District Court, the NBA's primary argument was based on Article XXXI, § 8 limiting appeals of discipline for "conduct on the playing court" solely to the Commissioner. The NBA insisted that misconduct "at or during a game" constituted "conduct on the playing court." By contrast, the players argued that the term only applied to conduct occurring as part of the game. The NBPA relied upon Article 35(h) of the NBA constitution, providing that any challenges to a Commissioner action taken under Article 35, except for those relating to wagering on games, shall be resolved in accordance with the grievance procedure. Since Article 35(d) provides for fines or suspension for player conduct during regular season games, indicating that punishment for in-game misbehavior was appealable under 35(h), the court rejected the NBA's broad reading of "conduct on the playing court," which would render review under Article 35(h) illusory. The court asserted that the Commissioner's authority throughout the CBA and NBA constitution was clearly defined, and that if the parties intended for the Commissioner to have broader powers, they would have explicitly granted them.

Boston Bruin Marty McSorley hit Vancouver Canuck Donald Brashear in the helmet with his hockey stick during the final three seconds of a game between the two teams. Brashear suffered a concussion after the helmet hit and fell to the ice, hitting his helmet once again. McSorley was not only suspended for the rest of the season (23 games) by Commissioner Gary Bettman, but he was also charged with and tried for assault in Vancouver. Following his conviction and 18–month probation sentence, McSorley's suspension was extended to a full year.

Should the arbitrator have reduced Sprewell's punishment? What effect, if any, might this have had on the legitimacy of the Commissioner's authority? Should McSorley have been tried in a court of law, or should the matter have been left to the NHL to police? What standard would you suggest ought to be applied to review the Commissioner's decisions for physical acts? What weight, if any, should be given to the context of the situation, e.g. during game play, during practice, or off the field?

Note that in the NBA, the league may promulgate rules governing player "conduct on the playing court" without NBPA approval, provided the league gives notice and consults with the NBPA.[10] Furthermore, it should be noted that "conduct on the playing court" has been broadly defined to include all activity a player engages in from the time he arrives at an arena for a game until he leaves. On the other hand, in MLB, playing and scoring rules that significantly affect terms and conditions of employment must be negotiated, as must a change in a player benefit under an existing rule or regulation.[11]

IV. DRUG USE

Recreational drugs and performance-enhancing drugs work in opposite directions—one diminishes the body's capacities while the other enhances them—but the use of both is regulated by each of the three leagues.

A. RECREATIONAL DRUGS

Consider and compare the following cases of Commissioner discipline for recreational drug use.

Following the arrest of Vida Blue, Willie Wilson, Jerry Martin, and Willie Aikens of the Kansas City Royals for cocaine possession in 1983, Commissioner Kuhn suspended each player for one-year. The players challenged the Commissioner's ruling under the "just cause" standard before a neutral arbitrator, who agreed with the Commissioner's conclusion that player drug use was a legitimate threat to the "best interests of baseball." The arbitrator noted that drug use risked physical harm to the players and increased the chance that dangerous criminals could gain control over players. Despite accepting the Commissioner's invocation of the "best interests" clause, the arbitrator still reduced Wilson's suspension to one-month because he had been imprisoned throughout almost all of the 1983 season.

Steve Howe had been suspended from baseball for drug use six times between 1982 and 1988. Although Howe did not test positive during a two-year period when Commissioner Fay Vincent ordered him regularly tested, Howe was arrested in 1991 for attempted possession of cocaine. Given

---

10. NBA Collective Bargaining Agreement Art. VI, § 12 (2005).
11. MLB Collective Bargaining Agreement Art. XVIII (2007).

Howe's history, Commissioner Vincent imposed a lifetime ban, which the MLBPA challenged. Citing the *Wilson* arbitration, Arbitrator Nicolau called for " 'careful scrutiny of the individual circumstances and the particular facts relevant to each case.' " Furthermore, Nicolau noted that the "need for scrutiny is at its zenith here simply because of the nature of the penalty at issue." Conducting a just cause review, the arbitrator determined that baseball had not done enough to justify the imposition of the penalty. For example, Nicolau argued that if Howe had been subjected to more stringent, year-round testing, he would not have engaged in the behavior that resulted in his arrest. The arbitrator ruled that the Commissioner should have examined Howe's circumstances more carefully, evaluating his condition and the adequacy of his treatment, before imposing discipline. Nicolau reduced the suspension to time served, a total of 119 days that cost Howe around $400,000.

Commissioner Rozelle punished Miami Dolphins Randy Crowder and Don Reese following their arrests for unlawful distribution of cocaine in 1977. After each player was sentenced to one year in jail, Rozelle launched his own disciplinary process. The Commissioner's ruling discussed at-length the high standard of conduct professional players owe the public as role models. However, given the fact that the players had already served a prison sentence, he decided to forego the imposition of a suspension, only ordering that the players each contribute $5,000 to a drug rehabilitation facility in the state of Florida. The NFLPA challenged the decision to test the scope of the Commissioner's authority. Noting that the CBA enabled the Commissioner to withdraw from the grievance procedure any "action taken against a player by the Commissioner for conduct detrimental to the integrity of, or public confidence in, the game of professional football," the arbitrator upheld the ruling.

The first ever appeal of an NFL Commissioner's disciplinary decision to the courts was brought by Dallas Cowboy Clayton Holmes. Holmes was suspended for four games and involuntarily enrolled in the NFL's Policy and Program for Drugs of Abuse and Alcohol (the "Drug Program") after testing positive for marijuana. Before signing with the Cowboys as a restricted free agent, Holmes visited the Detroit Lions. As a condition of potential employment, the Lions requested that Holmes submit to a drug test, for the purpose of detecting the use of steroids. After testing positive for marijuana, Holmes was enrolled in Stage 1 of the Drug Program, adopted as part of the collective bargaining process between the NFLPA and the Management Council. A player who is referred to Stage 1 moves into Stage 2, where he is subjected to unannounced testing. A player who tests positive during Stage 2 faces a four-game suspension and advances to Stage 3, where a positive test can yield a suspension of at least one year. Holmes tested positive on three occasions during Stage 2. After Holmes was fined and suspended for four games, he appealed to the Commissioner.

Commissioner Tagliabue determined that Holmes's appeals of his initial positive test and two of the subsequent Stage 2 tests were untimely, and that there was no evidence suggesting that the remaining test was suspect. Before the District Court, Holmes argued that his involuntary enrollment in the Drug Program breached the CBA and that his suspension was improper because he did not receive full due process rights, including the opportunities to confront his accusers, to cross-examine witnesses, and to present evidence. Holmes contended that the traditional judicial deference to resolutions of labor disputes by tribunal would be misplaced in this case because of the alleged due process violations. However, the District Court concluded that since the arbitration was a voluntary component of the labor contract, the arbitrator was not the equivalent of a government official, meaning that constitutional rights did not attach. Furthermore, the breach of contract claim was rejected because the arbitration ruling "drew its essence" from the CBA.[12]

Is the *Steve Howe* arbitration ruling "in the best interests of baseball"? How does it compare to the Randy Crowder/Don Reese NFL arbitration ruling? Which do you think protects the "best interests" of the league?

B.   PERFORMANCE ENHANCING DRUGS

Arguably more damaging to the game than player use of recreational drugs is player use of performance-enhancing drugs because use of such drugs undermines the authenticity of the game. Nowhere has the effect of such use been more acute in recent years than in MLB. MLB and its Commissioner Allan "Bud" Selig were hounded for years by reports into the allegedly widespread illegal use of steroids and other performance-enhancing drugs by players. While speculation and innuendo had shrouded the sport for years, allegations became firmly entrenched in public discourse after federal agents raided the offices of the Bay Area Laboratory Co–Operative (BALCO) in September of 2003.[13] The government officials discovered numerous documents linking players to BALCO, and, by the end of the year, Barry Bonds, Jason Giambi, and Gary Sheffield were called to testify before a grand jury conducting a probe into the company's illegal production and distribution of performance-enhancing drugs. The fallout from the BALCO investigation led to congressional hearings in 2005, where the House Committee on Government Reform took Selig and Donald Fehr, Executive Director of the MLBPA, to task for not doing more to curb the use of illegal performance-enhancing drugs in their sport.[14] Largely in response to Congress's criticism, MLB and the MLBPA negotiated enhanced penalties for steroid use that went into effect before the 2006 season.[15]

---

12.   Holmes v. National Football League, 939 F.Supp. 517, 519 (N.D. Tex. 1996).

13.   See Mark Fainaru–Wade & Lance Williams, Sports and Drugs: How the Doping Scandal Unfolded; Fallout from BALCO Probe Could Taint Olympics, Pro Sports, S.F. CHRON., Dec. 23, 2003, available at http://www.sfgate.com/cgi-bin/article.cgi?file=/chronicle/archive/2003/12/21/SPGSB3RQPT13.DTL.

14.   Jack Curry, Congress Fires Questions Hard and Inside, and Baseball Can Only Swing and Miss, N.Y. TIMES, Mar. 18, 2005, available at http://www.nytimes.com/2005/03/18/sports/baseball/18curry.html.

15.   Steroid Penalties much tougher with agreement, http://sports.espn.go.com/mlb/news/story?id=2224832 (last visited May 19, 2008).

On March 30, 2006, baseball began another process that would culminate in condemnation for both the players and management when Commissioner Selig tapped former Senate Majority Leader George Mitchell to conduct an investigation into the use of performance-enhancing drugs in baseball's recent past.[16] Released on December 13, 2007, the Mitchell Report blamed both MLB and the MLBPA for their collective failure to address the problem of steroid use and named eighty-six players, including Bonds, Giambi, Sheffield, and Roger Clemens, who used illegal performance enhancing drugs. In a subsequent hearing before Congress on January 15, 2008, Selig accepted Mitchell's criticisms for baseball's failure to act during the mid to late 1990s, but also pointed out that even if he had taken a harder line and proposed a more rigorous drug policy, the MLBPA would have prevented him from imposing a stronger testing regime.[17] As for the players named in the Mitchell Report, Selig's efforts to punish these players appear to have been stymied by union pressure.

Barry Bonds, now baseball's all-time home run king, faces indictments for fourteen counts of making false statements under oath and one for obstruction of justice stemming from his testimony before the grand jury in 2003.[18] Congress has also called for the Justice Department to investigate whether Roger Clemens lied under oath to Congress during hearings regarding his own alleged steroid use.[19] Finally, as of May 2008, it has been reported that federal authorities involved in the BALCO prosecution may subpoena each of the 104 players who anonymously tested positive for steroids in 2003, making it appear likely that soon even more players will be exposed as users of illegal performance-enhancing drugs.[20] The names on the list, which were supposed to be kept secret, have been leaked to the media one-at-a time in 2009.

Among the players listed were Alex Rodriguez, the $252 million dollar man for the Texas Rangers who was arguably known as the best naturally talented player in baseball. After Rodriguez's test result was released, he admitted to using a performance enhancing drug—he purportedly received from his cousin in the Dominican Republic—from 2001 to 2003. During spring training 2009, Rodriguez discovered a cyst in his hip and suffered a torn labrum, which warranted surgery. Though Rodriguez potentially has several years left on his career, unlike Barry Bonds, Rafael Palmiero, Mark McGwire, and others accused of performance enhancing drug use at the end of their careers, it remains to be seen how Rodriguez will perform upon his return to the game. Other high-profile players, including David Ortiz, continue to be implicated.

---

16. Mitchell report: Baseball slow to react to players' steroid use, http://sports.espn.go.com/mlb/news/story?id=3153509 (last visited May 19, 2008).

17. Steroid Use by Baseball Players: Hearing Before the H. Comm. on Oversight & Government Reform, 110th Cong. (statement of Allan H. Selig, Comm'r of Major League Baseball).

18. Michael S. Schmidt, Prosecutors Rework Indictment of Bonds, N.Y. TIMES, May 14, 2008, available at http://www.nytimes.com/2008/05/14/sports/baseball/14bonds.html.

19. Congress asks DOJ to prove whether Clemens lied under oath, http://sports.espn.go.com/mlb/news/story?id=3267163 (last visited May 19, 2008).

20. Michael S. Schmidt, Drug Test Results From 2003 Could Soon Be in Evidence, N.Y. TIMES, May 18, 2008, available at http://www.nytimes.com/2008/05/18/sports/baseball/18drugs.html.

Two famous Yankee pitchers, Roger Clemens and Andy Pettite, were also accused of using performance enhancing drugs. Clemens, who was known throughout his career for his work ethic, vehemently denied that his trainer, Brian McNamee, injected him with steroids. Pettite, by contrast, admitted to using human growth hormone to heal after injuring his elbow. In 2009, Miguel Tejada pled guilty to a count of perjury for lying in his testimony to Congress about whether or not teammate former Rafael Palmiero had used steroids. These famous cases have led commentators to dub the 1990s and part of the 2000s as the "steroid era" in baseball.

The MLBPA and the Commissioner's Office have agreed to a "Joint Drug Prevention and Treatment Program," designed "(1) to educate Players ... on the risks associated with using Prohibited Substances ...; (2) to deter and end the use by Players of Prohibited Substances; and (3) to provide for, in keeping with the overall purposes of the Program, an orderly, systematic, and cooperative resolution of any disputes that may arise concerning the existence, interpretation, or application of this agreement." Any disputes are resolved through the Grievance Procedure of MLB's Basic Agreement. An independent administrator oversees the program. The program prohibits the use of both "drugs of abuse," such as cocaine, LSD, marijuana, and opiates, and "performance enhancing substances," including anabolic androgenic steroids, designer steroids, and a list of 58 hormones, and "stimulants," such as amphetamine. Players are testing in spring training and are subject to additional random testing and reasonable cause testing. The most famous player to be suspended under the new policy is the Los Angeles Dodgers' Manny Ramirez. After a difficult period of off-season negotiations, in which Ramirez bargained for a two-year, $45 million contract, at the start of the 2009 season Ramirez tested positive for a women's fertility drug used to stimulate natural testosterone generation after using performance enhancing drugs. Ramirez apologized and disappeared from the limelight immediately after receiving a 50 game suspension. (In response, Selig wants to close "loophole" which permitted Manny to play in the minor league system, while still suspended from "MLB" games.)

Under the NFL's drug testing program, two to three independent contractor Drug Program Agents regularly rove each team's practice facilities and test players weekly. The players to be tested are selected at random. Players have four hours after notification that they have been selected to produce a sample. To avoid deception, players are observed as they urinate. This observation was initiated in response to players using the "Whizzinator," a device with an artificial bladder, to conceal clean urine.

Despite its stringent testing, the NFL still does have players who take the risk of taking prohibited substances. In 2006, a local newspaper reported six Carolina Panthers players had steroid prescriptions, though none had tested positive. San Diego Charger Shawne Merriman served a four-game without pay sentence for a positive test, even though he claimed that he was held strictly liable for substances he did not know were tainted. This strict liability policy, contained in the NFL Policy on Anabolic Steroids and Related Substances, was challenged in court in 2008. A Minnesota district court judge granted an injunction blocking the NFL from suspending five players who were taking "StarCaps," which contained a banned diuretic not listed on the label. The pills are designed for weight loss, but the banned diuretic they contained presumably could be used as a masking agent. The players first challenged their suspensions through the league's internal grievance system to NFL chief legal office Jeffrey Pash. The players complained that having Pash as their arbitrator and the NFL's failure to notify the players StarCaps were prohibited constituted a breach of fiduciary duty, endangered the health of the players, and "fatally tainted the suspensions [which] would unfairly punish the players and condone the improper behavior and breaches of duty by the NFL, in violation of public policy and the essence of the CBA." The judge criticized the NFL for taking two months to let the players know they were suspended. An NFL appeal of the ruling is pending and scheduled for the summer of 2009.

The NBA and NBPA "Anti-drug Program" prohibits "amphetamine and its analogs, cocaine, LSD, opiates, PCP, marijuana, and steroid." A "Prohibited Substances Committee" comprised of one member from the NBA, one from the NBPA, and three jointly selected members issue the definitive list of prohibited steroids, and a Medical Director oversees the program. Players who come forward voluntarily can seek treatment free of penalty the first time they come forward. Since its implementation in 1999, only three players have tested positive. The more pressing issue for the NBA has been recreational drug use. In 2001, veteran Charles Oakley claimed that sixty percent of players smoked marijuana. Prominent players such as Allen Iverson, Chris Webber, and Kareem Abdul–Jabbar have been charged with marijuana possession. In 2008, Dallas Maverick Josh Howard admitted to using marijuana in the off-season. Owner Marc Cuban said they would address the issue internally.

Is the use of performance enhancing drugs or recreational drugs more objectionable? Do you think that players ought to be permitted to opt into a treatment program for voluntarily coming forward?

Not only has athlete use of steroids and recreational drugs come under scrutiny, but athlete use of "dietary supplements" has as well. What role should the Commissioner and/or the courts play in regulating "dietary supplements" as referenced at pages 63 to 64 in *Weiler* in the Steve Bechler and Korey Stringer cases? What about over-the-counter supplements players may use? Should players be strictly liable if these supplements contain unlisted traces of prohibited substances?

Writing Exercise 1: Negotiate and Draft a "Hypothetical" Consent Decree between Alex Rodriguez and Commissioner Selig[21]

In light of the foregoing precedents, imagine the attorney for Alex Rodriguez and the general counsel for MLB Commissioner Bud Selig are

---

21. An "exemplar" student submission in response to this hypothetical can be found in the accompanying Teacher's Manual.

trying to reach a resolution of Rodriguez's outstanding issues with Commissioner Selig, who has reserved the right to punish Rodriguez. As you consider how to resolve the issues, bear in mind the Commissioner's treatment of Jason Giambi,[22] Barry Bonds, and Miguel Tejada. Further, assume the following facts:

1. Congress has required MLB and Rodriguez to work out their issues or else Congress will institute an investigation into steroid use among MLB players and consider revoking baseball's antitrust exemption.

2. Rodriguez has been advised that his records from 2001 to 2003 will be marked with an asterisk until he "tells the truth" about his drug use.

3. A majority of the owners—who have elected Commissioner Selig—have advised him that it is in the best interests of the game to resolve this matter.

Draft a proposed "consent decree," from the perspective of each side, pursuant to which Rodriguez will consider an apology and/or will make certain admissions against interest and Commissioner Selig will be instructed by MLB owners to make a deal—under any circumstances—to avoid Congressional intervention.

Be creative regarding Rodriguez's "cooperation" possibilities, including following Giambi's and Tejada's examples. On Selig's side, consider offering retroactive similar treatments to Mark McGuire's and Sammy Sosa's home run records, if Rodriguez cooperates.

What are each sides "must haves," "nice to haves," and "throw aways"? What is each side unwilling to agree to, such that it is will walk away if demanded by the other side? Draft a final agreement to which both sides agree.[23]

V. DIVERSITY IN SPORTS

Decisions made by the Commissioner affect not only the composition and treatment of league personnel, but also touch upon the rights and privileges of third parties. Athletes such as Jackie Robinson, Hank Greenberg, Hank Aaron and Roberto Clemente in MLB, Kenny Washington in the NFL, and Chuck Cooper and Nat "Sweetwater" Clifton in the NBA played a role in shaping how race and ethnicity are viewed in America. Moreover, actions by the Commissioner may, at times, touch upon and implicate important Constitutional issues, such as the First Amendment of free expression and rights under the Equal Protection and Due Process Clauses.

---

22. Selig presented Giambi with an ultimatum that Giambi must cooperate with George Mitchell's investigation, to which Giambi conceded. Giambi publicly apologized for his use of [?].

23. In response to each of the "hypothetical" Writing Exercises set forth throughout this book, "exemplar" student submissions can be found in the accompanying Teacher's Manual.

A. RACIAL, NATIONAL, AND ETHNIC MINORITIES IN SPORTS[24]

Today, African–Americans comprise approximately 79 percent of NBA players, 65 percent of NFL players, and 8.5 percent of MLB players. About 3 percent of NFL players and 2.5 percent of MLB players are Asian. About 28.7 percent of MLB players are Hispanic, as compared with 1 percent of players in the NFL.[25] While a significant percentage of athletes in the three major leagues are from various minority groups, there is still a dearth of minorities in coaching and managerial positions. As of the writing of this book, only seven of the 32 NFL head coaches were African–American.

In response to the disparity between the proportion of minority players versus the proportion of minority coaches, the NFL instituted the "Rooney Rule" in 2003.[26] The Rule requires NFL teams to interview minority candidates for the head coaching job. After the Rule was implemented, the number of African–American coaches rose from 6 percent to 22 percent in 2006.[27] In 2008, several commentators called for a similar rule to apply to the NCAA after only three African–American coaches remained at the end of the football season.

Do you agree with the use of the "Rooney Rule"? Should it apply to each league? If not, is there another policy you can design to encourage more minority applicants and to remove the specter of bias in hiring?

Fair treatment of the athletes who are members of racial and ethnic minority groups is also of concern. College basketball coach Keith Dambrot was fired from Central Michigan University for violating the University's discriminatory harassment policy after Dambrot used the word "nigger" in the locker room with his players, 11 of whom were African–American and three of whom were white.[28] Though Dambrot testified that he had asked and received permission from a player to use the term and that he intended to use the term in a "positive and reinforcing" manner, as he had heard the players using it themselves, and though the players, when interviewed, said that they had not been offended, the University discharged the coach. Dambrot's wrongful termination suit claimed the University's policy violated the First Amendment because it was overbroad and vague. Although Dambrot's First Amendment challenge to the policy was successful—and the policy was declared unconstitutional—

---

24.   For more information on racial integration of MLB and issues facing minority players, you may want to read JULES TYGIEL, BASEBALL'S GREAT EXPERIMENT: JACKIE ROBINSON AND HIS LEGACY (1997); JACKIE ROBINSON, I NEVER HAD IT MADE (1995); David Maraniss, CLEMENTE: THE PASSION AND THE GRACE OF BASEBALL'S LAST HERO (2006).

25.   NFL data from: N.F.L. Players Evaluate Their Coaches, William C. Rhoden, N.Y. Times. MLB data from: http://sports.espn.go.com/mlb/news/story?id=2891875.

Racial Composition of NBA, NFL and MLB teams and racial composition of franchise cities, Journal of Sport Behavior, Dec. 1997, William M. Leonard II.

26.   The Rooney Rule is named after Pittsburgh Steelers' owner Dan Rooney, chairman of the NFL's Diversity Committee.

27.   Tackling Unconscious Bias in Hiring Practices: The Plight of the Rooney Rule, Brian W. Collins, June 2007 NYU Law Review, Student Note.

28.   Dambrot v. Central Michigan Univ., 55 F.3d 1177 (6th Cir. 1995).

Dambrot could not properly claim wrongful termination because the particular speech he used was not protected by the First Amendment. Therefore, the court reasoned, Dambrot had not suffered any harm, and he was not wrongfully terminated.

Do you agree with the Court's analysis in *Dambrot*? Do you agree with the University's decision to fire Coach Dambrot in the first place, or should his players' interviews have absolved him?

First Amendment issues arise vividly on the playing field itself. When NBA player Mahmoud Abdul–Rauf refused to stand for the Star Spangled Banner before games—stating that the flag was a symbol of oppression and tyranny—the NBA suspended Abdul–Rauf for one game. The league and Abdul–Rauf reached a settlement, whereby he agreed to stand during the national anthem, but he was permitted to look down and not required to sing the words. By contrast, the Commissioner permitted Alan Iverson to sing a "gangsta rap" song on the grounds that the lyrics were similar to rap in general and that the song was artistic expression. MLB's Carlos Delgado refused to stand on the field when "God Bless America" was played as a symbolic gesture against the Iraq War and the bombing exercises on an island off Puerto Rico. As a symbolic gesture, when Mike Lowell played for the Florida Marlins, he declined to play to protest the treatment of Elian Gonzalez and his return to Cuba.[29]

Do you agree with the Commissioner's decision to suspend Abdul–Rauf? Should a different standard apply to Commissioner decisions that impinge on free speech? How does an athlete's off-field persona relate to his standing in the league?

B. WOMEN AND SPORTS

In this context, perhaps the most egregious example of a Commissioner exceeding his authority is *Ludtke v. Kuhn*. Challenged in *Ludtke* was the constitutionality of Commissioner Kuhn's policy of barring females from the Yankees locker room. Reporter Melissa Ludtke claimed the policy was discriminatory because male journalists were permitted in the locker room, but merely because of her gender, she was not. After finding that the Fourteenth Amendment applied because of a sufficient nexus between the stadium and the state, the court went on to invalidate the policy as contrary to the Equal Protection and Due Process Clauses.

If there had not been state action in this case, do you think Ludtke's constitutional challenge would have been successful? If not, on what other grounds could you invalidate the policy?

Legal Writing: "Tips" re: Drafting Brief Headings

As you consider the *Ludtke*-related "Hypotheticals" which follows re: consider the following brief writing "tips" in the sports law world:

---

29. Scott Wilson and April Witt, *For Elian, a Called Strike*, Washington Post, April 26, 2000, D01, available at http://www.latinamericanstudies.org/elian/called.htm (last visited May 1, 2009).

Put your best ("why I win") argument first. In drafting Brief Headings, you must attempt to assess the order of your arguments on the assumption that the judge (or clerk) reading your headings may well stop reading your headings after the very first one! Accordingly, you should always try to put your "best argument first," in as succinct and persuasive a heading as possible, without "going overboard" to the point where you are so dismissive of your opposition's best argument that you lose your credibility with the court.

In so doing, whenever possible, you should encapsulate your heading's facts within the "highest / most authoritative" legal precedent available to support your arguments. In other words, you should get to the "highest legal ground" on which you can stand, whether it be the U.S. Constitution itself, a relevant federal or state statute, or a directly controlling "on point" case precedent from the highest court in your jurisdiction.

"Honesty is the best policy" here, however. As indicated above, if you "overbid your hand" in your first Brief Heading, you may well lose your audience. Be certain, therefore, that any relevant "supporting authority" cited in the first Brief Heading cannot be undercut of effectively distinguished by the opposition. Similarly, in reciting the relevant supporting "facts of record," be certain that there are no "ellipses" or "omissions of material fact" that the opposition can exploit to destroy your credibility with the Court.

Your first few "narrative" Brief paragraphs, after the first Headings, should next flow naturally from the "introduction," which the reader has (hopefully) accepted. You can then provide a more thorough explication of this initial argument, while putting more "flesh on the bones" of the Heading's factual / legal skeleton. In so doing, your general rule should be "no surprises," lest the reader detect a deviation from the heading theme on which you have implicitly promised to deliver your narrative.

As you end the narrative of the first Brief section, you can begin to summarize again, without insulting the reader, "why I win," if the reader accepts only your first argument. In so doing, however, you should also begin gently directing the reader to your next "best argument," lest the reader (prematurely) compares the opponent's first "best argument," and decides the case (perhaps against you!). At a minimum, the reader must be convinced that he must read on in fairness to your client.

Put next-best ("why I win") argument second. After anticipating your next best argument at the end of the first Brief section, you will need to transition as seamlessly as possible by drafting your second "why I win" Brief Heading. In so doing, the same general drafting principles should apply as described above—get to your "highest ground" of legal/precedential authority, and tailor-make the ("fairly read") facts to fit within that framework. Again, any perceived "contortion" of the facts or law will count against you. So, too, would be an overly hyperbolic or otherwise exaggerated conclusion. Courts/clerks like to be "led to the water," but not "forced to drink" by Brief Headings/narratives that are overly self-righteous or self-assured.

After all, if there were not "another side of the story," the case would not be in litigation to begin with! *Suggesting* (irreversible) conclusions to the Court should be the target, leaving room for the Court to agree that you have hit the "bulls eye"—perhaps with (unanticipated) "arrows" that you did not even realize might be in your "quiver," but for the Court's citing of a case/legal authority that you might have missed.

As you tease out the narrative in support of your second Brief Heading, you can "assume a lot" and "incorporate by reference" much of the factual predicate of your preceding argument, to the extent it applies.

As to the legal predicates, eye-catching undeniably relevant "direct hits" should be imbedded in your narrative, as you attempt to guide the Court/clerk how to write an Opinion in your favor, without being pedantic or condescending. "String cites" are generally disfavored, unless accompanied by a short summary of the cited cases which add to, (i.e., do not simply "repeat") the prior cases' holdings.

If you take one "false/unsupportable step" at this point in your Brief-writing exercise, it could be fatal re: losing credibility. Accordingly, it may be appropriate at this point to begin to distinguish your opponent's (anticipated) "best case." In fact, you may even want to "concede" an opponent's best non-controlling counter-argument, if only to show that the Court's accepting it would still be consistent with an ultimate ruling in your favor. This evenhandedness will lend further credibility to the (favorable) conclusion which you trust the Court will ultimately arrive at on its own.

Put Best ("Why I Don't Lose") Counter–Argument Last. In concluding your Brief, you must "give the devil his due," and admit that the opposition's "best arguments" are worthy of consideration but, ultimately, should be rejected when contrasted with yours.

Accordingly, your Brief Heading here will often take the form of "even if you believe (some point of) my opponent's argument," you should not rule in his favor, for the following reasons.

Here, you will need to tread very carefully in "enemy territory," while conceding as few non-conclusive opponents' points as possible. In so doing, fresh legal and factual precedents may need to be invoked, again with as "neutral" an interposition that leads the Court to its own ineluctable conclusion that the opponent's "best argument" is, at the end of the briefing cycle, unavailing.

In certain "clear loser cases," however, this final part of the Brief may also have to do significant "damage control," by minimizing the opponent's recovery, should he win. Equitable/"unclean hands" types of arguments and/or "unjust enrichment" claims may be necessary, to avoid a catastrophic loss, as you throw yourself on the mercy of the Court to "personalize" your client to avoid a "punitive damages" award.

Conclusion. In closing, of course, in every type of case, you will return to your "why I must win—(and win big!)" mantra, harvesting the "seeds of victory" that you have been sowing throughout your Brief. As you do so, it can be helpful to "remind" the Court, in a non-threatening way, that ruling in your client's favor would simply be the (non-reversible) "right thing to do."

As a potential "iron fist" within that "velvet glove," though, you may also want to alert the Court (as an "officer" of same!), to the "reversibility consequences" that the Court would suffer if the Court flew in the face of your Brief's irrefutable logic and somehow ruled in favor of your opponent.

Finally, be very clear in your conclusion re: what relief you are seeking so as to "monetize" same for the Court. In effect, without being presumptuous, you can conclude with the equivalent of a "draft Order" which the Court/clerk can adopt if you have won the case.

Pre–Filing/Post–Brief Writing "Tips". After finalizing your Brief, if time permits, you should put it aside, and not review/revise it again for a pre-determined period of time. Then, before filing it, you should make sure that you have not "fallen in love with your own brief" because you got too close to it during the drafting process.

In so doing, you could, inter alia, read aloud your Brief Headings to a colleague familiar with the case, in a simulated "oral argument" environment. You can then call upon the colleague to make the best counterargument for the opposition. By working your way through the Brief Headings in seriatim fashion, you can ensure the optimal structure/ordering of your Brief Headings, and fine tune any perceived weaknesses in them. You can also begin to decide which of your weakest arguments could be conceded, if/when the opposition exploits them either at oral argument or in a responsive brief.

Finally, then, by testing your arguments against a "devil's advocate" colleague in this way, you can feel most confident that the essence of the Brief's best argument should withstand the most carefully crafted "frontal attacks" by the opposition.

Writing Exercise 2: Appellate Legal Briefs from Commissioner Kuhn and Ms. Ludtke[30]

In light of these "tips", now please consider the *Ludtke v. Kuhn* decision. Assume that Commissioner Kuhn refuses to drop MLB's appeal, and instructs his attorneys to begin to prepare an appellate brief. Correspondingly, Ms. Ludtke's attorneys must begin to anticipate MLB's best arguments, as they prepare the basic brief headings for their responsive appellate court brief.

---

30. An "exemplar" student submission in response to this hypothetical can be found in the accompanying Teacher's Manual.

Draft the basic "brief headings" for each side. Layer the arguments, presenting the best arguments first, followed by the arguments explaining why you should not lose. In the text of each brief heading, include reference to the most helpful case/arbitration citations referenced in the Chapter 1 reading materials. Be sure to distinguish the most damaging precedents. "Exemplar" briefs can be found in the Teacher's Manual.

Legal Writing: "Tips" re: Drafting a Client Memorandum

A different form of legal writing important in the "sports law" world is drafting a "privileged/confidential" memo to an otherwise (seemingly all-powerful) authority, such as the Commissioner of America's three "major leagues." When advising such a client, the first issue you should be concerned with is ensuring that you are giving legal advice, so that the attorney client privilege and/or work product doctrine will attach to the document produced. The attorney client privilege is a rule of evidence that prohibits courts from demanding the disclosure of legal advice given to clients. The privilege is designed to preserve the right to effective assistance of legal counsel by protection confidences between lawyers and clients. To attach, the communication must be between the client and the lawyer exclusively, and the communication must be for the purpose of securing a legal opinion, legal services, or assistance in a legal proceeding. Be sure to intersperse case citations and legal advice throughout your memorandum.

The work product doctrine protects certain documents prepared in anticipation of going to trial. Typically the doctrine protects memoranda reflecting "mental impressions, conclusions, opinions, or legal theories" developed by lawyers.

Your memo should be structured in such a way that you can communicate the "answer" to your commissioner-type client quickly and effectively. If your memo is long enough, you will want to begin with a "table of contents" that directs your client to the information therein.

The substance of your memo should begin with an executive summary that briefly explains the issue at hand, your conclusion of the issue, and the facts relevant to your conclusion. You should give firm/clear "precedent-based" "privileged" advice. The summary should be "legally sufficient" for the client to read and then take confident action, if at all possible. If you get to non-legal-based "suggestions," be sure to connect same somehow/some way to your "legal-based" advice, lest you lose the protection of the privilege. Avoid wishy-washy "maybe/maybe not" types of "advice"—try to be firmer and have the courage of your convictions, backed up by precedent. "Caveats" are, of course, necessary. But that does not mean you should leave the client "hanging" without your "expert" opinion on the law. Remember—you are the lawyer. Your client wants you to tell him if that case is or is not "determinative," and if so, what action he should take based thereon.

After the executive summary, in which you will alert the client to the important relevant facts and legal issues, you should delve into a more detailed discussion of your facts and the application of the law to those facts. For each discrete issue, create a separate subsection, using headings and subheadings where appropriate to aid your reader.

Finally, conclude your memo with your recommendation regarding the issue. You can encourage your client to make up his or her own mind, but should not eschew your responsibility to exercise your own judgment. In your recommendation, explain the reasons for your conclusion, and the possible consequences of following the avenue you describe. Then, you may want to explain alternative courses of action and the reasons why you find these courses less desirable than the route you have selected. You will want to arm your client with the information necessary so your client can make a well-reasoned, informed judgment.

Writing Exercise 3: Preparing a "Privileged" Memorandum Addressing the Legality of a Hypothetical Dress Code Policy and Foreign Reporters' Exclusive Post–Game Access Policy[31]

In light of the foregoing "tips", please consider the following "Hypothetical".

Assume the following variation on the fact pattern in *Lutdke vs. Kuhn*. Erin Andrews (and a similarly situated "class" of female MLB reporters) is claiming "discrimination" based on the new "Dress Code Policy" that Commissioner Selig has instituted, which states:

> "When engaging in locker-room reporting, all reporters, both male and female, must wear business casual attire. This standard requires, at a minimum, clothing that covers the entire torso up to the bottom of the neck, and pants, skirts or shorts that are long enough to cover the top of the kneecap. Under no circumstances may inappropriately tight clothing be worn by male or female reporters in the locker room."

Assume further that Selig has also instituted the following "non-English-speaking" MLB players and reporters policy, which has been challenged as being "discriminatory" by all other "English-only-speaking" MLB reporters:

> "Henceforth, in the best interests of the globalization of the MLB game to non-English-speaking countries beginning with Japan and Korea, the following rule will be instituted re: MLB reporters' access to foreign-born Japanese and Korean-speaking MLB players: for the first five (5) minutes of post-game interviews, such access will be provided exclusively to those MLB reporters who are fluent in the

---

31. An "exemplar" student submission in response to this hypothetical can be found in the accompanying Teacher's Manual.

foreign-born players' native language, for purposes of providing a 'first look' at the player's post-game reflections to his 'native market.'

After the initial five-minute exclusive period, all other reporters will be given access to such foreign-speaking players, on an open-ended basis, at the player's option.

To qualify for the initial exclusive access period, however, any reporter must pass the fluency test for Japanese or Korean, which will be administered by the MLB General Counsel's Office."

The Commissioner has stated that the primary purpose of this Policy is to help grow the MLB game in those foreign markets, as the Seattle Mariners and Boston Red Sox have done so effectively, for example, through the signing and marketing of Ichiro Suzuki and Daisuke Matsuzaka.

Please consider these hypothetical policies in light of the Chapter 1 readings regarding the Commissioner's Authority. Which legal precedents would be most relevant to upholding or striking down Selig's attempts to institute the foregoing policy rules as to which he has invoked his (ultimate) authority to act "in the best interests of baseball"?

Acting as General Counsel to Commissioner Selig, please prepare a confidential/privileged memorandum in which you cite which case and/or arbitral citations and MLB Collective Bargaining Agreement or Constitutional provisions would support or undercut the Commissioner's Authority to institute these two new "rules of the game." See the course study guide in Appendix B for additional guidance.

In particular, please advise whether the intervention of "the law" can be expected and would be "appropriate" in preventing or modifying the institution of either of the policy rules.

SUMMARY QUESTIONS

1. Consider the "review" of the Commissioners' decisions on appeal to courts and arbitrators. Based on that consideration, discuss which were the best legally-reasoned reviews of which Commissioners' decisions, and which were the worst legally-reasoned reviews of which Commissioners' decisions in each of the three major leagues. Consider the ways in which the Commissioner's various decisions were consistent with prior decisions or departed from precedent.

In general, where was it most beneficial in the "Best Interests of the Game," for a court or an arbitrator to intervene into the evolution of the game itself? Should Commissioners be given "plenary powers" which would not permit them to be overruled by Courts or arbitrators?

In MLB, for example, do the Commissioners' nearly "plenary powers" help to justify the antitrust exemption because the Commissioner can "protect" the fans' interest without being "reversed" by the MLB owners? In the exercise of such plenary powers, however, consider Commissioner Landis's seemingly contradictory rulings in the face of players' gambling (see, e.g.,

Landis' absolution of Ty Cobb and Tris Speaker versus treatment of Hal Chase and the Black Sox scandal's "Eight Men Out.")

2. Should the three major leagues adhere to the same evidentiary and procedural standards as courts, or should they be free to adopt their own rules? If they choose to adopt their own rules, what outer limits and review process ought to exist on this power?

3. How should NBA Commissioner David Stern have dealt with NBA referee Tim Donaghy's betting on NBA games? Should the target of gambling allegations, in this case, Tim Donaghy, be considered "innocent until proven guilty"?

At the sentencing stage of the Commissioner's decision, please consider whether the following factors should factor in as mitigating circumstances in the sentencing of Donaghy: (1.) Donaghy's claim that he has a gambling addiction, and is receiving medical treatment therefore; (2.) Donaghy's affliction with clinical depression, which led to his gambling addiction; (3.) Donaghy's claim that he is entitled to accommodation under the Americans with Disabilities Act (ADA), based on the foregoing;[32] and (4.) assume Donaghy claims that Commissioner Stern is discriminating against him personally, given that other NBA referees are involved in other forms for gambling, such as participation in March Madness pools, but are not facing disciplinary action.

How pro-active should Commissioner Stern have been, as the scandal was unfolding, before the criminal proceedings took on a life of their own?

Compare and contrast Commissioner Stern's handling of the Isaiah Thomas/New York Knicks' "sexual harassment" case. Thomas was accused of making sexual advances and suggestive comments towards an employee. The suit ultimately resulted in a $11.6 million judgment against Thomas and the Knicks. Is "public confidence in and/or the integrity of the game" at issue here, too?

4. What should NFL Commissioner Roger Goodell have done in response to the allegations, federal and state charges, and subsequent conviction and incarceration of Michael Vick for Vick's participation in a dog-fighting ring on his property? How would your advice to Commissioner Goodell change if Vick could, in good faith, say that he did not know what others were doing on his property? Accordingly, assume that Vick can claim that he did not intentionally do anything wrong, but that at worst, he is culpable for his gross negligence, for not better supervising his lifelong friends' use of his property? Should Commissioner Goodell reinstate Michael Vick upon the conclusion of his sentence?

Is Commissioner Goodell's creation of the NFL Player Conduct Policy and his subsequent handling of the Adam "Pacman" Jones situation—in which

---

32. In this regard, also consider Roy Tarpley's successful ADA claim based upon his addiction to cocaine and alcohol. Tarpley was banned for life and refused reinstatement by the NBA after his third failed drug test, pursuant to the rules in the NBA's collectively-bargained anti-drug policy. The Equal Employment Opportunity Commission agreed with Tarpley that the NBA ought to have reinstated him once he provided evidence that he was no longer using drugs and alcohol.

Commissioner Goodell suspended Jones without pay for the entire 2007 season for his off-field behavior, including several arrests—an overreaction to Vick? How should Commissioner Goodell treat Donte Stallworth, who was sentenced to 30 days in jail for a DWI manslaughter? Should he defer to the court's punishment, or render a harsher penalty? Should Commissioner Goodell suspend Plaxico Burress after he completes his jail sentence for having a gun in a nightclub, or is the penal sanction imposed by New York punishment enough?

5. How should MLB Commissioner Bud Selig have acknowledged Barry Bonds' breaking of Hank Aaron's home run record? Should the Commissioner require an asterisk placed next to Bonds' name because of Bonds' alleged use of performance-enhancing drugs during his career? Assume no MLB drug-testing policy existed until 2005. Assume further that Bonds has never tested positive since MLB's drug-testing policy came into effect. Also assume that Bonds' defense is that he did not knowingly ingest a controlled substance, but rather merely took what was prescribed by his trainer.

Further, consider the appropriate role of Commissioner Selig (and the MLB Owners and the MLBPA) before, during and after the Bonds and BALCO-related ordeal, including the related criminal proceedings and the eventual Congressional hearings (which led, in turn, to Roger Clemens' testimony). How could/should Commissioner Selig and/or his "constituents"/stakeholders (the Owners, the MLBPA, the MLB Legal Office/General Counsel, and the fans, themselves) have acted to avert these "disasters"?

6. Consider how you would have reacted, if you were the Commissioner, to the following situations:

- Miami Heat guard Mario Chalmers and Memphis Grizzlies forward Darrell Arthur getting caught for sneaking women into their hotel room and smoking marijuana during the rookie-transition program.

- Dallas Stars Sean Avery publicly commenting on how his fellow NHL stars continue to date his former girlfriends.

- NFL quarterback Brett Favre retiring and unretiring.

Writing Exercise 4: "Confidential and Privileged Memorandum" Analyzing the Scope of the Commissioner's Authority in Each League[33]

In concluding this Chapter, please review all of the MLB, NFL and NBA Commissioners' decisions referenced in the assigned reading materials for Chapter 1, as summarized in the Course Study Guide in Appendix B, and consider the review of these decisions on appeal to courts and/or arbitrators. Compare and contrast the powers of the Commissioner in each of the three leagues. Write a confidential and privileged memorandum comparing the scope of the Commissioner's powers in each league and answering the following questions.

---

33. An "exemplar" student submission in response to this hypothetical can be found in the accompanying Teacher's Manual.

1.   Do you agree or disagree with the conclusion that the NFL Commissioner model is preferable to the MLB or NBA model? Cite specific CBA and case law references in support of your Group's conclusions.

2.   In particular, also consider the cases and arbitration decisions in which the Commissioner has been "reversed." Consider whether it is ever "in the best interests of the game" for outside third-parties, such as an arbitrator or a court to be able to "overrule" a Commissioner. Provide specific case-citation authority in support of your conclusion.

CHAPTER 2

CONSTRUCTING A PLAYER'S MARKET FROM CONTRACT TO ANTITRUST LAW

■ ■ ■

Introduction

Arguably, the most critical part of a Commissioner's duties is to ensure labor peace so that the league can continue to operate. After all, without skilled players, professional sports could not thrive and attract a fan base. Today, skilled players are in high demand, and teams compete vigorously for their services. Player contracts set forth the rules governing player mobility. These rules are integral to the league's ability to sustain a robust pool of player talent and to purportedly maintain competitive balance among the teams.

Leagues are concerned not only with player movement intraleague, but also with players movement from one league to another, rival league. In that sense, teams within each league are not only competing with one another for player talent, but each league is competing with upstart leagues in the same sport. Moreover, leagues that play different sports are competing for rare two sport athletes, such as Danny Ainge.

I. MAJOR LEAGUE BASEBALL'S RESERVE SYSTEM: EQUITABLE RELIEF AND "UNCLEAN" HANDS

Challenges to baseball's "reserve system,"[1] which gave teams the right to claim exclusive rights to some players and to renew player contracts, began at the start of the 1900s. The diametrically opposed fates of Nap Lajoie and Hal Chase offer vivid examples of how a court's interpretation of a player's contract, and the team's right to seek equitable relief, can affect a player's ability to pursue his livelihood. In *Philadelphia Ball Club v. Lajoie*,[2] the Philadelphia Phillies sued the talented second baseman when he jumped to the Philadelphia Athletics in the upstart American League. According to Lajoie, his departure was prompt-

---

1. See Weiler & Roberts, p. 138, for a description of the reserve system.
2. 202 Pa. 210, 51 A. 973 (1902).

ed by the discovery that though he was promised equal pay to Ed Delahanty, he earned $400 less than his teammate.

The skill that helped Lajoie succeed on the field propelled the court's reasoning in his loss in court. In granting the Phillies' request for a negative injunction—preventing Lajoie from playing for any other team in the state—the court relied on principles of contract law that favor negative injunctions in breaches of contracts for the delivery of services involving special knowledge, skill, and ability. The court explained that Lajoie's "place would be hard to fill with as good a player" and that though "He may not be the sun in the baseball firmament ... he is certainly a bright particular star." Therefore, Lajoie's skills were so difficult to substitute for his absence would result in irreparable injury to the Phillies. The court rejected the argument that the contract lacked mutuality because the Phillies had the power to terminate Lajoie with 10 days notice and also the sole power to renew his contract; Lajoie's large salary was enough to make the contract mutually beneficial.

Hal Chase fared much better than Lajoie in his dispute with the Chicago White Sox. Chase, like Lajoie, was also motivated to terminate his contract to jump to a rival league, the Federal Baseball League. When the White Sox sued Chase, the court was alive to the effect the draconian reserve system had on players, arguing that under the reserve system, "the baseball player is made a chattel" and subjected to "involuntary ... servitude."[3] *Chase* revisited the mutuality issue raised in *Lajoie*; while under the uniform player contract, teams could terminate player contracts upon 10 days notice, players, akin to "quasi peon[s]," were bound to "many obligations under the remarkable provisions" of the agreement. Therefore, "the absolute lack of mutuality, both of obligation and of remedy, in this contract, would prevent a court of equity from making it the basis of equitable relief by injunction or otherwise. The negative covenant, under such circumstances, is without a consideration to support it, and is unenforceable by injunction." Given the absolute power the White Sox possessed, it lacked "clean hands," and could not come to court to enforce such an inequitable system.

A. MAJOR LEAGUE BASEBALL'S CURRENT UNIFORM PLAYER CONTRACT

After many years of inconsistent and unpredictable court interventions, the reserve system was ultimately enshrined, via the collective bargaining process, in baseball's Uniform Player Contract (UPC). (See Appendix A, Section 1, for the current version of the MLB UPC.) Major League Baseball's Basic Agreement justifies the use of UPCs, as opposed to individually negotiating player contracts on the following grounds, in Rule 3(b) in the Basic Agreement, which states, "To preserve among Major League players and to produce the similarity of conditions necessary

---

3. American League Baseball Club of Chicago v. Chase, 86 Misc. 441, 149 N.Y.S. 6 (1914).

for keen competition, the contracts between all Major League Clubs and their players on the Major League Reserve List shall be in the form prescribed by any Basic Agreement in effect between Major Leagues and the Major Leagues Baseball Player's Association." If a club wishes to enter into a contract that differs from the UPC, it must seek the written approval of the Commissioner.

The UPC begins with the term, or the number of years for which the player is committed to the club. Teams typically have options to extend the term for a stated consideration, which is set forth as an Addendum to the UPC.

The next paragraph describes the compensation the player is to receive. Unless stated otherwise, players are paid in semimonthly installments beginning in the season covered by the term. If a player joins a team after the start of the season, the club is only obligated to pay the player a prorated portion of his salary. The player's agent may try to negotiate for a certain amount of "guaranteed" compensation, which must be paid except in certain situations, such as if the player is injured because he engaged in an ultrahazardous activity or if the player retires. A player's contract may also contain bonus or incentive clauses. Player compensation may be structured in the following ways:

(a.) payments for performing services for a Club in addition to skilled services as a baseball player;

(b.) cash, lump sum, payments made in accordance with agreed upon special covenants to compensate for trading a Player, releasing a Player, etc.;

(c.) the value of individual property rights granted to a Player by a Club;

(d.) any compensation for post-active Major League Baseball playing career employment; or

(e.) other payments not specifically made for performance as a Major League Baseball Player.

Players cannot, however, get bonuses for statistical performance bonuses; this might create a perverse incentive for players to sit out games.

The UPC also obligates players to participate in all reasonable promotional activities that will promote the welfare of the club or professional baseball. Along with promotional activities, players are required to permit their pictures to be taken, to permit those pictures to be used, on a non-exclusive basis, to promote the club, and to restrict public appearances in season to that which the clubs have consented in writing.

Paragraph 4 contains player representations regarding a player's ability. Each player represents that he has "exceptional and unique skill and ability as a baseball player and that his services are of such special, unusual and extraordinary character which gives them peculiar value that cannot be adequately compensated by damages at law and that the player's breach of this contract will cause the club irreparable harm and damages." The UPC explicitly reserves for teams the right to seek injunctive relief. Players also represent that they will maintain themselves in playing condition and that they do not suffer from physical or mental defects. Finally, players represent that they do not have a financial interest in the club.

The next section of the UPC, Paragraph 5, binds players to participate exclusively in major league baseball, and not for other professional baseball clubs or in other ultrahazardous sports. The untimely death of Yankee pitcher Cory Lidle in a single-engine aircraft in Manhattan drew attention to the category of "ultrahazardous sports," whether its structure ought to be changed. In October 2006, Lidle, while on a flying lesson, lost control of the plane he was flying and crashed into a high-rise condominium. In the weeks prior to his death, Lidle had assured both the Yankees and the media that flying was safe. The Yankees were acutely aware of the dangers of a player learning to pilot a plane, as that is how catcher Thurmon Munson was killed in 1979. Though Lidle's contract provided that the team could forego payment on his $6.3 million salary if Lidle died while flying, because the crash occurred after the end of the regular season, the pitcher had already been paid in full.

Paragraph 6 covers assignment of player contracts. Players agree that they may be traded to other clubs, pursuant to the rules set forth. Players also agree to have their medical information shared in association with assignments. A player's salary may not be decreased upon assignment, unless a player fails to report. Players are also granted moving allowances.

The lack of mutuality at issue in *Lajoie* and *Chase* is enshrined in Paragraph 7, Termination. Clubs can terminate player contracts if a player shall "fail, refuse or neglect to conform his personal conduct to the standards of good citizenship and good sportsmanship or to keep himself in first class physical condition or to obey the club's training rules; or fail, in the opinion of the club's management, to exhibit sufficient skill or competitive ability to qualify or continue as a member of the club's team . . ."

Disputes must be resolved in accordance with Paragraph 9. All disputes must be resolved according to the grievance procedure outlined in Article XI of the Basic Agreement, the exclusive remedy for the parties. According to the Basic Agreement, "Any Player who believes that he has a justifiable Grievance shall first discuss the matter with a representative of his Club designated to handle such matters, in an attempt to settle it. If the matter is not resolved as a result of such discussions, a written notice of the Grievance shall be presented to the Club's designated representative," who must given a written opinion to the player within 10 days. The player then has the opportunity to appeal the decision to the Labor Relations Department. The decision at Step 2 can be appealed once more to arbitration. The arbitrator's decision "shall constitute full, final and complete disposition of the Grievance appealed to it." Further, the club, league or Commission can make the findings public.

Paragraph 10 governs renewal of contracts, at issue in *Flood*. Though today the provision is understood differently, during Flood's time, teams were essentially ensured unlimited renewals. Chapter 6 discusses the current rules regarding player movement, salary arbitration, and free agency.

While individual players have difficulty significantly altering the content of the uniform contract, the MLBPA has more strength to challenge contract provisions. In March 2009, the MLBPA filed a grievance for arbitration regarding a clause in player contracts that required players to make a charitable donation from their salary. Approximately 22 teams inserted the clause into what amounts to about 109 players' contracts. The MLBPA is arguing that the clause does not inure to the benefit of the player, and thus cannot be required.

SUMMARY QUESTIONS

Consider the contrasting results in *Lajoie* and *Chase*.

1. With which decision do you agree? Which decision do you think is better-reasoned?

2. Should "freedom of contract" override a seeming lack of mutuality, or should the court inquire into whether the party seeking relied has "clean hands"?

3. Do you think that high player salaries can justify a lack of mutuality in obligations and remedies? Consider the following statement in *Gardella v. Chandler*: "... if the players be regarded as quasi-peons, it is of no moment that they are well paid; only the totalitarian-minded will believe that high pay excuses virtual slavery."[4]

4. If you were the MLB Commissioner, which decision would you decide was in the "best interests of baseball," over the long run?

5. Do you think equitable relief ought to be available at all, given that teams suffer "irreparable harm," or should players who are able to "buy out" their contracts be permitted to breach and pay liquidated damages in the amount of the salary paid to date?

Danny Ainge, whose athletic talents made him a sought after basketball and baseball prospect, tried the latter. Ainge, who was signed by the Toronto Blue Jays, continued to play basketball for Brigham Young University. His 25–points per game caught the eye of the Boston Celtics, who drafted him despite his commitment to the Blue Jays. After struggling in baseball, Ainge tried to repay the Blue Jays and jump to the Celtics, who were offering a much richer contract. Ainge's Blue Jays contract contained the same language that bound Lajoie; he had agreed to play only for the Jays, and not only for no other baseball team, but also for no other basketball, football or hockey team. According to Ainge, "I know I told a lot of people I was going to play baseball,

---

4. 172 F.2d 402, 409–10 (2d Cir. 1949).

but there's a difference between saying, 'I have a contract to play baseball,' and 'I have a contract to play baseball but I really don't want to,' which is how I felt."[5] The Celtics ultimately bought out the contract. Ainge went to the Celtics, and is currently their President of Basketball Operations.

II. "UNCLEAN HANDS" IN THE NATIONAL FOOTBALL LEAGUE AND IN INTER-LEAGUE NFL COMPETITION

The doctrine of "unclean hands," discussed in *Chase*, also affected the remedies available in challenges to player mobility in the NFL. Prospective NFL players are developed in college as "amateur athletes," and their interaction with the professional league is governed by the NCAA. NCAA rules prohibit players who have signed with professional teams from playing college football. Therefore, teams and players eager to commit to one another prior to the end of the college bowl season must keep any deals secret if the player wants to maintain eligibility. Furthermore, unlike baseball, which was immune from antitrust scrutiny for most of the 20th century, in *Radovich v. National Football League*, the court ruled that the NFL was subject to antitrust laws until Congress said otherwise. This weapon—a claim that the NFL was violating antitrust law—added another arrow into the quiver for players challenging restraints on movement in contracts.

In 1959, the University of Mississippi's Charles Flowers wanted to play in the New Year's Day Sugar Bowl after signing with the New York Giants, and got the team to agree to keep the deal secret.[6] When the Los Angeles Chargers of the upstart AFL expressed an interest in signing Flowers for more money, Flowers reneged on his agreement with the Giants and returned the checks received. The Fifth Circuit denied the Giants' request for an injunction on the grounds that " 'he who comes into equity must come with clean hands.' " Therefore, given that the Giants had agreed to keep Flowers' contract secret so that he could deceive the NCAA, the Giants could not come to court seeking relief.

Though the Giants were precluded from seeking a remedy in the Fifth Circuit, the Oilers were successful in getting an injunction against Ralph Neely in the Tenth Circuit.[7] Neely, like Flowers, had agreed to a deal with the Oilers prior to the New Year but wanted the contracts to be kept secret until after the Gator Bowl. When Neely began to negotiate with Dallas and withdrew from the deal with Houston, Houston went to court seeking an injunction. Neely missed the Gator Bowl and signed with Dallas. The Tenth Circuit found that the agreements with Houston were enforceable, given that it is not "unlawful or inequitable for college football players to surrender their amateur status" and Houston did not

---

5. Anthony Cotton, "The Courting of Danny Ainge," Sports Illustrated (October 12, 1981).

6. New York Football Giants, Inc. v. Los Angeles Chargers Football Club, Inc. (Flowers), 291 F.2d 471 (5th Cir. 1961).

7. Houston Oilers, Inc. v. Neely, 361 F.2d 36 (10th Cir. 1966).

have a legal duty to keep the deal secret. The court's decision also seems to be influenced by what it saw as Neely's own "unclean hands," for "The scheme to mislead Neely's school, his coaches, his team, and the Gator Bowl opponents, no doubt would have succeeded but for Neely's own double dealing with Dallas." The Court rejected Neely's argument that *Flowers* warranted a finding for Neely.

Unlike Flowers and Neely, who were seeking entry into the professional ranks during their legal battles, Bill Bergey was looking to move from the NFL to the Virginia Ambassadors of the WFL when the Bengals sued their linebacker.[8] Bergey, while he was still playing with the Bengals, signed a deal to play with the Ambassadors upon the conclusion of the contractual term with the Bengals. The Ohio court, relying on *Barry* and *Cunningham*, described in Part III, rejected the Bengals' claim and held that "it is not illegal for either the player or the sports organization, at the time when the player is under a valid contract to one team, to negotiate and enter into a contract with a different, competing, team and league, under the terms of which the player agrees to render his services at the expiration of his current contract." The lack of a legitimate public interest in granting the injunction, given that "restraints on competition are not favored," also weighed a finding in favor of Bergey.[9]

III. LEAGUE JUMPING AND CONTRACT RENEWAL IN THE NBA

Bergey's attempt to jump from the NFL to the WFL is illustrative of the lucrative contracts players can get by leaving the dominant league to join an upstart league in the United States. Brian Shaw of the Boston Celtics also exploited the opportunities for higher pay from league's abroad. After playing out his one-year contract with the Celtics, Shaw agreed to go play basketball in Italy for two years.

Representatives from the Celtics visited Shaw—who was unrepresented at the time—in Italy, and coaxed him into a deal to return to the United States. Shaw agreed, but upon reflection, realized that he could probably have bargained for a higher salary from the Celtics. Shaw tried to renege on his deal with the Celtics and failed to send his Italian team a termination letter. The dispute first went to arbitration, in which the arbitrator found that the Shaw had improperly breached his deal with the Celtics. Interestingly, Shaw tried to rely on the argument that his contract with Italy was void, given that it was signed while he was still playing for the Celtics. On appeal, the Court upheld the arbitrator's decision to honor the Celtics' contract and the district court's decision to grant injunctive relief.[10] The First Circuit rejected Shaw's argument that the Celtics'

---

8. Cincinnati Bengals v. Bergey, 453 F.Supp. 129 (Ohio 1974).

9. For information on the current challenges facing college football players seeking to move into the NFL, you may want to read Geoffrey R. Scott, ed., FOOTBALL Rising to the Challenge: The Transition from College to Pro (2006).

10. Boston Celtics v. Brian Shaw, 908 F.2d 1041 (1st Cir. 1990).

hands were "unclean" because they had traveled to Italy and signed him in a moment of weakness, because Shaw was a sophisticated party who had graduated from college.

While Brian Shaw tried to jump from the United States to Italy, Dick Barnett tried to jump from the NBA to the American Basketball League (ABL). Barnett, the Syracuse National's first-round draft pick, had played two years for the team and agreed over the telephone to play a third. Before an agreement was memorialized in writing and the first check was cashed, Barnett agreed to play for the Cleveland Pipers in the ABL, prompting the Nationals to seek an injunction.[11] As in *Lajoie*, the court granted a negative injunction to prevent Barnett from leaving his team. After conflicting testimony regarding Barnett's unique talents and skills, the court rested its conclusion on the grounds that Barnett's high salary indicates that "he is an outstanding professional basketball player of unusual attainments and exceptional skill and ability, and that he is of peculiar and particular value to plaintiff." Moreover, the court reasoned, "Damages at law would be speculative and uncertain and are practically impossible of ascertainment in terms of money." Finally, the court rejected the argument that the contract is in restraint of trade and that the contract lacked mutuality because the team could terminate him and then prevent Barnett from moving to another club.

The *Barry* and *Cunningham* cases relied upon in *Neely* also had the affect of limiting player movement. In *Washington Capitols Basketball Club, Inc. v. Barry*,[12] the Ninth Circuit upheld an injunction preventing Barry from playing for anyone other than the Washington Capitols of the ABA and preventing the San Francisco Warriors of the NBA from enforcing a contract with Barry. Barry began his career with the Warriors, but them jumped to the Oakland Oaks in the ABA. The Warriors won an injunction preventing Barry from playing for the Oaks for a year—the length of an option the Warriors had the right to exercise—but could not get additional equitable or monetary relief. The Oaks thereafter left Oakland and became the Washington Capitols. Barry wanted to stay on the West Coast and resigned a contract with the Warriors. This time, the Capitols sought and won injunctive relief to keep Barry from playing with the Warriors, and the court rejected Barry's "unclean hands" argument against the Oaks, who had taken Barry from the Warriors, as transferring to the Capitols.

Similarly, in *Munchak Corp. v. Cunningham*,[13] the court again addressed what transfers upon assignment when a team changes ownership. Cunningham had a "no trade" clause in his agreement with the Carolina Cougars of the ABA. When the Cougars were sold, Cunningham argued that the "no trade" clause was violated, and therefore the assignment was void. The Fourth Circuit, however, reasoned that the clause meant Cun-

---

11. Central New York Basketball, Inc. (Syracuse Nationals) v. Barnett, 181 N.E.2d 506 (Ohio 1961).

12. 419 F.2d 472 (9th Cir. 1969).

13. 457 F.2d 721 (4th Cir. 1972).

ningham could not be traded to another team, not that the contract could not be assigned to a new owner of the same team. While acts amounting to "unclean hands" do not transfer, the team under new ownership is not different enough to amount to a change in violation of a "no trade" clause.

Summary Questions

1.   Which of the three "major leagues" has had the best legally reasoned court decisions, based on your review? Which of the three major leagues has had the worst legally reasoned decisions?

2.   Do you think that cases like *Flowers* and *Neely*, where players are making the transition from amateur to professional, ought to be treated differently than cases such as *Bergey* and *Shaw*, when professional players are switching from one league to another?

3.   Do you agree with the grant of negative injunctions because player skills are unique? Or, do you think that players, or interested teams, ought to be able to "buy out" contracts for a stipulated amount?

4.   Today, to avoid the problems that arise many of the cases above, collective bargaining agreements specify when teams and players can begin discussions with one another. Problems associated with amateur players retaining attorneys, financial (or other) advisors or agents and negotiating with professional teams still remain, and are heavily regulated by the NCAA. To close a loophole, the NCAA recently also deemed middle-school athletes "prospects," in addition to high school students, so that teams and agents could not contract with these young athletes. Do you think that Neely was properly found to be a sophisticated party? What if a high school athlete had signed a deal? A middle schooler's parents?

CHAPTER 3

THE BASEBALL "TRILOGY": *FLOOD V. KUHN* AND THE CREATION OF THE BASEBALL ANTITRUST EXEMPTION

■ ■ ■

Introduction

Major League Baseball developed for more than a century under the umbrella of a judicially-created antitrust "exemption," immunizing the league from many of the legal challenges faced by the NFL and the NBA. For nearly a hundred years, baseball player salary and movement was constrained by the reserve system.[1] When professional baseball first began, players could move from team to team freely at the expiration of a one-year contract.[2] To control their players, in 1879,[3] owners created a "gentleman's agreement" amongst themselves to permit each to reserve five of their own players.[4] By the 1880s, every player had the "reserve clause" in his contract,[5] permitting players to be "sold for as little as twenty five cents and traded for a bulldog, a bird dog, a turkey, and an airplane."[6] If a player tried to leave for another team, some courts were willing to grant negative injunctions prohibiting star players like Nap Lajoie from providing their services to anyone else.[7] This Chapter explores the creation, and subsequent judicial ratification, of the exemption. The Chapter concludes with the narrowing of the scope of the antitrust exemption with the 1998 Curt Flood Act. We will revisit the reserve system in Chapter 6, when we discuss the *Messersmith / McNally* arbitration decision.

Baseball's broad exemption from antitrust laws protected it from the reach of the Sherman Antitrust Act, enacted in 1890. Section 1 of the

---

1. Roger Abrams, The Money Pitch (2000), p. 26.

2. Thomas J. Hopkins, Arbitration: A Major League Effect on Players' Salaries, 2 SETON HALL J. SPORTS L. 301, 303 (1992).

3. Kenneth M. Jennings, Balls and Strikes: The Money Game in Professional Baseball 181 (1990).

4. Kevin A. Rings, Baseball Free Agency and Salary Arbitration, 3 OHIO ST. J. DISP. RESOL. 243, 245 (1947).

5. Id. at 303.

6. Kenneth M. Jennings, Balls and Strikes: The Money Game in Professional Baseball 181 (1990).

7. See e.g., Philadelphia Ball Club, Ltd. v. Lajoie, 202 Pa. 210, 51 A. 973 (1902)

Sherman Act states that any "contract, combination, or conspiracy in restraint of trade" is illegal.[8] Section 2 prohibits the effect to "monopolize or attempt or conspire to monopolize trade."[9] If a violation of the Sherman Act is found, the Clayton Antitrust Act (1914) provides the victorious plaintiff with the opportunity to get treble damages, and "shall recover threefold the damages by him sustained, and the cost of the suit, including a reasonable attorney's fee."[10] There are two standards of liability under the Sherman Act (which will be discussed in more detail in Chapter 4).

I.   FEDERAL BASEBALL CLUB OF BALTIMORE, INC. v. NATIONAL LEAGUE OF PROFESSIONAL BASEBALL CLUBS[11]

Prior to the merging of the American and National Leagues into Major League Baseball, the two leagues operated according to a "National Agreement." The Agreement provided that each league would honor the player contracts executed by the other. The leagues wanted to stop the destructive raiding of players. In 1913, the Federal League organized professional baseball games with players who were not under contract to American or National League. When the Federal League tried to join the National Agreement, the American and National Leagues refused to make the upstart league a party to the agreement. Barred from joining in the cooperative Agreement, the Federal League decided to engage in the type of practices the National Agreement was designed to prohibit. Federal teams began to induce players to jump to their league and signed players who were subject to the "reserve system" and obligated to play for their National or American league team for another year.

Seeking official sanction of its actions in the hopes of gaining legitimacy, and more talented players, the Federal League went to court and claimed that the National Agreement violated the Sherman Act. Had the Federal League prevailed, all player contracts subject to the National Agreement would have been void. As the judicial gears slowly turned, all Federal League teams except for Baltimore settled by entering into a "Peace Agreement" with the National and American leagues. The Federal League would be dissolved in exchange for a sum paid to each owner. Baltimore pursued the antitrust claim, and alleged that blacklists were used to preserve the reserve system, anchoring players to teams and restraining competition.

The dispute ultimately reached the Supreme Court. However, the Supreme Court refused to evaluate the reserve clause and the antitrust claims raised by Baltimore. Justice Holmes concluded that baseball was

8.   15 U.S.C. § 1.

9.   15 U.S.C. § 2.

10.   15 U.S.C. § 15.

11.   259 U.S. 200 (1922).

not interstate commerce. Though clubs crossed state lines when they competed against one another in games, the business of holding baseball games was purely a state affair. Player travel was found to be merely incidental to the business, and "personal effort, not related to production, is not a subject of commerce."[12] And thus, baseball was immunized from the application of the Sherman Act.

II.   TOOLSON v. NEW YORK YANKEES

Though courts may not have liked it, as evinced by the Second Circuit's statement that players are "quasi-peons" and that "it is of no moment that they are well paid,"[13] the Supreme Court was not willing to reverse itself and remove the antitrust exemption that it had created itself. In *Toolson v. New York Yankees*,[14] the Yankees successfully prevented George Toolson—who had been relegated to a minor league team he thought failed to maximize his chances to breaking into the majors—from playing for any other team. The Supreme Court stated that "if there are evils in this field which now warrant application to it of antitrust laws it should be by legislation."[15]

Toolson also states that baseball has developed in reliance on the antitrust exemption, and that it can not strip it of the exemption now. The court explained that in *Federal Baseball*, "The court held that the business of providing public baseball games for profit between clubs of professional baseball players was not within the scope of federal antitrust laws. Congress has had the ruling under consideration but has not seen fit to bring such business under these laws by legislation having prospective effect. The business has thus been left for thirty years to develop, on the understanding that it was not subject to antitrust legislation." As the Supreme Court's commerce clause and antitrust jurisprudence developed over the next twenty years, yet another challenge to the judicial holding that baseball was not interstate commerce was presented in *Flood v. Kuhn*.

III.   FLOOD v. KUHN[16]

The final courtroom battle over the reserve clause came in the 1972 decision *Flood v. Kuhn*.[17] Curt Flood was traded from the St. Louis Cardinals to the Philadelphia Phillies, but did not want to go play in Philadelphia. Despite his dissatisfaction with the trade, Flood was obligat-

---

12.   Id.

13.   Gardella v. Chandler, 172 F.2d 402, 409–10 (2d Cir. 1949).

14.   346 U.S. 356 (1953).

15.   Id.

16.   For more information on Curt Flood's long and tortured battle with the reserve system, you may want to read Brad Snyder, A Well–Paid Slave: Curt Flood's Fight for Free Agency in Professional Sports (2006).

17.   407 U.S. 258 (1972).

ed to go to the Phillies because of the reserve clause in the standard player contract. When the contract was assigned, the Phillies were also assigned the right to compel Flood to play the following season. Angered that he was traded from the St. Louis Cardinals in 1969, Flood recalled, "If I had been a food-shuffling porter, they might at least given me a pocket watch. But all I got was a call from a middle-echelon coffee drinking ... Was I not entitled to a gesture from the general manager himself? ... In the hierarchy of living things, [baseball players] rank with poultry."[18] But his legal petition, claiming that the reserve clause violated federal and state antitrust laws and also violated the Thirteenth Amendment's prohibition on involuntary servitude, was to no avail.

Though by this point the court recognized that baseball "is a business and it is engaged in interstate commerce,"[19] the five-justice majority, written by Justice Blackmun, declined to remove the archaic antitrust exemption because "It is an aberration that has been with us now for a half a century."[20] Congress had not yet reversed its position that "Experience points to no feasible substitute [to the reserve clause] to protect the integrity of the game or to guarantee a comparatively even competitive struggle."[21] Justice Blackmun's opinion concluded with the following explanation: "If there is any inconsistency and illogic [in baseball's antitrust exemption but football's and boxing's subjection to antitrust laws], it is an inconsistency and illogic of long standing that is to be remedied by the Congress and not by this court. If we were to act otherwise, we would be withdrawing from the conclusion as to Congressional intent made in *Toolson*.... Under these circumstances, there is merit in consistency though some might claim that beneath the consistency is a measure of inconsistency." According to one commentator, at least in the courts, "history had won out over logic and consistency."[22]

Justice Marshall wrote a dissenting opinion, in which Justice Brennan concurred. Justice Marshall acknowledged the reality that the "essence of [the reserve] system is that a player is bound to the club with which first signs a contract for the rest of his playing days." Consequently, a player "cannot escape from the club except by retiring, and he cannot prevent the club from assigning his contract to any other club." Justice Marshall could not find the same merit in consistency, noting that antitrust laws are just as "important to baseball players as they are to football players, lawyers, doctors, or members of any other class of workers." Therefore, Justice Marshall concluded, *Federal Baseball Club* and *Toolson* ought to be overruled.

---

18. KURT FLOOD, THE WAY IT IS (1971).

19. Id.

20. Id.

21. 1952 Report of the Subcommittee on Study of Monopoly Power, of the House Committee of the Judiciary, H.R Rep. No. 2002, 82d Cong., 2d Sess., 229.

22. JENNINGS, supra note 16 at 186.

SUMMARY QUESTIONS

1. Out of *Federal Baseball Club, Toolson,* and *Flood,* which is the worst legally reasoned decision? On what grounds?

2. Are you less convinced by the reasoning of *Federal Baseball Club,* which said that baseball was not interstate commerce but focused in particular states, or by the reasoning of *Flood,* which leans heavily on stare decisis and Congressional inaction?

3. Do you agree with the majority opinion or the dissenting opinion in *Flood v. Kuhn*? On what basis? Do you think that the Supreme Court's consistency within baseball justifies the inconsistent treatment given to basketball and football players?

4. From your understanding of *Federal Baseball, Toolson,* and *Flood,* do you think that the antitrust exemption applies to the "business of baseball" in its entirety, or merely to the reserve clause? We will return to this issue in the context of franchise relocation in Chapter 8.

Legal Writing: Renegotiating Contracts—Making Big Changes With Just a Few Words

When drafting and editing contracts, you will have the power to affect significant legal consequences with just a few words. Adding in "materiality" or "reasonableness" qualifiers can significantly alter the obligations under a contract. Similarly, requiring that a particular set of facts be known "to a party's [actual/constructive] knowledge [after reasonable inquiry]," such as the medical and physical defects players might have, may help to protect a party if a problem later arises.

Writing Exercise 1: Renegotiating the MLB Uniform Player Contract on behalf of Curt Flood[23]

Consider the state of the law re: MLB's "reserve clause" and Curt Flood's / the MLBPA's quest for free agency, as the facts existed while the *Flood* case was on appeal to the U.S. Supreme Court.

As of that time, in 1971–72, consider the standard form Major League Baseball Uniform Player Contract ("UPC"), Constitution, Player Agreement and amendments thereto which appears in the Weiler Third Edition Supplement.

In particular, pay attention to the clauses in that Uniform Player Contract (previously referenced in Chapter 2) which would most directly affect Curt Flood as he decided whether or not to accept his trade / "assignment" from the St. Louis Cardinals to the Philadelphia Phillies, rather than fight for "free agency" as the MLBPA prevailed upon him to do.

Specifically, at the time of Flood's making that decision and appealing his case to the Supreme Court, how would you negotiate and draft the following paragraphs in the Uniform Contract:

---

23. An "exemplar" student submission in response to this hypothetical can be found in the accompanying Teacher's Manual.

(a.) Paragraph 3 re: player loyalty and baseball promotion/public appearances;

(b.) Paragraph 4 re: player representations;

(c.) Paragraph 7 re: Termination;

(d.) Paragraph 9 re: disputes and publication; and

(e.) Paragraph 10 re: renewals.

Also consider the Sample A Addendum to the Uniform Player's Contract, Sections A and B, with particular attention being paid to Curt Flood's early 1970's "misconduct" and/or inability/incapacity to perform his baseball services at an MLB-acceptable level with the Washington Senators.

After you consider these clauses, consider what changes to the current Form's clauses Flood's counsel would require, while Flood considers whether to accept his trade / assignment to the Philadelphia Phillies in 1969, or to sit out a year and seek free agency on behalf of the MLBPA.

On MLB's side, consider what edits to the current language you would recommend to the MLB Commissioner / owners, in an attempt to avoid a reversal against MLB by the Supreme Court in *Flood v. Kuhn*. In so doing, assume fairly equal "bargaining power," because of the MLB's fear of losing the "antitrust exemption," if Flood should win his Supreme Court case.

Assume the role of General Counsel to the MLBPA, and prepare a "Confidential/Privileged" memorandum explaining what final black-line edits you believe the MLBPA should insist upon (or strike!), and why.

The following is an example of how students have addressed Writing Exercise 1: Renegotiating the MLB Uniform Player Contract on behalf of Curt Flood.

Table of Contents

e. (§ 4a) Player Representations (Ability): Modification of section.

f. (§ 5a) Service: No competition for other leagues until end of championship season.

g. (§ 6a) Assignment: Assignment and reassignment to other Clubs conditioned on player approval.

h. (§ 7) Termination: Modification of grounds for termination by both player and Club.

i. (§ 9a) Rules: Requirement of lack of abridgement by other provisions of contract itself.

j. (§ 9c) Publication: Prevention of publication of findings of any inquiry, investigation or hearing.

k. (§ 10a) Renewal: Requirement of Club to offer new contract based on fair market value for Player services.

l. Addendum: Modification of Addendum.

2. **Proposed UPC Black–Lined Edits by MLB General Counsel**

a. (§ 3b) Baseball Promotion: Prevention of Player involvement in Promotions which are harmful to the Club or the League.

b. (§ 5b) Service (Other Sports): Participation in Other Sports is grounds for contract termination and suit by Club.

c. (§ 7b) Termination: Modification of grounds for termination by Club.

d. (§ 10a) Renewal: Right of Club to match offers by other clubs.

3. **Memo to the MLBPA re: UPC**

Proposed Black–Lined Edits by Flood's Counsel:

The following are changes to the Uniform Player Contract proposed by counsel for Curt Flood in 1969. These changes would be required by Curt Flood in order for him to accept his trade to the Philadelphia Phillies in 1969.

Payment: Client desires to ensure that the minimum rate of payment for MLB players, referenced herein as set forth in Article VI(B)(1) of the Basic Agreement between the major league clubs and the MLBPA, is satisfactory to both the client and the MLBPA. Client's acceptance of the contract is therefore subject to approval of this minimum rate of payment by both Flood and the MLBPA.

Loyalty: Client wishes to modify the term "first-class physical condition" to "condition suitable for the playing of baseball." It has been well-established throughout baseball history by players such as Babe Ruth to Cecil Fielder to Bartolo Colon, that success on the baseball field does not necessarily require a player to be in first-class physical condition. Client also wishes to strike the term "pledges himself to the American public," as the term is very vague and the player should not be required to owe a duty to the American public when he is only signing a contract with the Club. (See Mahmud Abdul–Rauf case for dangers of including this language in the contract).

Baseball Promotion: Client desires to condition participation in "any and all reasonable promotional activities of the Club and Major League Baseball" upon the Player receiving reasonable compensation for such services. Clubs stand to derive incremental revenue from promotional activities, and it is reasonable for the Player to be compensated for his role in generating this revenue.

Further, with regard to the clause specifying compliance with "all reasonable requirements of the Club respecting conduct and service," client requests a specific delineation of the Club's requirements respecting conduct and service of the team and players.

Pictures and Public Appearances: Client desires to strike the clause in this section specifying that the Player must obtain written consent of the Club in order to make public appearances, participate in radio or television programs, permit his picture to be taken, or write or sponsor newspaper articles, magazine articles or commercial products. Client believes that as a citizen and free individual he should have the right to make such appearances and to sponsor such products as he sees fit. While the team may own the rights to the Club name and logo, the player should retain the right to publicize his own name and to derive the benefits associated with his individual good name.

Further, client requests the following addition to the end of the section: "The Player shall be permitted to write and publish autobiographical books and magazine articles and to receive full profits from such endeavors."

Player Representations:

Ability: Client desires to modify this section to read as follows: "The Player agrees that, in addition to other remedies, the Club shall be entitled to injunctive and other equitable relief to prevent material breach of this contract by the Player, only if such material breach would cause the Club irreparable harm which cannot be cured by the Player. Such injunctive and other equitable relief shall include, among others, the right to enjoin the Player from playing baseball for any other person or organization within Major League Baseball during the term of his contract." The Player believes that in some cases the Club can be compensated for the loss of the Player in damages at law, thus there is no need to entirely rule out the possibility of such an outcome as the original language would do.

Service: Client desires to modify this section to state that "The Player agrees that, while under contract, and prior to expiration of the Club's right to renew this contract, he will not play baseball otherwise than for the Club until the completion of the Club's playing season. The completion of the Club's playing season is defined as either the point in time when the Club terminates its regular season if the Club does not qualify for the playoffs, or the point in time when the Club either is eliminated from the playoffs or wins the World Series if the team qualifies for the playoffs. Upon completion of the team's season, the Player shall be free to play in other leagues or in other games. The player may also participate in post-season games under the conditions prescribed in the Major League Rules." As leagues such as the Dominican Winter League gain popularity, Player wishes to preserve his right to participate in such leagues and practice his profession when it does not interfere with his obligations to the Major League Club.

Assignment: Client desires to modify this section to read "Any assignment of the Player's contract by the Club and any reassignment by any assignee Club to any other Club in accordance with the Major League Rules shall be subject to approval by the Player. Upon the Player's showing of reasonable cause for such veto, any such assignment or reassignment shall be void. The Club and the Player may, without obtaining special approval, agree by special covenant to limit or eliminate the right of the Club to assign this contract." Client wishes to preserve his contractual expectation of performing his duties for the Club with whom he contracted. If he is assigned to another Major League Club or Minor League Club, he wishes to have input into the decision since he never contracted to play baseball with this new third-party entity.

Termination:

By Player: Client desires to add the following to the end of this section: "The Player may also terminate this contract due to any and all of the following occurrences: i) a material change in the Player's playing conditions, which shall include but not be limited to change in team ownership or change of the Club manager; ii) mistreatment of the Player by the Club manager, coaches, or the team owner(s); and iii) continued poor performance by the club (defined as the team having a winning percentage of less than .400 for a period of two years or longer)." This clause reinforces the Player's contractual expectation in signing a contract with the Club. If the circumstances change such that Player is not able to perform his duties in the circumstances under which the contract was made, the Player should have the ability to remove himself from the contract. The Club has the mirror image of this right with respect to the Club's contractual expectation of the Player under Section 7(b)(2).

Client also desires to add the following clause: "The Player may terminate this contract by buying out the contract in full. Contract buyout shall be defined as the Player's paying to the Club the full amount of salary remaining on the contract, upon which the Player shall be released from his contract and able to sign with other Clubs." This will in essence restore both parties to their pre-contractual state, with the Club receiving the money that it would have spent on the Player in the future.

By Club: Client desires to strike clause (1) of this section as a basis for termination of the Player's contract.

Rules: Client seeks to modify the first sentence of this section to read "The Club and the Player agree to accept, abide by and comply with all provisions of the Major League Constitution, and the Major League Rules, or other rules or regulations in effect on the date of this Uniform Player's Contract only if such provisions do not abridge or substantially modify the provisions of this contract . . ." The Player wishes to ensure that the understanding reached under this contract will remain intact, and that changes in the Major League Constitution or Major League Rules will not affect his rights as agreed to under this contract.

Publication: Client seeks to modify this section to read "Neither any member of the Club nor the Commissioner may make public the findings, decision and record of any inquiry, investigation, or hearing held or conducted concerning the Player, unless the Player provides express approval regarding such public disclosure." The Player has a right to privacy and the League and Club may not use any investigations it conducts as public leverage against the Player. Failure to modify the provision in such a manner may lead to further instances of club owners using private investigations to pressure or publicly humiliate players who have fallen out of favor with the Club, such as Yankees owner George Steinbrenner did with Dave Winfield by hiring a private investigator named Howard Spira to dig up dirt on Winfield.

Renewal: Client desires to modify 10(a) of this section to read: "If the Player has not exercised his right to become a free agent as set forth in the Basic Agreement, the Club may instruct the Office of the Commissioner to tender to the player a contract for the term of the next year . . . If the player's previous contract has terminated, and such contract tendered to the Player is a new contract, the Club and Player shall then enter into good faith negotiations to establish the final contract. If prior to the March 1 next succeeding said December 20, the Player and Club have not agreed upon the terms of such final contract . . . the Club shall have the right to renew this contract for the period of one year but only at fair market value for the player's services, to be validated at the player's request by an independent arbitrator . . . The Club shall have this ability to renew the Player's contract only once . . ." The current provision allows the Club to unilaterally determine the Player's salary for the following year, and to also perpetually renew the Player's contract provided he doesn't exercise his right to be a free agent. The modified provision allows an independent arbitrator to check that the Player is receiving fair compensation for his services, and gives the Club this ability to renew only once at the end of the Player's initial contract.

Addendum: Client desires to modify Section A to read "(1) Retirement as an active Player not due to pending litigation or a change in circumstances as defined in the 'Termination By Player' section" and "(5) Physical or mental incapacity or death." Player wishes to be protected in case he is forced out of baseball and is currently pursuing his rights in court. Player also does not wish to give Club additional reasons to void his contract, providing that he is physically and mentally capable of performing his duties as specified in the contract. Client wishes to strike the part of Section B that reads "provided, however, that the foregoing agreement to continue the Player's salary applies only in those situations where insufficient skill or competitive ability does not result from the Player's misconduct or the Player's unlawful or contractually prohibited acts, which include the following acts." If the Player has broken his contract, adequate legal remedies exist to enforce the contract and recover damages. The Player does not want the Club to be able to terminate his contract for reasons outside of the scope of the contract. The Club should not have additional means of terminating the contract if the Player is able to fulfill his duties under the contract.

Proposed Black–Lined Edits by MLB General Counsel:

The following are changes to the MLB Unifrom Player's Contract required by the MLB Commissioner and the Owners. These changes are intended to further the best interests of the game with regard to player compensation, performance, and the continued success of the major leagues.

In order of importance, the right of the Club to match offers from other Clubs upon the Player's exercising his right to free agency is most important to the MLB. This right enables Clubs to gauge market demand for a player and to resign those players who are most valuable to the Club, stemming the departure of players and the resulting negative impact upon the Club, the city and Club fans. The modification of secondary importance to the club is the addition of grounds for termination based on harmful or offensive behavior by players. Such behavior is detrimental to the game's best interests and reduces fan appreciation and support for the game. Of lesser priority to the league are limitations on baseball promotion and right of termination/lawsuit for participation in Other Sports.

Baseball Promotion: Client desires to add the following clause to the end of this section: "The Player expressly agrees not to participate in promotions which criticize, disparage, or reflect negatively upon the Club or Major League Baseball. Participation in such promotions shall be ground for sanctions being placed on the Player by the Club and/or the League." The Club's image is intimately tied to its overall value, thus the Player as an employee of the Club should not be able to tarnish that image and the overall value of the Club.

Other Sports: Client desires to add the following clause at the end of this section: "Such engagement without the written consent of the Club shall constitute material breach of the contract. Injuries sustained through participation in the activities referenced herein shall be grounds for termination of this Contract by the Club. The Club shall also reserve the right to sue for damages resulting from injuries sustained by the Player through participation in such activities, not to be limited by the amount of future compensation remaining on the Player's contract."

Termination: Client desires to add the following clause as section 7(b)(2) as a condition for termination: "(2) engage in behavior either on or off the playing field which is harmful or detrimental to the Club or Major League Baseball, including, but not limited to i) publicly disparaging other players, coaches or managers; ii) publicly disparaging fans; iii) committing a felony; iv) making racial slurs; v) engaging in lewd behavior; or vi) engaging in behavior detrimental to the best interests of the Club or Major League Baseball."

Renewal: Client desires to add the following section as section 10(c) within the Renewal section: "If the Player exercises his right to become a free agent, the Player shall have the right to seek contract offers from other Clubs between the conclusion of the championship season and January 15. Upon the earlier of the Player's having concluded this solicitation of offers from other clubs, or January 15, the Player shall submit such offers to the Club. The Club shall then have the right to substantially match such alternative offers. If the Club's offer is the same or better than the best of such alternative offers, according to a sum analysis of all material terms, the Club shall have the right to re-sign the Player. If the Club's offer is inferior to the best of such alternative offers, the Player shall have the right to sign with only the team which offered the best alternative offer." This would create a restricted free agency system similar to that currently employed by the NBA. This would allow the Club to retain the Player that it originally drafted, provided that it is willing to pay the market price for that Player.

Memorandum (Privileged/Confidential)

To: President of the MLBPA
Date: 9/20/1971
Re: MLB Uniform Player Contract

President of the MLBPA,

As requested, we have prepared a final recommendation regarding the modifications and additions to the MLB Uniform Player Contract which would be required for the MLBPA to sign the new contract in 1971. These changes are in the best interest of the players, the league and the game itself, and promote a sustainable framework which aligns incentives and ensures outstanding player and Club performance.

Executive Summary: The desired modifications to the UPC center upon the establishment of minimum pay scales for players of all levels, the establishment of the Player's right to approve assignment to another Club, the establishment of the Player's right to buy out his contract, and the Player's ability to exercise his right to free speech. The overall intention of these changes is to increase the level of mutuality between Players and Clubs, and to ensure that MLB Players, like employees in a range of other professions, have a say in for whom they work and how they are compensated.

The most important modification is the Player's right to approve assignment; this change to the existing reserve clause enables players to have a say in where they pursue their profession. The Player's right to buy out his contract is also important, because it provides mutuality in allowing the Player to move to a more desirable location, just as a Club can trade a player if in the Club's interest. Of lower priority, but still of significant importance to the League, are the establishment of minimum pay scales and the condition that Players be free to express their views on the Club and the MLB.

- **Payment:** The minimum rates of payment to major league players (Article VI(B)(1)), minor league players signing a second or subsequent Major League contract or having at least one day of Major League service (Article VI(B)(2)), and minor league players having no Major League service should be established at market rates which represent equitable rates for player services. In addition, binding scaled salary ranges (with wide bands to allow for flexibility) should be established for all player levels, which will serve as benchmarks for salary negotiations between players and clubs. As was illustrated in "A Well–Paid Slave," Brad Snyder, A Well–Paid Slave (2006) players ranging from All–Stars like Vida Blue to bench players and minor leaguers have been underpaid relative to their skill levels over a long period, due to their having no recourse but to sign with their current team. As in *Lajoie,* where the Philadelphia club successfully sued to enjoin its star player from joining another club for better contract terms, player contracts lack mutuality, and excellent players are particularly constrained because their unique skills have led courts to deem them irreplaceable for their current teams. The establishment of binding pay scales, which shall serve as floors for payment to players of a given skill level, increase the mutuality in contracts between players and teams and increase player incentive to perform well for the Club.

- **Loyalty:** The Player's agreement to conform to "high standards of personal conduct, fair play and good sportsmanship" should be conditioned upon the player's ability to exercise his right to free speech. As evidenced by Curt Flood's exercise of his right to free speech in *The Way It Is*, and the subsequent backlash against Flood from baseball men such as manager Ted Williams and commissioner Bowie Kuhn, a player's right to express his views has often been abrogated in Major League Baseball. This section should be amended by adding the following condition at the end of the section: "None of the foregoing shall be construed as to limit the Player's right to express his views in exercise of his First Amendment privilege."

- **Ability:** This section, as it currently reads, places Major League players in a position which is uniquely disadvantageous. Because of MLB's antitrust exemption, players do not receive rights which would be commensurate with that of a free labor market in which they can seek out the most beneficial place of employment. At the same time, due to their exceptional skill and ability which gives them peculiar value which cannot be adequately compensated at law, they are by default bound to their employer clubs, as was shown in the *Lajoie* case. At the same time, not all courts have given major league clubs unfettered ability to re-sign players. For example, in the *Chase* case the court sided with a player seeking to switch leagues, ruling that the player's contract lacked mutuality. This modified section (below) removes the default assumption that all players are irreplaceable because of their exceptional skill. Clubs seeking an injunction would be required to both i) show irreparable harm in the individual case, as in the *Barnett* case in the NBA, and ii) also show that the player's right to cure, in the form of buying out his contract, is not sufficient to repair the injury to the Club.

  This section should be modified to read as follows: "The Player agrees that, in addition to other remedies, the Club shall be entitled to injunctive and other equitable relief to prevent material breach of this contract by the Player, only if such material breach would cause the Club irreparable harm which cannot be cured by the Player. Such injunctive and other equitable relief shall include, among others, the right to enjoin the Player from playing baseball for any other person or organization during the term of his contract."

- **Assignment:** This section should be modified to read as follows: "Any assignment of the Player's contract by the Club and any reassignment by any assignee Club to any other Club in accordance with the Major League Rules shall be subject to approval by the Player. Upon the Player's showing of reasonable cause for such veto, any such assignment or reassignment shall be void. The Club and the Player may, without obtaining special approval, agree by special covenant to limit or eliminate the right of the Club to assign this contract." The right of a Major League Club to assign a player to another Club without his consent is a right which is unique to professional sports, which uniquely deprives a player of the right to pursue his profession in the manner in which he sees fit. When the Supreme Court decided *Federal Baseball* in 1922, holding that Major League Baseball was not interstate commerce and therefore was exempt from antitrust laws, and then affirmed its ruling in *Toolson* by holding that the doctrine of stare decisis required the Court to continue to honor baseball's antitrust exemption, it placed major league players in a situation where they are prevented from having the basic right to prevent relocation to another employment situation which is disadvantageous. This is a situation which violates basic principles of equity, and which, in Curt Flood's words, "violates my basic rights as a citizen, and is inconsistent with the laws of the U.S. and of the several states." Basic notions of contract law are also violated, as Players enter into contracts with Clubs with the expectation that they will perform their services for that particular Club under a particular set of circumstances. When the Club takes unilateral actions to materially change these conditions, it is fundamentally unfair under principles of contract law to hold the Player to the contract. Furthermore, courts have held that a Club's right to resign or assign a player is not absolute, as in the *Chase* case. Therefore, this section should be modified to subject any assignment or reassignment to approval by the player. If the player is able to show cause for vetoing such assignment, such as a significant detrimental impact on player performance, such assignment shall be void.

● **Termination:** This section should be modified to read as follows: "The Player may terminate this contract by buying out the contract in full. Contract buyout shall be defined as the Player's paying to the Club the full amount of salary remaining on the contract." This modification serves to increase the mutuality in the Uniform Player Contract, which as currently written is significantly weighted in favor the league. While the club may terminate the contract based on multiple grounds, such as the player's failing to adhere to Club and league standards, failing to exhibit sufficient skill, or neglecting to render services, the player's grounds for termination are primarily the narrow avenue of the club defaulting on payment, which is subject to remedy. Courts in cases such as the *Chase* case, the *Haywood* case in the NBA and the *Neely* case in the NFL have all affirmed a player's right to play for a chosen team and have limited a Club's ability to restrict player movement. A buyout provision, which provides the club full compensation for the value of the player's services, is sufficient to provide the club with full benefit of its bargain while enabling the player to retain his basic rights as an employee.

Conclusion: These changes are required for the MLBPA to achieve sufficient representation of players' rights within the UPC, and to ensure that players are able to pursue their profession in a manner which is commensurate with their skills and abilities.

Writing Exercise 2: Brief to the Supreme Court in Flood v. Kuhn[24]

Imagine that instead of agreeing to a new contract, Curt Flood decides to pursue his case to a "Super Supreme Court," which will review the decision in *Flood v. Kuhn*. As a clerk to the justices on the "Super

---

24. An "exemplar" student submission in response to this hypothetical can be found in the accompanying Teacher's Manual.

Supreme Court," you have been assigned to review the case and draft an opinion.

Draft a section of the judicial opinion presenting the best arguments as to why the reserve system ought to be abolished. Address the arguments raised by Justice Marshall in his dissent.

Also draft a section of the judicial opinion presenting the best arguments in favor of Commissioner Kuhn and against Flood. Address the arguments raised by Justice Blackmun in his majority opinion.

Finally, conclude the opinion with a decision in favor of either Flood or Commissioner Kuhn. Explain the basis of your decision, and why you reject the losing party's arguments.

As usual, "exemplar" responses to these drafting exercises are set forth in the Teacher's Manual.

CHAPTER 4

THE CREATION OF THE "NON-STATUTORY LABOR EXEMPTION" AND ITS APPLICATION TO THE NFL AND NBA

■ ■ ■

Introduction

Unlike MLB, which developed under the shelter of an antitrust exemption, the NFL and the NBA had to ensure they complied with the prohibition on conspiracies in restraint of trade. As explained at the start of Chapter 3, in *Radovich v. National Football League*, the court ruled that the NFL was subject to antitrust laws until Congress said otherwise. Similarly, in 1971, the year before *Flood v. Kuhn* was decided, the Supreme Court held in *Haywood v. NBA* that the NBA does not have an exemption from antitrust laws.

Recall from Chapter 3 that Section 1 of the Sherman Act states that any "contract, combination, or conspiracy in restraint of trade" is illegal.[1] Section 2 prohibits the effect to "monopolize or attempt or conspire to monopolize trade."[2] If a violation of the Sherman Act is found, the Clayton Antitrust Act (1914) provides the victorious plaintiff with the opportunity to get treble damages, and "shall recover threefold the damages by him sustained, and the cost of the suit, including a reasonable attorney's fee."[3] There are two standards of liability under the Sherman Act. First, a restraint may be found to be *per se* illegal. If a court cannot determine as a matter of law than a restraint is *per se* illegal, it then engages in a "rule of reason" analysis to determine if the restraint is "unreasonable," i.e. whether a practice's anticompetitive effects outweigh its procompetitive effects.

Between 1966 and 1991, the NFL had to defend over sixty antitrust suits.[4] But to view each team as a separate entity is to oversimplify the picture. The three major leagues are a unique amalgamation of competitors—each team competes for skilled players and fan attention—and

---

1. 15 U.S.C. § 1.

2. 15 U.S.C. § 2.

3. 15 U.S.C. § 15.

4. J. Gerba, Instant Replay, A Review of the Case of Maurice Clarett, the Application of the Non-Statutory Labor Exemption, and its Protection of the NFL Draft Eligibility Rule, 73 FORDHAM L. REV. 2383 (2005).

cooperators—each team needs to operate according to the same rules, agree on a schedule, etc. Consequently, the jurisprudence governing the sports industry could not merely treat the teams as competitors, but recognizes the interest labor and employers have in creating certain league-wide policies. These league-wide policies pertain to issues such as age eligibility, salary caps, player drafts, and free agency. This labor interest is protected by the statutory and non-statutory labor exemption, and defended by player's unions.

The 1950s and 1960s witnessed the creation of players' unions: the NBPA in 1954, the NFLPA in 1956, the MLBPA in 1965, and the NHLPA in 1967. Protected by the statutory labor exemption in the Clayton Act, these groups were able to organize and perform activities such as coordinated strikes. When antitrust suits began to riddle leagues, however, it was the leagues who invoked the nonstatutory labor exemption, with they hoped would protect practices included in their collectively bargained agreements from antitrust scrutiny. The cases in this chapter discuss how courts have applied this exemption to these agreements, provided that certain requirements are met. Court's have been driven by the aim to encourage parties to resolve issues—such as the appropriate restrictions on player movement—through arm's length collective bargaining.

I.   THE STATUTORY AND NON–STATUTORY LABOR EXEMPTIONS

Before Congress added provisions establishing the statutory exemption, courts viewed unions as groups of competitors pursuing common goals. Therefore, union activity constituted a combination in restraint of trade under the Sherman Act.[5] In 1908, the Supreme Court held that a union violated the Sherman Act by organizing a nationwide boycott of nonunion-made hats, ancillary to an organizational strike against a hat manufacturer.[6] Enduring labor strife and unrest prompted Congress to include, as part of the 1914 Clayton Act, specific exemptions from antitrust laws for particular conduct arising out of a labor dispute. The statutory exemption is found in section 6, which states the following:

> "The labor of a human being is not a commodity or article of commerce. Nothing contained in the antitrust laws shall be construed to forbid the existence and operation of labor, agricultural, or horticultural organizations, instituted for the purposes of mutual help, and not having capital stock or conducted for profit, or to forbid or restrain individual members of such organizations from lawfully carrying out the legitimate objects thereof; nor shall such organizations, or the members thereof, be held or construed to be illegal combinations or conspiracies in restraint of trade, under the antitrust laws."

---

5. Id.

6. Loewe v. Lawlor, 208 U.S. 274 (1908).

This explicit statutory exemption for employee unions was designed to provide employees with sufficient leverage to bargain at arm's length with management. Allowing this labor policy to trump antitrust laws would, according to the Supreme Court, put "equality before the law in the position of workingmen and employer as industrial combatants."[7] Putting it more directly in *Connell Construction Co. v. Plumbers & Steamfitters*,[8] the Supreme Court stated, "these statutes declare that labor unions are not combinations or conspiracies in restraint of trade, and exempt specific union activities, including secondary picketing and boycotts, from the operation of antitrust laws." Thus, the statutory exemption protects employee unions from the scrutiny of antitrust laws.

The statutory exemption does not, however, mention anything about the agreements that result from this bargaining. Thus, the Supreme Court complemented the statutory labor exemption with the nonstatutory labor exemption to protect collectively bargained agreements from antitrust scrutiny, so long as certain conditions are met. The Court articulated its rationale for this exemption in *Brown v. Pro Football*[9] (discussed in further detail below), stating the following:

> "As a matter of logic, it would be difficult, if not impossible, to require groups of employers and employees to bargain together, but at the same time to forbid them to make among themselves or with each other *any* of the competition-restriction agreements potentially necessary to make the process work or its results mutually acceptable. Thus, the implicit exemption recognizes that, to give effect to federal labor laws and policies and to allow meaningful collective bargaining to take place, some restraints on competition imposed through the collective bargaining process must be shielded from antitrust sanction."

Therefore, while the statutory exemption protects the formation and activity of unions, the nonstatutory exemption protects the agreements reached between unions and employers. Both have played an important role in the development of the NFL and the NBA, neither of which benefited from the antitrust exemption that shielded MLB. As you read the discussions below in the remainder of Chapter 4, consider how the application of antitrust laws and the labor exemptions have shaped the development and strength of the players' unions in these leagues, as compared with MLB. Further consider the chronology of the cases, and how prior precedents affected subsequent outcomes.

In addition to the protection of the non-statutory labor exemption, the three major leagues have also benefited from protection from antitrust scrutiny in their television broadcasting. The 1961 Sports Broadcasting Act, codified at 15 U.S.C. § 1291, enacted in reaction to a Supreme Court

---

7. Duplex Printing Press Co. v. Deering, 254 U.S. 443 (1921).

8. 421 U.S. 616 (1975).

9. 518 U.S. 231 (1996).

decision holding that the NFL's pooling agreement to broadcast games with CBS violated antitrust laws, reads:

> The antitrust laws ... shall not apply to any joint agreement by or among persons engaging in or conducting the organized professional team sports of football, baseball, basketball, or hockey, by which any league of clubs participating in professional football, baseball, basketball, or hockey contests sells or otherwise transfers all or any part of the rights of such league's member clubs in the sponsored telecasting of the games of football, baseball, basketball, or hockey, as the case may be, engaged in or conducted by such clubs. In addition, such laws shall not apply to a joint agreement by which the member clubs of two or more professional football leagues, which are exempt from income tax under section 501(c)(6) of the Internal Revenue Code of 1986 [26 U.S.C.A. 501(c)(6)], combine their operations in expanded single league so exempt from income tax, if such agreement increases rather than decreases the number of professional football clubs so operating, and the provisions of which are directly relevant thereto.

Note that the Act as drafted applies only to television broadcasts, not cable, satellite, internet, or other new media broadcasts. When Congress begins to investigate the NFL for its internal governance, including its treatment of the New England Patriots upon discovery that the team had been taping opponents' practices in violation of league rules, it is the protection of the Sports Broadcasting Act that it threatens to revoke.

Interest in the Act was revived after the NFL announced the creation of the NFL Network, which is shown in many fewer homes than the channels on which games were previously broadcast. Senator Arlen Specter raised complaints that the NFL's antitrust exemption ought to revoked. Currently, NFL officials have various deals with CBS, NBC, FOX, and Disney, and a six-year, $24 billion broadcast and cable rights contract that end in 2011. Additionally, DirecTV will pay $700 million every year through 2010 for its "Sunday Ticket" package. The NFL has an eight-game Thursday-to-Saturday night package in-house, on its NFL Network.

FOX Sports and Turner Broadcasting System paid for the rights to Major League Baseball broadcasts through 2013, including exclusive national television rights for the World Series and All-Star Game to FOX and recasting MLB coverage on TBS to a broader, league-wide focus. The rights deal with FOX Sports grants the network rights to up to 26 regionalized Saturday baseball games of the week; the American League Championship Series in 2007, 2009, 2011 and 2013; and the National League Championship Series in 2008, 2010 and 2012. The deal with Turner Broadcasting grants the network the rights to air MLB Division Series Playoff games exclusively beginning next year—a first for a cable network.

NBA games are played on a variety of networks. For the 2008–2009, ABC has the right to air 30 regular season games, TNT paid for the 52 games, including the season opener, ESPN and ESPN2 have the right to multiple games, and NBA TV can broadcast 96 games. According to an article on the TNT and ABC deals, signed in 2007, "The NBA's new television contracts with ESPN/ABC and TNT include rights to technologies that have yet to be invented, an indication of the importance the deals place on newer forms of media."[10] ESPN/ABC and TNT will each be able to simulcast and offer video on-demand for games that air on its networks. These deals extend through the 2015–2016 season. In return for the broadcast rights, the NBA will receive about $930 million a year, an increase of more than 20 percent from the previous average of $767 million.

Before turning to an analysis of the relevant precedents in the sports industry, it is worth discussing the legal analysis that shaped these precedents. The discussion begins with two non-sports precedents handed down on the same day in 1965: *Local Union No. 189, Amalgamated Meat Cutters & Butcher Workmen of North America, AFL–CIO v. Jewel Tea Co.*[11] and *United Mine Workers of America v. Pennington.*[12] These two plurality opinions formally established the nonstatutory labor exemption, though the precise contours of the exemption still remain uncertain.

The litigation at issue in *Jewel Tea* arose out of the 1957 contract negotiations between the representatives of 9,000 Chicago retailers of fresh meat and seven union petitioners. During the bargaining sessions, the employer group presented several requests for union consent to a relaxation of the existing contract restriction on marketing hours for fresh meat, which forbade the sale of meat before 9 a.m. and after 6 p.m. in both service and self-service markets. The union rejected these suggestions. In turn, the union's own proposal retaining the marketing-hours restriction was ultimately accepted at the final bargaining session by all but two of the employers, National Tea Company and Jewel Tea Company. Jewel Tea Company asked the union to present to its membership, on behalf of it and National Tea, a counteroffer that included provision for Friday night operations. On the recommendation of the union negotiators, the union rejected the Jewel Tea offer and authorized a strike. Pressured by the impending strike, Jewel Tea accepted the contract previously approved by the rest of the industry. The jilted company then sued the union.

The Court was asked to decide whether the collective bargaining agreement between a butcher's union and grocery stores in the greater Chicago area was exempt from antitrust laws. In its landmark ruling, the Supreme Court held that the alleged violations were exempt from the antitrust laws because the particular hours of the day and days of the week were within the mandatory subjects of collective bargaining, as defined by the National Labor Relations Act. The Court stated that

---

10. http://www.usatoday.com/sports/basketball/2007–06–27–3096131424_x.htm

11. 381 U.S. 676 (1965).

12. Id.

"the marketing-hours restriction, like wages, and unlike prices, is so intimately tied to wages, hours and working conditions that the union's successful attempt to obtain that provision through bona fide, arm's-length bargaining in pursuit of their own labor union policies, and not at the behest of or in combination with non-labor groups, falls within the protection of the national labor policy, and is therefore exempt from the Sherman Act."[13]

Thus, given that the agreement between the butchers and the grocers touched upon an aspect intimately related to wages, hours and working conditions, it was protected from the scrutiny of federal antitrust laws.

In its next breath, the Court declined to extend exemption to the claim at issue in *Pennington*. A coal workers union agreed to abandon its efforts to control the working time of miners, not to oppose increases in mechanization, to help fund those increases, and to impose these terms "on all operators without regard to their ability to pay." In return, the union garnered higher wages resulting from increases in productivity due to mechanization. According to disgruntled miners, however, the objective of the agreement was to drive small operators out of business though a conspiracy between the union and the large operators to impose the agreed-upon wage and royalty scales upon the smaller, nonunion opera- tors, regardless of their ability to pay and regardless of whether or not the union represented the employees of these companies. In denying the application of the just created *Jewel Tea* exemption, the Court stated "[w]e have said that a union may make wage agreements with a multiem- ployer bargaining unit and may in pursuance of its own union interests seek to obtain the same terms from other employers.... But we think a union forfeits its exemption from the antitrust laws when it is clearly shown that it has agreed with one set of employers to impose a certain wage scale on other bargaining units."[14] Not only was the application of the agreement to other employees problematic, but the Court also took issue with the alleged conspiracy, stating that "[o]ne group of employers may not conspire to eliminate competitors from the industry and the union is liable with the employers if it becomes a party to the conspiracy. This is true even though the union's part in the scheme is an undertaking to secure the same wages, hours or other conditions of employment from the remaining employers in the industry."[15]

Ten years later, the Court similarly refused to apply the exemption to the agreement at issue in *Connell Construction Company, Inc. v. Plumbers and Steamfitters Local Union No. 100*.[16] In *Connell Construction*, a steamfitters union engaged in a campaign to convince general contractors to hire subcontractors that had a collective bargaining agreement with the union. When Connell Construction refused to sign, the union held a single

---

13.   Jewel Tea, 381 U.S. at 690.

14.   *Pennington*, 381 U.S. at 665.

15.   Id. at 666.

16.   421 U.S. 616 (1975).

picket that led 150 workers to walk off a job and halt construction. Faced with a dearth of employees, Connell Construction signed the agreement under protest and subsequently sued under the Sherman Act. In declining the apply the exemption, the Court found that "[l]abor policy clearly does not require . . . that a union have freedom to impose direct restraints on competition among those who employ its members."[17] The Court further found that the antitrust immunity offered by the statutory exemption for unilateral union activity was not offered by the nonstatutory exemption "when a union and a nonlabor party agree to restrain competition in a business market."[18] In both *Connell Construction* and *Pennington*, the Court upheld the exemption but declined to apply it to agreements between parties other than labor unions and employers, or to the extent that the agreement affects third parties that are not privy to the agreement.

II.   ANTITRUST ATTACKS AND LABOR UNREST IN THE NFL

Without the protection of an antitrust exemption, the NFL relied upon the protection of the nonstatutory labor exemption to shield practices put in place by the league. The NFL not only has a player's union, but the league operates through it's Management Council, founded in 1971. The Management Council is the "multiemployer bargaining unit" of the NFL, and it represents the NFL in setting the working conditions of the players. For example, the Management Council sets the salary, benefits, squad size, length of season, etc., though negotiations with the player's union. It is the agreement between the Management Council—the employer—and the Player's Association—the employees—that receives protection under the nonstatutory labor exemption.

The NFLPA and the NFLMC have had a storied history of labor disputes. At the expiration of each collective bargaining agreement, the NFLPA has attached the NFL's system for player acquisition in retention. The NFLPA went on strike in 1970 for two days, in 1974 for forty days, in 1982 for seven games, and in 1987 for three games.

Application of the nonstatutory exemption to the NFL was first tested in *Mackey v. NFL*[19] in 1976. The Eighth Circuit was asked to decide whether the Rozelle Rule should be exempt from antitrust scrutiny. The Rozelle Rule provided that when a player's contract with one time expired, any other team that wished to sign that player must pay compensation to his former team. If the teams could not agree on such compensation, the Commissioner was empowered to mandate compensation in the form of one or more draft picks. While the rule was unilaterally imposed by the

---

17. Id. at 622.

18. Id. at 623.

19. 543 F.2d 606 (8th Cir. 1976).

NFL on member clubs in 1963, it was incorporated by reference into the 1968 collective bargaining agreement.

The Eighth Circuit created a three-part test to determine whether the relevant labor policy deserves preeminence over federal antitrust policy; absent application of the nonstatutory labor exemption, this rule would be a clear illegal restraint on trade. The Court stated that the restraint must: (1.) primarily affect only parties to the related collective bargaining agreement; (2.) reflect a mandatory subject of collective bargaining, such as wages, hours, and other terms and conditions of employment; and (3.) result from bona fide, arm's-length bargaining. Under this analysis, the Court struck down the Rozelle Rule. Although it fulfilled the first two prongs of the test, it failed the third prong because there was no bona fide arm's length bargaining of a rule that predated the collective bargaining agreement, and the Court could find no quid pro quo for its inclusion into the collective bargaining agreement. Thus, while the nonstatutory labor exemption was held to apply to such collectively bargained agreements, this particular rule did not satisfy all of the Court's requirements under its tripartite test.

A year after *Mackey*, James "Yazoo" Smith challenged the NFL's draft system as an unreasonable restraint on player salaries.[20] Smith, an all-American defensive back for Oregon, was selected twelfth in the draft by the Washington Redskins in the 1968 draft. Smith suffered a serious, career-ending neck injury in the last game of his first professional season. He argued that but for the draft, he would have earned a market-rate salary for his services. Smith challenged the "no tampering" rule, which provides that no team is allowed to negotiate before the draft with any eligible player and teams cannot sign another team's pick. The district court found that the NFL draft was a "group boycott" in *per se* violation of antitrust laws, awarded him the difference between his actual compensation and the compensation he would have received on the free market.

The Circuit court began its analysis of the NFL's practice by examining whether or not the draft is a *per se* illegal "group boycott." Acts rising to the level of a *per se* restraint are those which "because of their pernicious effect on competition and lack of any redeeming virtue are conclusively presumed to be unreasonable and therefore illegal without elaborate inquiry as to the precise harm they have caused or the business excuse for their use."[21] The court explained that a "classic group boycott is a concerted attempt by a group of competitors at one level to protect themselves from competition from non-group members who seek to compete at that level.... the hallmark of the 'group boycott' is that effort of competitors to 'barricade themselves from competition at their own level.' " Essentially, the boycotting group blocks competitors from entering the market. The Circuit Court declined to find that the NFL draft fell into the group boycott category for two reasons: (1.) NFL teams are a joint

---

20. 593 F.2d 1173 (D.C. Cir. 1978).

21. Smith, quoting Northern Pacific Railway Co. v. United States.

venture, and do not compete economically, and (2.) NFL teams have not combined to exclude competitors from their market. In sum, the Court noted, "The draft, indeed, is designed not to insulate the NFL from competition, but to improve the entertainment product by enhancing teams' competitive equality," and it "may serve to regulate and thereby promote competition in what would otherwise be a chaotic bidding market for the services of college players."

The Court next analyzed the draft to see whether it violated the rule of reason, i.e. whether the restraint's "anticompetitive evils" outweigh the "procompetitive virtues" resulting in a "net effect" that substantially hinders competition. Though the Court determined that the draft is not "nefarious," it nevertheless found that it was substantially anticompetitive. The Circuit Court rejected the NFL's argument that the draft was procompetitive because it promoted " 'competitive balance' and playing-field equality" during games as failing to focus on the correct aspect of the issue at hand. Though the draft might preserve a high-caliber of on-field competition, it "does not increase competition in the economic sense of encouraging others to enter the market and to offer the product at lower cost." Therefore, the procompetitive and anticompetitive effects the parties were arguing over were not comparable, and in fact, could not be properly balanced. Thus, the draft was anticompetitive in purpose and effect, and consequently, an unreasonable restraint of trade. The Court held that "a player draft can survive scrutiny under the rule of reason only if it is demonstrated to have positive, economically Procompetitive benefits that offset its anticompetitive effects, or, at the least, if it is demonstrated to accomplish legitimate business purposes and to have a net anticompetitive effect that is insubstantial."

The dissenting judge in *Smith* vigorously argued that the majority's internally consistent analysis had failed to examine the draft in the context of professional sports, which are uniquely organized in the sense that the success of the joint venture depends heavily on the cooperation of all the member clubs. Judge MacKinnon reanalyzed the antitrust issue, starting with the premise that the product offered is the league sport, whose value depends upon competitive balance among the teams. Thus, the draft is an essential instrument for giving teams the opportunity to be competitive and "insuring the vitality of the NFL's product." The dissent also recognized that players do have some leverage to negotiate their salaries, in that they choose a particular to fulfill a particular role and need that player to sign. The dissent would have upheld the NFL's draft under the rule of reason analysis. After the double blow of *Smith* and *Mackey*, the NFL realized that it needed the protection of the nonstatutory labor exemption for its practices to survive antitrust scrutiny.

Before turning to subsequent antitrust suits in the NFL, it is worth pausing to explore other cases in which *Mackey* was applied. Litigation of the nonstatutory exemption moved on to challenges by players to terms contained in existing collective bargaining agreements that unions had agreed to and supported. In *McCourt v. California Sports, Inc.*,[22] the Sixth Circuit applied the three-prong *Mackey* test to determine that the exemption protected an NHL procedure memorialized in the 1976 collective bargaining agreement requiring that an "equalization payment" be made by the signing team to the team losing a free agent. Unlike the Eighth Circuit in *Mackey*, the Sixth Circuit found that all three prongs were satisfied, as "the NHLPA used every form of negotiating pressure it could muster," and failed to negotiate a better deal for players.[23] While the union was unable to get the NHL to budge on this particular issue, the NHL had "yielded significantly on other issues."[24] The Court found that this type of good-faith, arm's-length bargaining—that achieved its ultimate objective of a mutually acceptable agreement—to be a classic case in which relevant federal labor policy deserved to trump federal antitrust policy. After *McCourt*, the NHL's reserve system was substantially overhauled through collective bargaining. More importantly, no subsequent antitrust suits were filed by hockey players against the NHL's restraints on free agency—though the NHL has still suffered its share of labor strife, namely in the 2004 to 2005 lockout—providing strong support for the courts' belief that the parties are better situated to resolve labor issues on their own and not in the courtroom.

In 1982, upon expiration of the 1977 NFL collective bargaining agreement, the NFLPA demanded (a.) that players be paid 55% of the NFL's gross revenues, and (b.) that players become free agents every third year of their career. After the owners rejected the players' demands, the NFLPA called a strike after the second game of the 1982 season. The parties ultimately resolved their dispute, extended the current collective bargaining agreement with modified compensation standards, and resumed play after seven games were cancelled. Competition from the now-defunct United States Football League, however, drove player salaries even higher between 1983 and 1985. In 1987, the NFLPA again demanded free agency, this time at the expiration of each player's contract. After the second game of the season, the NFLPA went on strike and the NFL called in replacement players. With dwindling funds, players reluctantly returned to work.

Nevertheless, the weakened NFLPA filed suit attacking the current compensation system. The "Right of First Refusal / Compensation" system provided that a team could retain a veteran free agent by exercising a right of first refusal and by matching a competing club's offer. If the prior team decided not to match the offer, the prior team would receive compensation from the new team in the form of additional draft choices. In *Powell v. NFL*, the NFLPA filed suit in Judge Doty's court in Minnesota, claiming that the labor exemption expired when the 1982 collective bargaining agreement was terminated and the parties then reached impasse. The Supreme Court defined impasse as a temporary deadlock or

---

22.   600 F.2d 1193 (6th Cir. 1979).

23.   McCourt, 600 F.2d at 1202.

24.   Id.

hiatus in negotiations "which in almost all cases is eventually broken, through either a change of mind or the application of economic force."[25] At trial, Judge Doty ruled in favor of the players, saying that the bargaining impasse ended the nonstatutory labor exemption. While *Powell* was on appeal to the Eighth Circuit, the NFL implemented a new player retention system, known as "Plan B" free agency, in which a club could protect 27 players, while allowing the remaining players to test free agency. In November 1989, the Eighth Circuit overturned Judge Doty and ruled that the NFLPA was precluded from filing an antitrust lawsuit so long as a "collective bargaining relationship" existed between the union and the NFL. The Court stated that "[a] rule withdrawing immunity because the previous contract expired before a new agreement was reached is contrary to national labor law. The parties would be forced to enter into a collective bargaining agreement to avoid antitrust sanctions, when labor law is opposed to any such requirement. On the hand, the employer cannot alter its stance subsequent to an impasse in negotiations and unilaterally impose a package different from that which has been on the bargaining table. Such action would be a refusal to bargain and an unfair labor practice by the employer."[26]

In response to the Eighth Circuit's ruling, the NFLPA attempted to end the "collective bargaining relationship" by renouncing its status as a labor union. After the renunciation of union status, several players filed their own personal antitrust lawsuits against the NFL owners, most notably *McNeil v. NFL. McNeil*, filed in 1990, attached "Plan B" free agency on the grounds that it was unilaterally imposed by the NFL in violation of the Sherman Act. The District Court in Minnesota applied the three-prong *Mackey* test and found that "Plan B" failed prongs one and three; therefore, the nonstatutory labor exemption did not apply. The jury found that Plan B violated the Sherman Act because while it promoted competitive balance, it was more restrictive than necessary. A heavy damages award was levied, and trebled, against the NFL on the basis that players were restricted from attaining salaries that reflected their true market value. Following *McNeil*, Keith Jackson and nine other plaintiffs filed an action seeking an injunction to allow them to freely negotiate with other teams. All ten plaintiffs were allowed at least a five-day window to negotiate and sign with other teams.

The NFL, at a crossroads, negotiated with McNeil's attorneys to settle the dispute. The settlement included a Salary Cap and free agency after four years. Subsequently, *White v. NFL* was filed to settle, on a class-wide basis, the claims of all other players. The NFL offered $115 million in compensation to players affected by Plan B, and after 95 percent of the players approved, Judge Doty approved the settlement as reasonable.

Twenty years after *Mackey*, in *Brown v. Pro Football, Inc.*, the Supreme Court upheld the nonstatutory labor exemption in the collective

---

25.   Charles D. Bonanno Linen Service, Inc. v. NLRB, 454 U.S. 404 (1982).

26.   Powell v. NFL, 930 F.2d 1293 (8th Cir. 1989).

bargaining agreement context and stated that it continues to apply to an agreement among several employers bargaining together to implement post-impasse the terms of their last best good-faith offer. After the NFL collective bargaining agreement expired in 1987, the NFL presented a plan that would establish six-player development squads for each team at a league-mandated salary for each player of just $1,000 per week. The system was designed to eliminate the practice of teams "stashing" players who had not made the regular roster on their injured reserve list. While the NFLPA approved of the new program, it insisted that the development players be given benefits and protections similar to those provided to regular players, and that they leave individual squad members free to negotiate their own salaries. When the negotiations reached impasse two months later, the NFL unilaterally implemented the development squad program. The NFLPA filed suit, asserting that the agreement to pay a $1,000 weekly salary did not fall within the nonstatutory exemption and without that exemption, violated the Sherman Act.

Justice Breyer's majority opinion began by upholding the nonstatutory labor exemption from federal labor statutes, and that the exemption requires "good-faith bargaining over wages, hours, and working conditions."[27] The majority acknowledged that in order to give effect to collective bargaining, federal labor laws must support some reasonable restrictions on competition which result from the bargaining process. It stated that the exemption exists not only to prevent the courts from usurping the NLRB's function of "determin[ing], in the area of industrial conflict, what is or is not a 'reasonable' practice," but also to "allow meaningful collective bargaining to take place" by protecting "some restraints on competition imposed through the bargaining process" from antitrust scrutiny.[28] Unilateral implementation of a plan after a negotiations impasse is an example of such a reasonable restriction.

By applying to both employers and employees "the implicit exemption recognizes that to give legal effect to general labor laws and policies and to allow meaningful collective bargaining to take place, some restraints on competition imposed through the bargaining process must be shielded."[29] The Court then rejected the NFLPA's claim that this exemption applies only to labor-management agreements, stating that employers, after impasse, may engage in considerable joint behavior such as joint lockouts and replacement hiring. Specifically, applying *Mackey*, it upheld the system unilaterally implemented by the NFL because (1.) the collusive conduct took place during and immediately after a collective-bargaining negotiation; (2.) it grew out of, and was directly related to, the lawful operation of the bargaining process; (3.) it involved a matter that the parties were required to negotiate collectively; and (4.) it concerned only the parties to the collective bargaining relationship. The Court concluded that antitrust courts are not in the best position to make decisions about

---

27.   Brown, 518 U.S. at 234.

28.   Id. at 237.

29.   Id. at 236.

the adequacy of collective bargaining processes. The argument that professional sports are "special" or different enough from other labor situations to warrant special treatment under federal and antitrust laws was rejected.

The dissent, by contrast, focused on the anticompetitive nature of the flat wage scheme, stating that the nonstatutory labor exemption does not "support a rule that would allow employers to suppress wages by implementing noncompetitive agreements." According to Justice Stevens, the competitive sports arena is not unique enough to warrant a revised application of the nonstatutory labor exemption. Further, the dissent highlighted the historical precedent of individual salary negotiations and challenged the notions that it is appropriate for a single party to unilaterally implement terms and that a genuine impasse was reached following a bona fide negotiations process between the NFL and NFLPA.

Writing Exercise 1: Renegotiation of Selected Clauses in NFL Uniform Players Contract[30]

Consider the NFL Uniform Players Contract ("UPC"), which is included in Appendix B.

Imagine that you are representing John Mackey and the NFLPA. Be cognizant of whether any conflicts of interest arise between your two clients.

Also consider this issues from the perspective of a representative of the NFL and Commissioner Pete Rozelle, as of the time (1976) that John Mackey's case could be appealed to the U.S. Supreme Court.

As you did with the MLB Uniform Player's Contract while Curt Flood's case was on appeal to the U.S. Supreme Court, consider the NFL Uniform Player's Contract, and possible "edits" thereto, including the following clauses:

Paragraph 3: "Other Activities"

Paragraph 4: "Publicity and NFLPA Group Licensing Program."

Paragraphs 11–12: "Skill, Performance and Conduct;" and "Termination"

Paragraph 15: "Integrity of the Game"

Paragraph 19: "Disputes"

Paragraph 23: "Waiver and Release"

Paragraph 24: "Other Provisions"

Pay particular attention to the "termination-related" clauses, in light of John Mackey's likely "leverage" from his anticipated "win" in the Supreme Court (as in the Curt Flood pre Supreme Court "Hypothetical").

---

30. An "exemplar" student submission in response to this hypothetical can be found in the accompanying Teacher's Manual.

Consider each side's respective "gives" and "gets" re: the negotiation of the above-referenced clauses. For example, should "restrictions" on unfettered "free agency" be traded off for other NFLPA "benefits"?

Begin to "black-line" three to four selected clauses of the UPC, based on the foregoing Hypothetical negotiation. During your negotiation, consider the impact of the *Powell, McNeil, White* and *Jackson* decisions, as well as the threat of treble damages.

After making your Group's "final edits," as General Counsel to the NFLPA (and <u>not</u> John Mackey!), write your "confidential/privileged" memorandum to the NFLPA detailing the specific language you would recommend changing and the reasons therefor. In your memorandum, include your legal conclusion, regarding whether NFL's proposed edits would (or would not) be ordered by a Federal Court, if a negotiating impasse were reached. Finally, recommend whether the edits that you are proposing to the NFLPA, if not accepted by the NFL, should result in a further recommendation to the NFLPA to "go on strike," or to "decertify."

Writing Exercise 2: Oral Argument Questions and Answers on "Super Appeal" of Brown—Creating the Record[31]

Consider the Majority and Dissenting Opinions in the *Tony Brown* (1996) Supreme Court case. Imagine you are an appellate judge preparing to hear oral argument on "Super Appeal" of *Brown*. Formulate four to five questions you would ask to challenge the lawyers for Brown and the lawyers for the NFL. When creating your set of questions for each side, pretend that you are a judge who sympathizes with the opponent's point of view. For example, the questions asked of Tony Brown should challenge him to explain why the NFL's position is erroneous. The questions should be in the order of "best questions first," and "why I don't lose" questions last. In so doing, please consider "remand" options, in case there are facts you still need.

Once you have formulated questions for each side, imagine you are the lawyer answering the set of questions during oral argument. Write out answers to the questions, explaining why your client should win. Be sure to establish the facts and introduce the legal precedents necessary to enable the judges to reach the legal conclusion you seek.

III. NFL COLLECTIVE BARGAINING AGREEMENT

The NFL's Collective Bargaining Agreement reflects the understanding between the NFL's Management Council and Player's Association. The current collective bargaining agreement is set to expire after the 2010

---

31. An "exemplar" student submission in response to this hypothetical can be found in the accompanying Teacher's Manual.

season. To encourage the parties to reach a resolution before the final league year, in the final league year, there will be no salary cap and heavy restrictions on player movement and free agency.

Pursuant to the current NFL CBA, player salaries can be between a floor and a cap set as a function of league revenues. In any given year, players are guaranteed a minimum percentage of the League's revenue each year.[32] Teams cannot spend more than a certain on player salaries in any given year.[33] This salary cap is determined as a percentage of the League's projected total revenue minus the projected benefits for the season. If a team exceeds the "hard cap," it will face a penalty. When calculating team salary, teams must consider the minimum salary guaranteed to players based upon the number of seasons played.

NFL players did not formally achieve the right to free agency until the negotiation of the 1993 CBA. Under the current regime, there are four types of free agents: unrestricted free agents, restricted free agents, exclusive rights players, and franchise and transition players.[34] Players who are not under contract with at least four seasons played are unrestricted free agents. After four years of play in the league, unrestricted free agents are are free to negotiate with any team. Given that the average NFL career lasts only three and a half years, most players never become unrestricted free agents. Players who have played three seasons may be restricted free agents. As the title indicates, these players have less freedom to determine their salaries and team than unrestricted free agents. These players may negotiate with any team, but their previous team holds a (i.) right of first refusal to match the offer of a new team on all material terms or (ii.) the right to receive draft-pick compensation from the signing team if they decline to match. Exclusive rights free agents—players whose contracts expire with less than three seasons of play—may not negotiate or sign with new teams if the player's previous team offers him at least the minimum salary. Finally, franchise or transition players are "tagged" as such when the team tenders an offer making the player one of the highest paid players at his position; once a player is tagged as such, the player cannot move to another team.

Teams select players during a rookie draft that occurs annually in April. During the seven-round draft, teams have the right to select one eligible player—who must wait at least three collegiate football seasons after high school or obtain a waiver from the Commissioner to enter earlier—per round. Teams select from the pool of prospective players in order of worst to best record from the prior season. If selected, the rookie's salary is limited by the amounts in the CBA.

---

32. See Collective Bargaining Agreement Between the NFL Management Council and the NFL Player's Association ("NFL Collective Bargaining Agreement"), March 8, 2006, Article XXIV § 4 (available at http://www.nflpa.org/CBA/CBA_Complete.aspx) (last visited on January 5, 2009).

33. See id. at § 5.

34. NFL Collective Bargaining Agreement, Article XIX §§ 1–4.

Writing Exercise 3: Confidential/Privileged Memorandum Regarding a Revised NFL Draft[35]—"Create a Draft" Hypothetical

Consider *Smith v. Pro Football, Inc.* (at Weiler, p. 186, et seq.). From the perspective of counsel to Yazoo Smith counsel for the NFL Owners / Commissioner, summarize the best arguments, as contained in the majority and dissenting opinions.

Based on the foregoing, create a draft system that would overcome the antitrust violation conclusions reached by the majority opinion in *Smith*, but which would also accommodate as many of the dissenting opinion's concerns as possible.

Based on the foregoing, prepare an Executive Summary "privileged/confidential" memorandum to the NFL Commissioner advising him, as of 1978 (immediately after *Smith* was decided) why you can opine that the newly devised draft system will pass "rule of reason" antitrust scrutiny (or not).

IV. PLAYER CHALLENGES TO NBA PRACTICES

The courts opened the door to antitrust challenges to NBA practices in 1971. In *Denver Rockets v. All–Pro Management, Inc. ("Haywood")*, 325 F.Supp. 1049 (C.D. Cal. 1971), the Court found that the NBA's rule requiring graduating high school players to wait four years before playing in the league violated antitrust laws. The NBA did not require that players must go to college during those four years or place a specific age restriction on when players could enter the NBA, but rather stated that a player had to wait four years. Spencer Haywood, who began playing professionally after his sophomore year of college with the American Basketball Association, was signed by the NBA's Seattle SuperSonics. The six year, $1.5 million deal, however, ignored the four-year waiting period, and the NBA threatened to void the contract. Like Yazoo Smith who came after him, Haywood argued that the NBA's conduct and draft policy was a "group boycott" in violation of the Sherman Act. The Central District of California awarded Haywood an injunction, finding that:

> "If Haywood is unable to continue play professional basketball for Seattle, he will suffer irreparable injury in that a substantial part of his playing career will have been dissipated, his physical condition, skills and coordination will deteriorate from lack of high-level competition, his public acceptance as a super star will diminish to the detriment of his career, his self-esteem and his pride will have been injured and a great injustice will be perpetrated on him."

On appeal, the Supreme Court upheld the District Court's ruling, and Haywood and the league subsequently settled the case. The NBA also created an exception the age eligibility rule to allow players to enter the NBA directly from high school upon the showing of an economic hardship.

---

35. An "exemplar" student submission in response to this hypothetical can be found in the accompanying Teacher's Manual.

While Spencer Haywood's claim chipped away at the NBA's restrictions, Oscar Robertson's case demolished them.[36] Robertson, like Haywood, had played with the American Basketball Association and The Big "O" was a stellar athlete. When the ABA and NBA decided to merge, then NBPA President Robertson brought a slew of claims, and sought to block the merger, to end the option clause that bound a player to a single NBA team in perpetuity, to end the NBA's college draft binding a player to one team, and to end restrictions on fee agency signings. The court stated that the nonstatutory labor exemption did not apply to these employer actions, but only to joint actions of employers and unions. Further, the court remained unconvinced by the NBA's arguments about the necessity of these restraints, stating "[b]ecause survival necessitates some restraints . . . does not mean that insulation from the reach of the antitrust laws must follow." The class-action suit was ultimately settled. In the settlement, the NBA agreed to modify or eliminate practices "so as to increase the number of teams with which NBA players may negotiate and sign player contracts." Pursuant to the settlement terms, teams had rights to drafted players for two years, the option clause was eliminated, and a $4.3 million settlement fund was established.

Thus, like the NFL, the NBA needed a shield from antitrust laws for its practices to withstand legal challenge. The applicability of the nonstatutory labor exemption was litigated in the NBA by Leon Wood, who filed suit over the league's newly imposed salary cap, which permitted any team that was over the cap to offer a new player just the minimum $75,000 salary in a one-year contract. Noting that "federal labor policy thus allows employees to seek the best deal for the greatest number by exercise of the collective rather than individual bargaining power," the Second Circuit upheld the league practice by applying the nonstatutory exemption.[37] Judge Winter, writing for the Second Circuit, explicitly declined to apply the *Mackey* test and instead balanced the relevant labor policy against the federal antitrust policy, as was done in *Jewel Tea*. In so doing, Judge Winter declared that "once an exclusive representative has been selected, the individual employee is forbidden by federal law from negotiating directly with the employer absent the representative's consent."[38] Judge Winter went on to state that the "gravamen of Wood's complaint, namely that the NBA–NBPA collective agreement is illegal because it prevents him from achieving his full market value, is therefore at odds with, and destructive of, federal labor policy."[39] Judge Winter concluded that if Wood believed that the collective bargaining agreement unjustifiably discriminated against rookie players, the proper course of legal action was to charge the union with unfair representation of new employees under the National Labor Relations Act.

---

36. Robertson v. National Basketball Association, 556 F.2d 682 (2d Cir. 1977).

37. Wood v. National Basketball Ass'n, 809 F.2d 954, 959 (2d Cir. 1987).

38. Id. at 958.

39. Id. at 959.

In 1995, two additional antitrust cases against the NBA were decided, both in the Second Circuit. In *NBA v. Williams*, the NBA sought a declaratory judgment against the NBPA regarding the ongoing collective bargaining negotiations that the continuation of the prior collective bargaining agreement did not violate antitrust laws because of the nonstatutory labor exemption. The NBPA demanded the elimination of the college draft, teams' right of first refusal, and the revenue sharing / salary cap program, and refused to negotiate further until the previous collective bargaining agreement expired, and argued that the NBA ought not to be shielded by the exemption. In ruling for the NBA, Judge Winter noted that multiemployer bargaining with a union was a well-established practice, and that employers needed flexibility in negotiations; the employers were just as entitled as the unions to bargain hard and use economic force to resolve disputes. The NBPA could not challenge the terms and conditions upon impasse under antitrust laws.

In *Caldwell v. The American Basketball Association, Inc.*, the Second Circuit held that Joe Caldwell's antitrust claim against the ABA was precluded by the nonstatutory labor exemption. Caldwell was suspended by his team, the St. Louis Spirits, after the team determined that Caldwell had deceived them regarding a teammate's whereabouts. Caldwell appealed his suspension to the commissioner, but ultimately decided to litigate the action and recovered his full salary. After the merger, Caldwell never played basketball again, and he claimed he was blacklisted for refusing to approve the terms of a collective bargaining agreement when serving as union president. The defendants predictably claimed that Caldwell never played again because he was not as athletic because of his age, a torn ligament, and a car accident. The Court cited *Wood* for the proposition that because a collective bargaining relationship existed, what would otherwise be a violation of the Sherman act was resolved on summary judgment because the claims would "subvert fundamental principles of federal labor policy." Thus, not only employee collective action, but also employer collective action is seen as essential to the collective bargaining process.

SUMMARY QUESTIONS

When answering the questions below, focus on antitrust laws' impact on the NFL and the NBA. (N.B. no MLB-related cases, due to *Flood v. Kuhn* "antitrust exemption").

1.   "Rank" the NFL (and NBA)-related cases, according to "best reasoned" versus "worst reasoned."

2.   How important was Oscar Robertson's winning his fight for free agency versus Curt Flood's losing his fight in the Supreme Court?

3.   Consider the impact of the above-referenced decisions on each of these two "major leagues" re, e.g., the owners', Commissioners' and the Player Associations' reactions thereto.

4.   Which decisions ended up being "in the best (or worst?) interests" of the games?

5.   Compare the non-statutory "labor exemption" from the antitrust laws versus MLB's (Court-created) "antitrust exemption." What difference does it make, if any?

6.   Consider the *Mackey* treatment of the "labor exemption's" application to the "Rozelle Rule." Should "incorporation by reference" from prior CBA's qualify for the "exemption"? (Consider same in context of *Clarett* case, discussed in Chapter 5.) In that context, what role must "arms-length bargaining" take, in order for the "exemption" to apply between the NFL and the NFLPA?

7.   What should happen "post-impasse" in the NFL/NFLPA CBA negotiations? (See, e.g., Judge Doty's view at page 238 of *Weiler*.)

8.   Is NFLPA "decertification" a fair response to every "impasse"? (See, e.g., *McNeil* opinion by Judge Doty, at page 240 of *Weiler*.) Compare NBA-related Second Circuit decision by Judge Winter in the *Williams* case re: "post-impasse" freedom of owners to unilaterally implement terms and conditions, etc. (See *Weiler* at p. 257.)

9.   Compare *Tony Brown* (*Weiler*, at page 244) re: NFL's "post-impasse" options. Consider "terms" vs. "tactics" distinction in connection with same. Which is the more persuasive opinion in the *Tony Brown* opinion—Justice Breyer's majority opinion, or Justice Stevens's dissent?

CHAPTER 5

AGE ELIGIBILITY RULES

■ ■ ■

Introduction

The age at which prospective professionals can enter into the major leagues differs depending on the league in question and this restriction on entry has been the focal point of controversy regarding athletes' autonomy and maturity. MLB arguably has the most lax restrictions, though by convention teams do not sign foreign players before the age of sixteen. Players can be drafted immediately out of high school. The NBA currently has a "one and done" rule, requiring players to wait one year until after their high school graduation to join the league. The NFL mandates that players must be three years out of high school prior to entry. Whether this age floor is a legitimate restriction, and whether the floor is protected from antitrust laws by the nonstatutory labor exemption discussed in Chapter 4, has been the subject of much debate.

As you consider the cases below, separate out the reasons offered by the leagues to justify the age limits. Which do you think are the most plausible? Is the paternalistic rationale offered by the NFL convincing enough to impede upon the freedom of young players and interested teams to contract?[1] Should the Commissioner consider whether players are both physically and mentally mature enough to play in the league?

I. AGE ELIGIBILITY

Both the NFL and the NBA have age eligibility floors for those who want to play in these professional leagues. MLB permits athletes to be drafted immediately out of high school. If a player opts to go to college, that player must wait three years before being eligible for the draft.

A. AGE ELIGIBILITY IN MAJOR LEAGUE BASEBALL

Each June, Major League Baseball teams gather via teleconference to participate in the First Year Player Draft, which is also known as the Rule 4 Draft. The procedures governing the Rule 4 draft were modified during the negotiations for the current MLB CBA, whose terms extend from 2007

---

1. For a detailed treatment of this issue, see Michael A. McCann and Joseph S. Rosen, *Legality of Age Restrictions in the NBA and the NFL*, 56 Case Western Reserve L. Rev 731 (2006).

to 2011. Teams—in order of worst to best past season record—select players from the vast pool of players from the United States, a United States territory, or Canada, or players enrolled in a United States high school or college—regardless of nationality—who have never signed a major league contract. Thus, the draft pool of first-year players is essentially comprised of (a.) high school graduates not yet in college, (b.) college students who have completed at least their junior year or are 21–years–old, and (c.) junior college players, regardless of age or year in school. Teams generally begin scouting players before they finish high school, around age 16, the age at which players are welcome to attend open scouting sessions by the league or a particular member club. Once drafted, the team retains the right to draft a player until before midnight on August 15 or until the player enters or returns to a four-year college. If the player does not sign with that team, the team cannot reselect that player the next year without the player's consent. Teams earn compensation usable towards the following year's draft for unsigned draft picks. Clubs also earn draft pick compensation when they trade away Type A or Type B free agents. Unlike in the NFL and NBA, therefore, MLB teams can pick players immediately after high school. However, MLB draftees typically enter the minor league baseball system, whereas the NFL and NBA do not have similar minor league systems of the same scope; rather, these leagues use the years during which players are in the NCAA to scout their talent. Another distinguishing feature is that the MLB draft lasts as long as teams wish to participate, and has lasted as long as 50 rounds. The NBA draft consists of only two rounds, and the NFL draft consists of seven rounds.

Though MLB teams are free to select high school players immediately after graduation, the trend in recent years has been to select college players, if it is possible to wait until that time without another team snatching a prospect first. Statistics have shown that college players were more successful in the league. Since the trend has shifting towards selecting more college players, those high school players who are selected have closed the statistical gap in the performance of the two cohorts.

MLB teams do not rely only on the pool of talent available in the United States, however. Clubs also heavily recruit in Latin American countries, signing players as young as 15 years old. Several teams, including the Pittsburgh Pirates, Boston Red Sox, and St. Louis Cardinals, have "academies" in Latin American countries where young prospects can show off their talents and be observed by teams for an extended period of time. Scouting of Latin American players is largely unregulated.[2] In 2008, the infamous "Latin American skimming scandal" was exposed. The Major League Baseball Department of Investigations and the FBI began to investigate the skimming by scouts and other official personnel of signing bonuses given to young prospects from Latin America. After the malfeasance was exposed, the Los Angeles Angels of Anaheim fired their interna-

---

2. See Arturo J. Marcana & David Fidler, STEALING LIVES: THE GLOBALIZATION OF BASEBALL AND THE TRAGIC STORY OF ALEX QUIROZ (2003).

tional supervisor of scouting, Clay Daniel; the Chicago White Sox fired the team's senior director of player personnel, David Wilder; the New York Yankees fired two scouts; and the Washington Nationals went as far as firing their General Manager Jim Bowden. Scouts have to contend with local *buscones*, or searchers, who bring young players to teams and seek a finder's fee.

Players are not the only ones at risk of exploitation and fraud, however. Several MLB teams discovered that players had fabricated their ages in order to come to play in the United States. Miguel Tejada's age discrepancy was famously broadcast on television, with a visibly jarred Tejada ending the interview early. Rafael Furcal and Bartolo Colon were older than teams had originally listed, as well. A top Washington Nationals prospect, Esmailyn Gonzalez, claimed to be twenty when in fact he was only sixteen, using doctored hospital records and birth certificates. Thus, MLB has two wells from which to dip—the regulated world of US athletes and the "wild west" of international scouting that is, as of yet, still largely unregulated.

B. AGE ELIGIBILITY IN THE NFL

Before a prospective NFL player may enter into the rookie draft, he must wait three collegiate football seasons from the date of his high school graduation.[3] The Commissioner has the authority to waive the NFL age eligibility rules, as Commissioner Tagliabue did for Larry Johnson. When Ohio State's Maurice Clarett wanted to enter the NFL after his freshman year, he sued the league under Sections 1 and 2 of the Sherman Act. Clarett led Ohio State to an undefeated 2002–2003 season and a national championship, earning accolades such as "Big Ten Freshman of the Year" and best running back in college football according to *The Sporting News*. Clarett was suspended for filing a false police report by the school and the NCAA for the 2003–2004 season, thus prompting him seek early entry into the NFL.

The Southern District of New York Court rejected the NFL's three arguments that (1.) the rule was collectively bargained, (2.) Clarett lacked standing under antitrust laws, and (3.) that the rule is reasonable. The District Court adopted for the Second Circuit the *Mackey* test, found that the three-years out of high school rule failed that test. Recall from Chapter 4 that the *Mackey* test has three prongs: (1.) that the rule concern a subject of mandatory collective bargaining, (2.) that the rule affects the parties to the collective bargaining agreement, and (3.) that the rule is a byproduct of good faith, arm's length negotiations. The Court found that the rule regarding age eligibility is not a mandatory subject of collective bargaining because "Nowhere is there a reference to wages, hours, or conditions of employment." Rather, the Court reasoned that the rule makes a "class of potential players *unemployable*." The Court distin-

---

3. NFL CBA Article XVI § 2(b).

guished away *Wood*, *Williams*, and *Caldwell*, on the grounds that the players challenging the restraints had been drafted or were playing for the league and then challenged the agreement. The Court went on to state that that the rule only affected non-employees, "players, like Clarett, who are complete strangers to the bargaining relationship." Finally, the Court completed the *Mackey* analysis by reasoning that the NFL failed to prove the rule resulted from arm's length negotiations. According to the Court, the rule was adopted after the 1925 draft, but the NFLPA was not formed until 1956 and the first collective bargaining agreement was not adopted until 1968. Moreover, the collective bargaining agreement itself does not state the rule, but rather states that players waive the right to bargain over or sue regarding provisions of the Constitution and Bylaws.

Further, the Court found that Clarett had standing "because his injury flows from a policy that excludes all players in his position from selling their services to the only viable buyer—the NFL." Playing in the NFL, with its uniquely high salaries, "represents an unparalleled opportunity for an aspiring football player in terms of salary, publicity, endorsement opportunities, and level of competition."

The Court concluded by finding that the NFL could not prove that the rule was reasonable. The NFL argued that the rule protected four groups: (1.) young athletes who are not psychologically mature to play professional football, (2.) teams who might sign these young athletes and lose money upon injury, (3.) the league and its entertainment product, and (4.) young athletes who might over-train or use performance enhancing drugs to speed up their development. The Judge, however, rejected all these proffered rationales and found that the rule was a "naked restraint," reasoning that "It harms competition because some players are simply not permitted to compete."

Clarett's victory, however, was short lived. On appeal, the Second Circuit reversed and remanded the District Court holding that the age eligibility rule was a "naked restraint" in violation of antitrust law.[4] The Second Circuit approached the issue differently. It framed the legal issue as whether federal labor laws protecting the collective bargaining process trumped the application of antitrust laws to the NFL's eligibility rules. The Court declined to apply *Mackey*, as the District Court had, and instead applied its own precedent in *Caldwell*, *Wood*, and *Williams*, in light of *Brown*. The Second Circuit interpreted *Brown* as holding that the nonstatutory labor exemption applied to any claims brought by professional athletes against their employers arising out of mandatory subjects of collective bargaining. The Court explained:

> Our analysis in each [Second Circuit] case was rooted in the observation that the relationships among the defendant sports leagues and their players were governed by collective bargaining agreements and thus were subject to the carefully structured regime established by federal labor laws. We reasoned that to permit antitrust suits against

---

4. See Clarett v. National Football League, 369 F.3d 124 (2d Cir. 2004).

sports leagues on the ground that their concerted action imposed a restraint upon the labor market would seriously undermine many of the policies embodied by these labor laws, including the congressional policy favoring collective bargaining, the bargaining parties' freedom of contract, and the widespread use of multi-employer bargaining units.

The Court relied on *Wood* for the specific proposition that new union members often find themselves disadvantaged relative to more senior members, but that is no reason not to insulate the agreement.

Contrary to the finding of the District Court, the Second Circuit found that the age eligibility rule was a mandatory subject of collective bargaining because it influenced the terms of initial employment, wages, and working conditions. The Court explained that "simply because the eligibility rules work a hardship on prospective rather than current employees does not render them impermissible." Therefore, it was the responsibility of the NFLPA to bring the issue up during the next negotiations, not the responsibility of the Court to invalidate the rule.

Finally, the Second Circuit found that the rules were collectively bargained for, giving the union's acceptance of the terms. The Court stated that "The eligibility rules, along with a host of other NFL rules and policies affecting the terms and conditions of NFL players included in the NFL's Constitution and Bylaws, were well known to the union, and a copy of the Constitution and Bylaws was presented to the union during negotiations.... the union or the NFL could have forced the other to the bargaining table if either felt that a change was warranted." The Court relied upon the declaration of NFLMC Vice President of Labor Relations, Peter Ruocco, as sufficient uncontroverted evidence that the rule was bargained for.

In the aftermath, Clarett participated in the 2005 NFL Combine but his athletic skills had deteriorated. Though he was drafted in the third round of the 2005 draft by the Denver Broncos, Clarett was released on waivers in August. After his release, Clarett had difficulty staying out of trouble. He is currently serving a jail sentence after he pled guilty to armed robbery and resisting arrest.

Writing Exercise 1: Document Requests and Deposition Questions of Maurice Clarett and the NFL Commissioner[5]

Assume the following facts regarding document production requests and deposition questions to be presented from counsel for Maurice Clarett to NFL Commissioner Paul Tagliabue, and from counsel for Commissioner Tagliabue to Maurice Clarett: (1.) the NFL is appealing the District Court's Order to the Second Circuit; (2.) in advance of the Oral Argument on appeal, counsel for Clarett and counsel for the Commissioner are

---

5. An "exemplar" student submission in response to this hypothetical can be found in the accompanying Teacher's Manual.

permitted to take the depositions of Clarett and the Commissioner, and to obtain (the most relevant) documents in advance thereof to supplement the record on appeal.

As counsel for each side, you must submit a pre-deposition request for four or five categories of documents, for review by the Second Circuit. Also, each counsel must submit a list of four to five questions to be asked at a deposition. In general, your deposition questions should result in "admissions," which can then be used to support your appeals court brief, when the admissions are used as "factual predicates" for the application of the relevant precedents. Create a "record" by conducting a mock deposition for each side to see if you can elicit the necessary admissions.

"Exemplar" student responses are, as usual, set forth in the Teacher's Manual.

Summary Questions

1. Compare the *Clarett* Opinion in the District Court versus the Second Circuit Court of Appeals' Opinion. Which Opinion is better legally reasoned and why?

2. In so doing, please consider whether "arms length bargaining" truly occurred in *Clarett* between the NFL and NFLPA, per the *Mackey* test. Also, is "age," a "term and condition of employment," per *Mackey*?

3. Is a unilateral "memo" (sent February 1990) from the NFL Commissioner to the NFLPA regarding "age eligibility" sufficient "bargaining," per *Mackey*? How about Peter Ruocco's November 2003 "declaration" that "bargaining had occurred" re: "age eligibility"?

4. Is the "incorporation by reference" of "prior history" (into the NFL Constitution and Bylaws) sufficient? How about the argument that the NFLPA "waived" any objection thereto, as accepted by the *Clarett* Second Circuit Opinion? Is this reasoning legally sufficient, per *Mackey*?

5. What "standing," if any, should a "prospective" NFLPA union member like Clarett be granted?

6. Was it appropriate for the NFLPA to "oppose" Clarett's "challenge" to the "age eligibility" rules?

C. AGE ELIGIBILITY IN THE NBA

As discussed in Chapter 4, Spencer Haywood successfully challenged the NBA's rule that a high school graduate had to wait four seasons before playing in the NBA. Recall that Haywood won on the grounds that the rule was a group boycott, and therefore, a *per se* violation of antitrust laws. Prior to 2006, players could be drafted directly out of high school. Most famously, 18–year old Lebron James was selected first in the 2003 draft, inking a professional contract and several lucrative endorsement deals.[6]

---

6. James signed a $90 million deal with Nike even before he was drafted.

Under the current iteration of the NBA's collective bargaining agreement, players must be nineteen during the draft year and at least one NBA season must elapse after that player's high school graduation. In 2007, the first year of the new age floor, five of the first 10 draft picks had only spent one year in college. In 2008, five of the first seven picks had only attended college for a year. This "one and done" rule results in freshman playing one year with universities with basketball programs before hopping to the NBA. Players are unable to take advantage of the professional salary and endorsements that Lebron James was able to earn. Though it did not reach the amounts James earned, O.J. Mayo—who spent a year at the University of Southern California from 2007 to 2008— allegedly received about $30,000 in cash and benefits including clothes and a big screen television during his collegiate season.

In response to the Mayo incident, NCAA President Myles Brand defended the "one and done" rule, staying that "hundreds, maybe even thousands, of young men each year . . . are now taking their high school studies more seriously rather than thinking, 'I can blow off high school and go right into the NBA.' . . . That's going to put them in good stead for their lives." Not only does the rule purportedly benefit students, but Gary Roberts, dean of Indiana University law school, thinks the rule is good for the universities as well. "I think it's good for the college game to have a Kevin Durant, or that caliber of player even for one year . . . rather than not at all." Roberts supported the rule, but questioned, however, whether the rule was good for all students. "There's probably a tiny percentage of kids who would be better off if they could quit the pretense of being a college student and go straight to the pros, but I'm not sure if the NBA should make its rules based on a tiny handful of kids who are eventually going to be in the NBA anyway."

Rather than spend a year playing college basketball, high school students may follow Brandon Jennings and opt to go to Europe to play professionally for a year before returning to the United States. Jennings, who averaged 38.7 points per game in his senior year of high school and won several accolades including 2008 Naismith High School Player of the Year went to go to play for the Italian league instead of playing for the University of Arizona. His contract was $1.65 million, and he also inked a $2 million contract with Under Armour. If he had been in college, not only would he have had to forego the player salary, he also would have not have been able to sign the endorsement deal. Jennings will be eligible for the 2009 NBA Draft.

Though Commissioner David Stern lost the battle against the NBPA to have prospective professional players wait two years after high school, he may push the issue again once the collective bargaining agreement expires. Commissioner Stern has said that the age limit is good for business, explaining:

This was not a social program, this was a business issue. There was a serious sense that this was hurting our game. Having an 18–year–old player not playing, sitting on the bench, is not good for basketball. If we could have these kids develop for another year, either (a) they'd see that they weren't so good, and we'd see that they weren't so good, or (b) they would get better, and when they came, they would be able to make a contribution. And that would improve the status of basketball.

Therefore, for Commissioner Stern, the age eligibility rule is a reflection of his view about what is in the "best interests" of the game.

SUMMARY QUESTIONS

1.   Compare MLB, NBA and NFL "age eligibility" rules. How does the MLB's 1998 Flood Act impact "minor league" baseball players' ability to "challenge" MLB's age eligibility rules à la *Clarett*?

2.   What are the NFL's justification for age eligibility rules? What are the NBA's? Which do you find more plausible?

3.   If you were Commissioner, at what age would you permit prospective players to be eligible for the draft? Would the age differ depending upon the sport at issue?

4.   Do you think that the NFL and NBA's eligibility rules have turned collegiate programs into a de facto minor league system?

5.   Alan Milstein and Michael McCann, who were part of the legal team representing Maurice Clarett, have argued against the age floor. Mr. Milstein has said that the age eligibility rule does not affect wages, because the same number of players would be drafted and the same wage scale would still apply. The only perceptible difference would be that younger players would be selected. Professor McCann has argued that players, like Clarett, are not represented at the bargaining table and that veteran players have an incentive to keep out amateurs. Both also pointed out that professional hockey and boxing, games that are just as physical as football, do not have age eligibility rules. Do you agree with their views?

6.   Do you think that a plausible solution is to permit college athletes to get paid? To engage in endorsement deals? Both of these practices are currently prohibited by the NCAA.

7.   Does your view of the legitimacy of the NFL, NBA, and NCAA rules change with the information that college baseball players can play in the minor leagues but still remain eligible for college football under the NCAA's "two sport exception"?

CHAPTER 6

MLB COLLECTIVE BARGAINING AGREEMENT ISSUES: FREE AGENCY AND COLLUSION

■ ■ ■

Introduction

While players in the NFL and NBA went to the courts to challenge restrictions on player movement and salary, MLB players were forced to do so through MLB's internal grievance system. MLB has two important and distinct arbitration procedures: grievance arbitration and salary arbitration. A player can file for grievance arbitration if a dispute "involves the existence or interpretation of, or compliance with, any agreement, or any provision of any agreement, between the Association and the Clubs or any of them or between a Player and a Club ..."[1] The Commissioner has a trump card over disputes that involve "the preservation of the integrity of, or the maintenance of public confidence in, the game of baseball."[2] Disputes regarding player photographs and public appearances, discussed in further detail in Chapter 7, are also excluded from the grievance procedure.

I. FREE AGENCY AND SALARY ARBITRATION

A. WINNING FREE AGENCY THROUGH GRIEVANCE ARBITRATION

After Curt Flood lost the battle for free agency at the Supreme Court level, Andy Messersmith and Davy McNally sought to win what Flood could not through arbitration. MLBPA Executive Director, Marvin Miller, had successfully introduced the right of players to appeal to an impartial arbitrator to mediate grievances in the 1970 collective bargaining agreement. Andy Messersmith, who had a one-year contract with the Dodgers in 1974, could not agree on new terms with the Dodgers for 1975.

---

1. MLB Basic Agreement, Article XI § A(1)(a).
2. Id. at Article XI § A(1)(b).

Messersmith wanted a no-trade guarantee or at least approval rights over where he could traded. The parties reached a stalemate, and Messersmith played 1975 without a contract. Messersmith explained, "It was less of an economic issue at the time of than a fight for the right to have control over your own destiny." McNally, a veteran pitcher at the end of his career, was traded from the Baltimore Orioles to the Montreal Expos. When McNally refused to sign a new deal, he returned home.

When Messersmith approached Miller about going to arbitration, he was optimistic about taking the dispute to Peter Seitz, who had granted Catfish Hunter free agency earlier when the Oakland A's failed to fulfill a contractual obligation. Miller recruited McNally to join in the dispute.

Messersmith and McNally argued that they were free agents because the "reserve clause," embodied in Paragraph 10(a) of the Uniform Player Contract, was effective for only one year. The Dodgers and Expos claimed that the reserve clause operated in perpetuity.

Arbitrator Seitz first addressed the question of whether he had jurisdiction to hear the dispute. Seitz was empowered to interpret where ambiguous and apply the collective bargaining agreement, but the collective bargaining agreement stated that

> ... this agreement does not deal with the reserve system. The Parties have differing views as to the legality and as to the merits of such a system as presently constituted ... During the term of this Agreement neither of the Parties will resort to any form of concerted action with respect to the issue of the reserve system, and there shall be no obligation to negotiate with respect to the reserve system.

However, Article III of the Agreement incorporated the Collective Bargaining Agreement and the Major Leagues, and therefore also what the owners saw as the "core" of the reserve system, Major League Rule 4–A(a) (the reserve list of up to 40 players), Rule 3(g) (the no tampering rule) and paragraph 10(a) of the Uniform Player Contract. Seitz seized on this ambiguity, and said he could not understand how "the Basic Agreement could state that it does not 'deal' with the Reserve System, when, at the same time, its own provisions and the provisions of the Players Contract and the Major League Rules which are absorbed into the Agreement patently do 'deal' with such rules." Seitz narrowed the reading of the language that said the agreement does not deal with the reserve system by interpreting it to be a reaction to the possible effects of the *Flood* case.

Next, Seitz turned to interpret paragraph 10(a) of the UPC. Paragraph 10(a) read, in part, that the "Club shall have the right by written notice to the Player to renew this contract for a period of one year on the same terms ..." Seitz reasoned that for a renewal option to be interpreted as providing for successive renewals, such intent must be manifested explicitly in the contract. For instance, Seitz explained, renewals of real estate leases are not presumed to be in perpetuity. The fact that the contract was for personal services weighed heavily against finding that the renewals are perpetual. Though other terms are incorporated from year to year, this clause was unique in that it concerned the existence of the contract itself.

Arbitrator Seitz also referred to *Barry*, discussed in Chapter 2. In *Barry*, the Court interpreted the renewal provision in the NBA standard player contract as applying for only one year. MLB unsuccessfully argued that Major League Rules 4–A(a) and 3(g) ought to apply even though there was no contract. Seitz reasoned that "absent a contractual relationship . . . the Club's action in reserving his services for the ensuing year by placing him on its reserve list was unavailing and ineffectual in prohibiting him from dealing with other clubs in the league and to prohibit such clubs from dealing with him."

Finally, Seitz addressed the League's concerns that abolition of the reserve system would create tumult and upheaval in the league. Seitz hoped that the parties could "reach an agreement on measures that will give assurance of a reserve system that will meet the needs of the clubs and protect them from the damage they fear this decision will cause, and, at the same time, meet the needs of the player."

Though Seitz was immediately fired as baseball's arbitrator thereafter, his decision was upheld on appeal to the Eighth Circuit. Courts are under instruction from the Supreme Court, as stated in the *Steelworkers Trilogy*, to defer to arbitrator decisions and to favor arbitrability of disputes. In *United Steelworkers of America v. American Manufacturing Co.*,[3] the Supreme Court determined that where all questions of contract interpretation are governed by an arbitration agreement, a court can only play the limited role of "ascertaining whether the party seeking arbitration is making a claim which on its face is governed by the contract." In the second *Steelworkers* decision, the Supreme Court held that "an order to arbitrate the particular grievance should not be denied unless it may be said with positive assurances that the arbitration clause is not susceptible to an interpretation that covers the asserted dispute. Doubts should be resolved in favor of coverage."[4] In the third *Steelworkers* case, the court held that where it is clear and unmistakable that the parties have authorized the arbitrator, the courts will not readily overturn the arbitrator's ruling on that issue.[5]

In *Kansas City Royals Baseball Corp. v. Major League Baseball Players Ass'n*,[6] the Eighth Circuit court refused to hear the owner's legal argument, which had been foreclosed by arbitration. The Eighth Circuit explained that "[t]he question of interpretation of the collective bargaining agreement is a question for the arbitrator . . . because it was arbitrator's construction which was bargained for."[7] Commissioner Bowie Kuhn,

---

3. 363 U.S. 564 (1960).

4. Id. at 1353.

5. 363 U.S. 593 (1960).

6. 532 F.2d 615 (8th Cir. 1976).

7. Id.

reflecting back on his career, said that though he had not invoke his best interests power at the time in fear of a strike over free agency, "In hindsight, my greatest regret about my sixteen years as commissioner is that I did not take the grievance and head off Seitz."

B.   BARGAINING AWAY FREE AGENCY

After players won free agency in *Messersmith/McNally*, they used it as a bargaining chip in the next collective bargaining agreement negotiations to secure salary arbitration for younger players, thereby preserving the biggest paychecks for the veterans. Before the development of final offer arbitration or free agency, players either had to take a team's offer or hold out for more money. With the reserve system securely in place, player salaries were reduced from their free market value because of monopsonistic exploitation. Holdouts were costly for players not only in that they made relationships with teams tense, but they also cost players valuable playing time.[8] Players had to balance these costs against the promise of a higher salary, and, according to pitcher Sandy Koufax, "dignity" and "bargaining power."[9] Koufax and fellow star pitched Don Drysdale jointly held out against the Dodgers, and the settlement made them the highest paid players in baseball at the time.[10] The Koufax–Drysdale holdout was part of the reason why the owners voted 22 to 2 to amend the collective bargaining agreement to include salary arbitration in 1973, effective starting with the 1974 contracts.[11] Two years later, the owners also pushed for inclusion of a prohibition on joint player action. The 1976 agreement included the prohibition, but applied it to both players and clubs.[12]

In 1995, the owners made an unsuccessful attempt to ignore salary arbitration during heated negotiations over the Collective Bargaining Agreement, but were blocked by the National Labor Relations Act. In *Silverman v. Major League Baseball Player Relations Committee, Inc.*,[13] the owners were enjoined from unilaterally eliminating salary arbitration because wages are a mandatory subject of collective bargaining and because the action would contravene the Basic Agreement.

Originally, players with two years of major league service were eligible for arbitration.[14] Today, most players must have more than three but less than six years of service to be able to file for salary arbitration.[15] In certain cases, a player with between two and three years of service is eligible if he is a "super two." Super twos are players who have played for

---

8. ABRAMS, supra note 9 at 29.

9. Id. at 28.

10. Id. at 29.

11. Id. Charles Finley of the Oakland A's and Augie Busch of the St. Louis Cardinals voted against the proposal.

12. Id.

13. 67 F.3d 1054, 1057–58 (2d Cir. 1995).

14. Paul L. Burgess & Daniel R. Marburger, Bargaining Power and Major League Baseball, in DIAMONDS ARE FOREVER, ED. PAUL M. SOMMERS, 51 (1992).

15. MLB Basic Agreement, art. VI(F)(5) (1997).

two years in the major leagues, have accumulated 86 days of major league service time in the prior season, and rank in the top 17 percent in total service among similarly situated players.[16]

Once a player files for arbitration, neither arbitrators nor the parties know who will hear which case.[17] During the hearing, each party has one hour to make a presentation and a half-hour for rebuttal and summation before a three-arbitrator panel.[18] After a hearing, the arbitration panel "may render the decision on the day of the hearing, and shall make every effort to do so not later than 24 hours following the close of the hearing."[19] The panel does not offer any written explanation of its decision, but rather merely writes the winning award onto a standard player contract. Arbitration awards are final and binding for one-year contracts only.[20] Arbitration awards do not include creative solutions that can come forth during negotiations, such as bonuses, no trade clauses, or multiyear deals.[21]

The panel is permitted to consider the following when making its decision:

> (1) the quality of player contribution to the team during the past season, including overall performance, leadership, and public appeal;[22]
>
> (2) the length and consistency of a player's career;
>
> (3) a player's past compensation;
>
> (4) salaries of comparable players;
>
> (5) team performance; and
>
> (6) player mental and physical defects.[23]

The Basic Agreement does not specify how much weight to accord each criterion. The following evidence is prohibited

> (1) the financial position of the player or team;
>
> (2) press comments, testimonials, or similar material describing player or team performance;

---

16.   Id.

17.   Id. at 148.

18.   MLB Basic Agreement, Art. VI (F)(9) (1997). The time limitations may be increased by the arbitration panel if there is a lengthy cross-examination or for "good cause."

19.   MLB Basic Agreement, Art. VI (F)(5).

20.   Burgess & Marburger, supra note 41 at 51

21.   See Elisa M. Meth, Final Offer Arbitration: A Model for Dispute Resolution in Domestic and International Disputes, 10 AM. RE. INT'L ARB 383, 390 (1999). Meth explains that benefits include bonuses, guaranteed contracts, no trade clauses, single occupancy rooms on road trips, requiring a team to pay charges incurred upfront rather than through reimbursement, locker room benefits, and arrangements for families.

22.   Some say that Rick Cerone won arbitration in 1981 because "a group of shrieking women showed up at his hearing and requested his autograph." JENNINGS, supra note 16 at 207.

23.   MLB Basic Agreement Art VI(F)(12)(a) (1997). After a stint in a rehabilitation center for treatment for addiction to cocaine, pitcher Steve Howe returned to baseball. Howe opted for salary arbitration, and lost, "undoubtedly" because of his drug use. ABRAMS, supra note 9 at 62. At Orel Hershiser's 1985 hearing, the team brought up that he had spina bifida as a child. JENNINGS, supra note 16 at 209.

(3) offers made prior to arbitration;

(4) the costs of representation; and

(5) salaries in other sports or occupations[24]

to ensure that the salary is commensurate with that of like baseball players.

The jump in salary for rookies to arbitration eligible players is enormous. From 2006 to 2007, Ryan Howard's salary nearly tripled from $355,000 to $900,000.[25] When the Phillies' first baseman was finally eligible for arbitration after the 2007 season, he took Philadelphia to a hearing and won the highest salary ever awarded in arbitration: $10,000,000.[26] Unlike the reserve system of old, through which teams could dictate player salary and mobility throughout a player's career, the Basic Agreement provides players with an opportunity through arbitration to have a neutral third party decide what is a "fair" rate of pay, before these players are eligible for free agency and able to have the "free market" determine their worth.

C. THE CURT FLOOD ACT OF 1998

After nearly 80 years of silence, Congress finally spoke on the issue of MLB's antitrust exemption. In 1998, Congress Passed the Curt Flood Act to "state that major league baseball players are covered under the antitrust laws (i.e., that Major League baseball players will have the same rights under the antitrust laws as do other professional athletes, e.g., football and basketball players)." The Act expressly limited the removal of the exemption to MLB players, and stated that it does not apply to the relationship between MLB and Minor League baseball, "franchise expansion, location or relocation, franchise ownership issues, the marketing or sales of the entertainment product of organized professional baseball and the licensing of intellectual property rights owned or held by organized professional teams . . .", or umpires. Only Major League baseball players have standing to sue under the Act.

A group of senators objected to the Act on the grounds that it "takes the potentially counterproductive step of engaging in a piecemeal approach to the issues confronting baseball by addressing only the application of the antitrust laws to Major League baseball labor relations." The minority senators identified "important issues" such as "league expansion and franchise movement, taxpayer-financed stadiums, revenue sharing, player salaries, and fan access to television coverage" that warranted addressing. We will visit some of these issues in Chapter 8.

---

24. MLB Basic Agreement art. VI (F)(12)(b) (1997).

25. Ryan Howard Stats, News, Photos. http://sports.espn.go.com/mlb/players/profile?statsId= 7437

26. Associated Press, Howard's $10M win in arbitration sets new high-water mark (Feb. 22, 2008). http://sports.espn.go.com/mlb/news/story?id=3256452. Alfonso Soriano was also awarded $10 million in arbitration, but sought $12 million. Twenty years ago, Don Mattingly held the record arbitration award of $1.975 million.

SUMMARY QUESTIONS

1. Note that in Messersmith / McNally, Arbitrator Seitz relied on *Barry*. Consider the MLB reserve clause's history in *Chase*, *Lajoie* and *Flood*, as opposed to the Court's treatment of the NFL's equivalent clause in *Mackey*.

2. Consider the Messersmith/McNally 1976 Arbitration Decision, pursuant to which "free agency" was achieved for the MLBPA, in a way that Curt Flood could not achieve it in the Supreme Court. (See: Weiler, at pp. 278–287.) In so doing, consider how the Commissioner's Authority was eroded, and why, to the point where an Arbitrator (arguably) was empowered to render this landmark decision, rather than the Commissioner himself?

3. Consider Arbitrator Seitz's "reasoning" in ruling in favor of the plaintiffs, and compare same with the companion NFL-related decision in the John Dutton arbitration. (Weiler, at p. 286). In 1980, John Dutton filed a grievance to determine if the option clause contained in § 17 of NFL player contracts was perpetually renewable. Arbitrator Luskin said that although under the *Mackey* test the players would win this claim in a court of law, under the collective bargaining agreement, the option is perpetually renewable. The rest of the player contract contained provisions that said all veteran free agents are subject to the right of first refusal and only denied this right in cases of extreme personal hardship. This collectively bargaining for provision is protected by the nonstatutory labor exemption, and Dutton could not try to win through arbitration what the NFLPA had bargained away.

4. During *Kansas City Royals*, an MLB counsel Louis Hoynes testified that Marvin Miller said during collective bargaining agreement negotiations that "[The reserve system] is going to be outside the Agreement. It will not be subject to the Agreement, but we will acquiesce in the continuance of the enforcement of the rules as house rules and we will not grieve over those house rules." Miller denied the statement. Consider that Marvin Miller's underlying agreement with the Commissioner to "play by house rules" during the preceding collective bargaining agreement negotiation is true. Is there a case by MLB for possible "fraud in the inducement" against Miller?[27]

5. Analyze Seitz's Opinion regarding remaining within "the four corners" of the collective bargaining agreement, as opposed to "admitting into evidence" the Owners' contrary testimony that there was never any intention to allow for "the end of the reserve clause," during the prior CBA negotiations.

6. Consider the Eighth Circuit Appeals Court decision re: the foregoing Arbitration Decision. In particular, consider the "Commissioner's Authority," as referenced in footnote 2 of the Appeals Court's decision, in which Commissioner Kuhn claimed that he could have invoked his "ultimate authority" to withdraw the case from Arbitration.

---

27. Though the elements differ from jurisdiction to jurisdiction, to prove "fraud in the inducement," a plaintiff generally needs to show that (1.) the defendant made a false statement of material fact, (2.) that the defendant knew or should have known was false; (3.) that was made to induce the plaintiff to enter into a contract, and (4.) that proximately caused injury to the plaintiff when acting in reliance on the misrepresentation. See William Herbert Page, The Law of Contracts 435–578 (1920).

7. Could or should Commissioner Kuhn have intruded upon the Messersmith/McNally arbitration or Eighth Circuit litigation by, *inter alia*, invoking the MLB Commissioner's authority to act in the best interests of the game (discussed in Chapter 1)? Consider Footnote 2 in the Eighth Circuit Opinion re: Commissioner Kuhn's opinion that he had the "authority" to remove the arbitration to his jurisdiction, but had "chosen" not to do so, for a variety of reasons. (In Bowie's autobiography, he called that his "worst decision" ever! (per *Weiler* text)).

8. Was the CBA's grant of grievance arbitration jurisdiction to an arbitrator, instead of the Commissioner, in the "best interests of baseball?"

9. Is the non-statutory labor exemption implicated here? How is that same exemption implicated differently in the NFL *Dutton* case?

Writing Exercise 1: Confidential and Privileged Memorandum advising Commissioner Kuhn as to whether he should invoke "best interests" powers in Messersmith/McNally[28]

Commissioner Kuhn is considering invoking his authority to act in the "best interests" of the game to usurp Arbitrator Seitz's jurisdiction. Advise Commissioner Kuhn as to whether he should take this action. What are the strongest arguments as to why "reserve clause" dispute should remain in the Arbitrator's jurisdiction, after the Supreme Court had already arguably ruled on it in *Flood v. Kuhn*?

In so doing, consider the following principles regarding contract interpretation:

(1.) the arbitrator should give effect to plain language of the collective bargaining agreement, and where the agreement is ambiguous, the interpretation that makes the agreement lawful and valid should prevail;

(2.) the arbitrator should use normal and technical usage in interpreting words;

(3.) the agreement should be viewed as a whole;

(4.) the arbitrator should avoid harsh, absurd, or nonsensical results;

(5.) the arbitrator must remember to expressly state something is to exclude another;

(6.) where general words follow specific words, the general words should cover only things of a general nature as those listed;

(7.) specific language trumps general language;

(8.) custom and past practice of the parties should be considered;

(9.) industry practice should be considered; and

---

28. An "exemplar" student submission in response to this hypothetical can be found in the accompanying Teacher's Manual.

(10.) the arbitrator should interpret the language in favor of the party who did not draft the agreement.[29]

Consider these principles, as related to the facts giving rise to the Messersmith / McNally arbitration and the history of the reserve system, when giving your advice to the Commissioner.

II. OWNER COLLUSION

MLB owners did not easily accept the players winning free agency, and consequently earning higher salaries. In the mid 1980s, player movement came to a sudden halt. At an owners meeting in 1985, MLB management distributed a memorandum encouraging the teams to "exercise more self-discipline in making their operating decisions and to resist the temptation to give in to the unreasonable demands of experienced marginal players."[30] The MLBPA, suspecting foul play, filed a grievance alleging that the owners were violating Article XVIII of the collective bargaining agreement, which prohibited either players or clubs from acting in concert with one another. The provision was originally included after Sandy Koufax and Don Drysdale and Larry Bowa and Mike Schmidt had negotiated in tandem with teams. In the first collusion hearing, arbitrator Thomas Roberts found that the owners had acted in concert in their treatment of free agents, and specifically that the clubs had waited until free agents were released by their prior teams and that team had indicated that it did not care to resign the player before pursuing the free agent. Based upon the evidence, Roberts concluded that the MLB owners had colluded, in violation of the same "Koufax Drysdale" clause that had (ironically) been applied reciprocally to the MLB owners. Note the "irony" of the Koufax/Drysdale language, when applied "mutually" to the owners; ended up "pantsing" the owner—one of Marvin Miller's greatest "Rope-A-dopes"!

As the first collusion grievance was undergoing arbitration, the 1986 free agent season had commenced and the MLBPA was concerned that the owners were still colluding, prompting the PA to file a second claim. This time, arbitrator George Nicolau would hear the case. After receiving Arbitrator Roberts' decision and the new evidence before him, Nicolau concluded that MLB had once again colluded based upon "the evidence taken as a whole that tells us where a common understanding exists."[31]

After a still frustrating 1987–88 free agency season, the MLBPA filed a third grievance, and prevailed once again, though on slightly different facts. This time, the MLBPA alleged that the owners had formed an "Information Bank" that stored and shared each team's information regarding free agent bids. The goal, according to the MLBPA, was to depress player salaries by sharing full information and preventing compe-

---

29. F. Elkouri, How Arbitration Works 342–65 (1985).

30. Grievance No. 86–2.

31. Grievance No. 87–3.

tition. Arbitrator Nicolau once again found in favor of the players because the clubs were impermissibly acting in concert.

After the third collusion ruling, MLB and the MLBPA reached a settlement of $280 million. As part of the settlement, the MLBPA agreed not to sue for collusion after the subsequent season, and sixteen players were given a second chance to test the free market. To this day, MLB management continues to deny that the owners impermissibly colluded.[32]

In subsequent litigation regarding the collusion award, *MLBPA v. Garvey*,[33] the Supreme Court reiterated the policy of judicial deference to arbitration decisions. Pursuant to the settlement of the collusion claims, the MLBPA designed a "Framework" to evaluate player claims. Players denied recovery could seek review through arbitration to determine whether "the approved Framework and the criteria set forth therein have been properly applied." Steve Garvey's claim for $3 million was denied, and the arbitrator denied Garvey's claim citing the need for more evidence. Garvey sought to vacate the award, and convinced the Ninth Circuit to review the decision because, according to the Court, "the arbitrator's refusal to credit [Padres' President and CEO Ballard Smith] was 'inexplicable' and 'bordered on the irrational.'" In a decision reversing the Ninth Circuit, the Supreme Court stated that "the fact that 'a court is convinced [the arbitrator] committed serious error does not suffice to overturn his decision.' It is only when the arbitrator strays from the interpretation and application of the agreement and effectively 'dispense[s] his own brand of industrial justice' that his decision may be unenforceable."

Though the Information Bank created by the MLB owners was held to be impermissible collusion, a similar information bank created by NFL agents was deemed to be permissible. In *Five Smiths, Inc. v. National Football League Players Ass'n*, 788 F.Supp. 1042 (D. Minn 1992), the NFL filed suit against the now decertified NFLPA and agents arguing that sharing information about player contracts violated the Sherman Act. The Court relied on *Container Corp.*, which held that exchange of price information, without an agreement to fix prices, raises antitrust concern of if the following conditions exist: (1.) a highly concentrated market with few sellers, (2.) a fungible product, (3.) competition that is based primarily on price, and (4.) inelasticity of demand. In *Five Smiths*, the court found that these four conditions do not apply to the NFL. There are over 1,500 players selling their services, each with unique skills. Player salary is driven by negotiations, not price, and there is no inelasticity of demand because buyers do not buy only to satisfy immediate needs. Moreover, the court reasoned, information can make the process more fair because it will clear up misunderstandings and misrepresentations. More importantly, sharing information was also procompetitive, because it allowed players to compete more equally with owners, who had such information.

---

32. See Marc Edelman, Moving Past Collusion in Major League Baseball: Healing Old Wounds, and Preventing New Ones, 61 The Wayne L. Rev. 601 (2008).

33. 532 U.S. 504 (2001).

SUMMARY QUESTIONS

1.   Why didn't the antitrust exemption protect the MLB owners from liability, or in the context of the information bank arbitration ruling?

2.   Why was Judge Doty's NFLPA agents' similar information bank case decided differently?

3.   How did the 1998 Flood Act change the judicially-created antitrust exemption?

4.   How does the territorial antitrust exemption (discussed in detail in Chapter 8) continue to create inequities in MLB payrolls? How do "regional networks" like YES and NESN create an "uneven playing field" for "mega-market teams" versus "smaller-market teams" like Kansas City and Cleveland?

CHAPTER 7

COLLECTIVE BARGAINING AND INTELLECTUAL PROPERTY DISPUTES REGARDING PLAYER, TEAM, AND LEAGUE RIGHTS

■ ■ ■

Introduction

As professional athletes garner fame (or notoriety), their personas gain commercial value. An athlete's persona can be extremely valuable and a lucrative source of income. To protect this economic interest, courts have recognized a "right of publicity." The "right of publicity" protects an individual's interest in controlling the commercial use of that individual's identity. If this right to pecuniary gain from one's fame were exclusive, however, it would always trump the right of others to use one's person, thereby consistently stifling free expression. Therefore, one's own right to publicity uncomfortably coexists with others' right to free expression. Courts have struggled to define a clear boundary between these two rights and to determine how to resolve disputes that arise when these two rights seem to overlap. The first part of this Chapter describes the contours of the still blurry right of publicity, and the rights that players have against third party advertisers or artists who try to appropriate their identity.

Teams and leagues, eager to use their superstar players to market themselves, are also interested in using players' personas. Each league has collectively bargained for a grant of the right of publicity from the player to the league for marketing purposes, though when the league can use the players' identity varies from league to league, as explained in part II.

I. DEVELOPMENT OF THE RIGHT OF PUBLICITY

In what might seem like an odd origin, the right of publicity sprang from the doctrine of the "right of privacy."[1] When writing about the right of privacy, William Prosser identified four distinct torts that might befall a victim: (1.) intrusion upon physical solitude; (2.) public disclosure of

---

1. Samuel Warren and Louis Brandeis first named the right of privacy in 1890 in an eponymous article. See Samuel Warren and Louis Brandeis, The Right to Privacy, 4 HARV. L. REV. 193 (1890).

private facts; (3.) depiction in a false light in the public eye; and (4.) appropriation of name or likeness.[2] It is from this last tort that courts grasped and grafted into their jurisprudence the right of people to "block the use of their names and likenesses in advertisements without their consent."[3]

The specific contours of the right of publicity developed slowly and haphazardly across state lines. Some courts had difficulty accepting that any tortuous interference of a subcategory of one's right of privacy—as identified by Prosser—could have occurred when the alleged victim was a celebrity, someone who had voluntarily made himself or herself a public figure. For instance, in *O'Brien v. Pabst Sales*,[4] one-time All–American quarterback Davey O'Brien objected to Pabst beer company's use of his image juxtaposed with a glass of beer in its annual football calendar. The court dismissed the claim on the grounds that O'Brien had no reasonable expectation of privacy given his celebrity and that the calendar's use of his image did not contain or constitute O'Brien's explicit endorsement of Pabst beer. All-star athletes who reached the height of fame prior to the acceptance of the right of publicity, including Joe DiMaggio, Joe Louis, and Babe Ruth, were never able to profit from the commercial use of their identities, as licenses for use by third parties were unnecessary.[5]

Finally, in 1951, about a half-century after the right of privacy had been identified, *Haelan Laboratories, Inc. v. Topps Chewing Gum, Inc.*[6] explicitly recognized a right of publicity. Drawing upon state common law, the court not only identified a cognizable "publicity value of one's name and picture," it also determined that this right is assignable by its holder.[7] Thus, the court reasoned, Topps could not sell baseball cards with player photographs because those players had already granted an exclusive license for this use to a Topps competitor. According to the court,

> [I]t is common knowledge that many prominent persons (especially actors and ballplayers), far from having their feelings bruised through public exposure of their likenesses, would feel sorely deprived if they no longer received money for authorizing advertisements, popularizing their countenances, displayed in newspapers, magazines, buses, trains and subways. This right of publicity would usually yield them

---

2. William Prosser, Privacy, 48 CAL. L. REV. 383, 389 (1960).

3. See Pavesich v. New England Life Insurance, 122 Ga. 190, 50 S.E. 68 (1905). But see Roberson v. Rochester Folding Box, 171 N.Y. 538, 64 N.E. 442 (1902) (denying the right of privacy). New York's legislature later passed §§ 50 and 51 of the Civil Rights Law, which provides a claim for the unauthorized use of the "name, portrait or picture of any living person . . . for advertising purposes, or for the purposes of trade . . ."

4. 124 F.2d 167 (5th Cir. 1941).

5. Paul Weiler & Gary Roberts, SPORTS AND THE LAW 473 (3d ed. 2004).

6. 202 F.2d 866, 868 (2d Cir. 1953). Haelan Laboratories is no longer valid law in New York. See Pirone v. MacMillan, Inc., 894 F.2d 579 (2d Cir. 1990) (acknowledging that Haelan Laboratories no longer stated the law regarding the right of publicity in New York, and that the only claims could arise from statutes).

7. Id.

no money unless it could be made the subject of an exclusive grant which barred any other advertiser from using their pictures.[8]

Valuable economic gains, the *Haelan* court stated, would be diverted from players if the players were unable to control the use of their photographs. The Restatement (Third) of Unfair Competition also focuses on the economic losses that could stem from the violation of the right of publicity, defining the right as the appropriation of "the commercial value of a person's identity by using without consent the person's name, likeness or other indicia for purposes of trade."[9]

Zacchini v. Scripps–Howard Broadcasting[10] is the only opinion the Supreme Court has rendered on the right of publicity. After considering the case brought by a "human cannonball," the Court ultimately agreed that the right of publicity was indeed violated when a new report broadcast the entire fifteen-second performance.[11] Analogizing to the incentive-laden regimes of patent and copyright law, the Court reasoned that the right of publicity also "focus[es] on the right of the individual to reap the reward of his endeavors and ha[s] little to do with protecting feelings or reputation."[12] In distinguishing from acceptable uses by the media, or seemingly, a less troubling type of violation of the right of publicity, the Court noted that "the broadcast of petitioner's entire performance, unlike the unauthorized use of another's name for purposes of trade or the incidental use of a name or picture by the press, goes to the heart of petitioner's ability to earn a living as an entertainer."[13] According to the Court, economic interests are paramount in the inquiry of whether the right of publicity has been violated.

Precisely what is protected, and when it is violated, is still not clear. Looking at various precedents can help elucidate the parameters of the right of publicity. In *Carson v. Here's Johnny Portable Toilets, Inc.*,[14] the court held that the use of the phrases "Here's Johnny" and "The World's Foremost Commodian" violated comedian Johnny Carson's right of publicity. Even though Carson's name was not used, it was clear the public would identify those phrases with his identity. Similarly, in *Ali v. Playgirl, Inc.*,[15] the Court held that a drawing in a man in a boxing ring with the

---

8. Id. at 868.

9. Restatement (Third) of Unfair Competition § 46 (1995). "The name, likeness, and other indicia of a person's identity are used 'for purpose of trade' under the rule stated in § 46 if they are used in advertising the user's goods or services, or are placed on merchandise marketed by the use, or are used in connection with services rendered by the user. However, use 'for purposes of trade' does not ordinarily include the use of a person's identity in news reporting, commentary, entertainment, works of fiction or nonfiction, or in advertising that is incidental to such uses." Id. at § 47.

10. 433 U.S. 562 (1977).

11. Id. at 563–64. The Court rejected the argument that the First Amendment, as applied through the Fourteenth Amendment, always trumps the right of publicity. Id. at 564.

12. Id. at 574.

13. Id. at 576.

14. 698 F.2d 831 (6th Cir. 1983).

15. 447 F.Supp. 723 (S.D.N.Y. 1978).

phrase "The Greatest" above the drawing was sufficiently associated with boxer Muhammad Ali to violate his right of publicity. The use of the name "Crazylegs" for a woman's shaving cream violated famous football player Elroy Hirsch's—whose nickname was Crazylegs—right of publicity.[16] In *Doe v. TCI Cablevision*,[17] the Court found that hockey player Tony Twist's right of publicity was violated by a cartoon's use of his name for one of its characters. Unauthorized use of Bette Midler's distinctive voice through a sound-alike in a Ford commercial,[18] of a famous race car driver's distinctive car that implicated his identity,[19] and of a robot dressed and posed like Vanna White[20] were all found to violate the celebrity's right of publicity.

Players do not have intellectual property rights in the broadcasts of their performances. In *Baltimore Orioles v. MLBPA*,[21] the Seventh Circuit held that players do not own the broadcasts, but the clubs do, because the broadcasts are created as "works for hire." Further, copyright law trumped any state law publicity claims the players might have. After players sent letters to clubs and television and cable companies with which the clubs had contracts alleging that the broadcasts misappropriated player publicity rights, the clubs filed an action for declaratory judgment. The Court first analyzed whether the player's telecasts were "works for hire" under Section 201 of the Copyright Act. Works for hire are not owned by the authors, but rather by the employer. The Seventh Circuit explained that "an employer owns a copyright in a work if (1) the work satisfies the generally applicable requirements for copyrightability ..., (2) the work was prepared by an employee, (3) the work was prepared within the scope of the employee's employment, and (4) the parties have not expressly agreed otherwise in a signed written instrument." Though the telecasts are copyrightable audiovisual works, i.e. original works in a fixed medium, the players created the works as employees within the scope of their employment. The Court rejected the argument that merely because revenues from broadcasts were shared with players that meant there was some question as to ownership. This federal copyright preempted the players' state right of publicity claims. State law can only give protection to unfixed performances, not to performances that are otherwise fixed elsewhere. The Court noted that "the Players have attempted to obtain ex post what they did not negotiate ex ante," and they could not use publicity rights to do so.

Professional athletes also do not have rights in statistics stemming from their performances. Early in the litigation regarding these attributes, where a board game company used player names and statistics without player permission the Court upheld the players' claim, noting that "[p]layer names and statistics are valuable only because of their past public

---

16.   See Hirsch v. S.C. Johnson & Son, Inc., 90 Wis.2d 379, 280 N.W.2d 129 (1979).

17.   110 S.W.3d 363 (Mo. 2003).

18.   Midler v. Ford Motor Co., 849 F.2d 460 (9th Cir. 1988).

19.   Motschenbacher v. R.J. Reynolds Tobacco Co., 498 F.2d 821 (9th Cir. 1974).

20.   Vanna White v. Samsung Electronics America, Inc., 989 F.2d 1512 (9th Cir. 1993).

21.   805 F.2d 663 (7th Cir. 1986).

disclosure, publicity, and circulation ... To hold that such publicity destroys a right to sue for appropriation of a name or likeness would negate any and all causes of action, for only after disclosure and public acceptance does the name of a celebrity have any value at all to make its unauthorized use enjoinable."[22]

Subsequently, however, courts have narrowed the scope of the right of publicity with respect to such names and statistics alone. In *National Basketball Ass'n v. Motorola, Inc.*,[23] the Second Circuit found that statistics from NBA games are uncopyrightable facts and that Motorola was legally transmitting live information about NBA games to handheld pagers. Motorola's pager, "SportsTrax," displayed updated information about ongoing professional baseball games. Though the Second Circuit recognized a narrow "hot news" protection under state law, it protected Motorola's transmission of real time NBA scores and information. In support of its holding, the Court noted that Motorola was using a company whose reporters watched the games and translated the data to the pagers, not taking information already tabulated by the NBA. Claims for misappropriation of "hot news" are limited to situations in which "(i) a plaintiff generates or gathers information at a cost; (ii) the information is time-sensitive; (iii) a defendant's use of the information constitutes free-riding on the plaintiff's efforts; (iv) the defendant is in direct competition with a product or service offered by the plaintiffs; and (v) the ability of other parties to free-ride on the efforts of the plaintiff or others would so reduce the incentive to produce the product or service that its existence or quality would be substantially threatened."

Five years later, in *Gionfriddo v. Major League Baseball*,[24] former players alleged that their names, statistics, photographs and video images were unauthorizedly used in All–Star game and World Series programs, on Major League Baseball's websites, and in videos and television broadcasts. The Court dismissed the lawsuit, holding that the information used "may fairly be characterized as mere bits of baseball history ... [the use of which] is a form of protection due substantial constitutional protection." The Court went on to say that the "public interest favoring free dissemination of information regarding baseball's history far outweighs any proprietary interests at stake." Finally, the players' statistics and likenesses were being used to "promote the product of baseball," not to endorse an unrelated commercial product. Advertisements violate the right of publicity when "the plaintiff's identity is used, without consent, to promote an *unrelated* product."[25]

Not only is appropriation of statistics or historical information protected, but if a work is sufficiently transformative, it may warrant protection under the First Amendment as well. The Restatement (Third) of

---

22. *Uhaelander*, 316 F. Supp. at 1282–1283.

23. 105 F.3d 841 (2d Cir. 1997).

24. 94 Cal.App.4th 400, 114 Cal.Rptr.2d 307 (2001).

25. Gionfriddo.

Unfair Competition, in a comment to its definition of the right of publicity, states that the right "as recognized by statute and common law is fundamentally constrained by the public and constitutional interest in freedom of expression."[26] The law attempts to achieve a balance between the right of publicity and freedom of expression where both are implicated. As such, courts attempt—sometimes awkwardly—to weigh the competing interests of publicity and free speech and to determine which seems stronger in a particular case. Unfortunately, the Supreme Court has yet to provide a specific way to accomplish this task. Incorporating ideas from more developed fields with similar underlying policies (such as copyright and trademark law) has proven somewhat helpful, but has also been somewhat confusing, given that these other doctrines do not readily translate into the arena of publicity rights. This has led to an interrelated collection of doctrines inconsistently adopted by different jurisdictions across the country. Generally, speech is thought to exist on a spectrum where on one end purely non-commercial speech receives the highest protection and on the other end wholly commercial speech garners much less, though still significant, protection.

"Parodies," works that appropriate elements of an original work to make a commentary on the original or on society, receive full protection. Though parody has arisen only a few times in publicity rights, its protection in other fields requiring First Amendment balancing is well-established. In *Cardtoons, L.C. v. Major League Baseball Players Association*,[27] a company produced baseball cards featuring easily recognizable caricatures of players. Though the defendant appropriated the identity of baseball players, he also arguably provided humorous and insightful commentary by transforming each individual athlete. After weighing Cardtoons' parody as a "vital commodity in the marketplace of ideas," the Court examined the effect of infringing upon the publicity rights. It stated that unlike other types of appropriation, parody does not seem to provide celebrities with any additional income because rarely, if ever, will a celebrity give permission for a parody of himself or herself. Thus, parody rarely acts as a substitute for an original work and does not economically affect the market for non-parodist works that a celebrity might license. Additionally, the Court reasoned that the market for parodies is sufficiently small that celebrities would not lose the incentive to enter the industry. Finally, and perhaps more importantly, the Court expressed concern that celebrities given control over their appropriation in parodies would "use that power to suppress criticism, and thus permanently remove a valuable source of information about their identity from the marketplace."

This creative element of products featuring appropriated celebrity identities, coined "transformative use," has become its own First Amendment defense to publicity rights claims. Articulated by the California Supreme Court in *Comedy III Productions, Inc. v. Gary Saderup, Inc.*,[28]

---

26. Restatement (Third) of Unfair Competition, § 47, Comment c.

27. 95 F.3d 959 (10th Cir. 1996).

28. 25 Cal.4th 387, 106 Cal.Rptr.2d 126, 21 P.3d 797 (2001).

and adopted by the Sixth Circuit in *ETW Corp. v. Jireh Publishing, Inc.*, the transformative use doctrine gives protection to expression that has added significant creativity to an appropriation of identity. The California Supreme Court summarized the test as "whether the celebrity likeness is one of the 'raw materials' from which an original work is synthesized or whether the depiction or imitation of the celebrity is the very sum and substance of the work in question." To receive protection, the defendant must transform the product featuring the celebrity likeness to the extent that the expression becomes primarily the defendant's. The artistic creativity is added to the First Amendment side of the scale against the publicity rights. In *Comedy III*, the Court found that lithographed and silkscreen tee shirts depicting the Three Stooges lacked enough creativity to trump the right of publicity.

In *Jireh*, artist Rick Rush created paintings commemorating Tiger Woods' first Masters victory featuring multiple depictions of Woods on the Augusta National course. Though the images of Woods occupied most of the picture, and one looked identical to Woods engaged in his "signature swing"—the use of which had been licensed to Nike to make a poster—the Sixth Circuit refused to find a violation of Woods' publicity rights. The Court found that "Rush's work consists of a collage of images in addition to Woods' image which are combined to describe, in artistic form, a historic event in sports history and to convey a message about the significance of Woods' achievement in that event." The Court concluded that what it saw as the substantial creative and informative content of Rush's work outweighed Woods' right to publicity—despite the existence of an expert's "survey evidence" indicating "consumer confusion" over Woods' endorsement (or not) of the Rush "collage".

II. BARGAINING AWAY THE RIGHT OF PUBLICITY

Haelan Laboratories not only stands for the important principle that professional athletes have a right of publicity, but also that such right is assignable. Athletes who join the MLB, NFL, and NBA grant away some of these rights to the player's union in each league. Moreover, players' ability to pursue endorsement opportunities may be limited per the terms of their player contracts.

A. MAJOR LEAGUE BASEBALL PUBLICITY RIGHTS

If a player so chooses, upon joining the MLB, it can grant the MLBPA the right to that player's attributes. Aggregating these grants, the MLBPA currently holds the "exclusive, worldwide right to use, license and sublicense the names, numbers, nicknames, likenesses, signatures and other personal indicia (known as 'publicity rights') of active Major League Baseball players who are its members for use in connection with any product, brand, service or product line *when more than two players are involved*." As an example of these rights, the MLBPA explains that it alone can license the right of three players to appear on a single product or when players are used to sponsor products. The MLBPA touts its "Players Choice" program as protecting "the rights of players from exploitation by unauthorized parties" and providing "marketing services few players could provide for themselves . . ." Under this regime, players receive a pro rata share—determined by days of Major League service in a given season—of licensing revenue. The MLB requires "players to confirm to high standards of personal conduct," presumably diminishing the universe of endorsement opportunities available.

The MLB's use of player rights was first challenged with baseball cards. In 1986, the dispute over who could produce baseball cards between Topps, Fleer, and the MLBPA came to a head in *Fleer Corporation v. Topps Chewing Gum, Inc.*[29] Topps had obtained the rights through exclusive licenses from individual players. To obtain the licenses, Topps approached players while still in the minor leagues to acquire rights to publish the player's "name, picture, signature and biographical sketch" and to sell cards along with bubble gum. Simultaneously, players who played for major league teams also granted their publicity rights to the MLBPA, to enable the MLBPA to convey group licenses. The MLBPA could not, however, execute a group licensing contract with "merchandisers for rights covered by players' contracts respecting competing products," and therefore the MLBPA could not license others to sell baseball cards in competition with Topps, i.e. player cards sold alone of in combination with gum, candy, and other confections. Fleer, a competing baseball card manufacturer, sued Topps for violation of antitrust laws because Topps had obtained an exclusive license agreement with every professional baseball player. The court, however, rejected the antitrust challenge on the grounds that Fleer could enter the market by competing for minor league players, that the group license was procompetitive because it facilitated the sale of baseball items, and that Topps and the MLBPA were not horizontal competitors who had joined together. Rather, the court reasoned, Topps was a consumer of the player licensing rights, whereas the MLBPA was the distributor of those rights.

Topps upheld the MLBPA's right to collectively license player attributes to baseball card manufacturers, and the MLBPA enjoyed licensing these rights for lucrative contracts until 2008. By that time, the shape of the market for publicity rights had changed dramatically. No longer was licensing baseball cards the principal source of revenue; rather, the fantasy sports market had burgeoned into a multi-million dollar industry. In 2009, it was estimated that over 27 million people participated in fantasy sports leagues and the industry earned about $1 billion annually.

C.B.C. Distribution and Marketing, Inc. ("CBC") was licensing player names and statistics from the MLBPA for use in CBC's fantasy baseball

---

29.   658 F.2d 139 (3d Cir. 1981), *cert. denied*, 455 U.S. 1019 (1982).

league. The parties had nearly a ten year relationship until CBC's license expired, and Major League Baseball Advanced Media ("MLBAM") declined to renew the license to reserve the right to run fantasy games for itself on MLB.com. CBC, worried about the legality of running fantasy games without a license, sued seeking a declaratory judgment that it could permissibly run its website. The Eighth Circuit ruled in favor of CBC, finding that in fantasy sports games, the First Amendment trumped player publicity rights.

The Eighth Circuit began its analysis with an examination of the right of publicity. The Court stated that under Missouri law, the elements of a right of publicity action are that the defendant used the plaintiff's name as a symbol of his identity without consent and with the intent to obtain a commercial advantage. After the expiration of the license agreement, CBC was indeed using the player's names without consent, the names referred to actual major league baseball players, and that CBC used "baseball players' identities in its fantasy sports for purposes of profit," fulfilling the "commercial advantage" prong of the analysis. In total, the players had made a claim for violation of the right of publicity.

Nevertheless, the First Amendment trumped the violation of the right of publicity. The Eighth Circuit, relying on *Gionfriddo*, was persuaded by the argument that the dissemination of player statistics was in the public interest. Further, the Court found that players would not suffer an economic disincentive to play baseball because they are already "rewarded, and handsomely too, for their participation in games and can earn additional large sums from endorsements and sponsorship arrangements."

The Court concluded its analysis by (incredibly) finding not that CBC had breached its agreement with MLBAM, which had provided that CBC would not challenge the title of the rights granted and that CBC would not use the rights upon expiration, but rather that MLBAM had ("after the fact") breached the agreement because it had represented that it owned the rights.

B. NATIONAL FOOTBALL LEAGUE PUBLICITY RIGHTS

The NFL has a similar group licensing program. NFL players who note "opt-out" ability in all three leagues agree to the NFL Group Licensing Form give the NFLPA the right to use that player's attributes in licensing agreements for products with six or more players. The grant in contained in the NFL's standard Player Contract, and reads as follows:

4. PUBLICITY AND NFLPA GROUP LICENSING PROGRAM.

(a) Player grants to Club and the League, separately and together, the authority to use his *name and picture* for publicity and the promotion of NFL Football, the League or any of its member clubs in newspapers, magazines, motion pictures, game programs and roster manuals, broadcasts and telecasts, and all other publicity and advertising media, provided such publicity and promotion does not constitute an endorsement by Player of a commercial product. Player will cooperate with the news media, and will participate upon request in reasonable activities to promote the Club and the League. . . .

(b) Player hereby assigns to the NFLPA and its licensing affiliates, if any, the *exclusive right to use and to grant* to persons, firms, or corporations (collectively "licensees") the right to use his name, signature facsimile, voice, picture, photograph, likeness, and/or biographical information (collectively "image") in group licensing programs. Group licensing programs are defined as those licensing programs in which a licensee utilizes a total of six (6) or more NFL player images on or in conjunction with products (including, but not limited to, trading cards, clothing, videogames, computer games, collectibles, internet sites, fantasy games, etc.) that are sold at retail or used as promotional or premium items. Player retains the right to grant permission to a licensee to utilize his image if that licensee is not concurrently utilizing the images of five (5) or more other NFL players on products that are sold at retail or are used as promotional or premium items. If Player's inclusion in a particular NFLPA program is precluded by an individual exclusive endorsement agreement, and Player provides the NFLPA with timely written notice of that preclusion, the NFLPA will exclude Player from that particular program. In consideration for this assignment of rights, the NFLPA will use the revenues it receives from group licensing programs to support the objectives as set forth in the Bylaws of the NFLPA. The NFLPA will use its best efforts to promote the use of NFL player images in group licensing programs, to provide group licensing opportunities to all NFL players, and to ensure that no entity utilizes the group licensing rights granted to the NFLPA without first obtaining a license from the NFLPA. . . . The terms of this subparagraph apply unless, at the time of execution of this contract, Player indicates by striking out this subparagraph (b) and marking his initials adjacent to the stricken language his intention to not participate in the NFLPA Group Licensing Program. Nothing in this subparagraph shall be construed to supersede or any way broaden, expand, detract from, or otherwise alter in any way whatsoever, the rights of NFL Properties, Inc. as permitted under Article V (Union Security), Section 4 of the 1993 Collective Bargaining Agreement ("CBA").

The NFLPA has used this grant to license player attributes to tee shirts, posters, trading cards, stickers, board games, toys, and other products. Note that the NFLPA promises to use its "best efforts" to promote the use of the images. Further, players have the power to opt out of a particular program that conflicts with a player's own endorsement, if that player gives the NFL timely notice. When players are pursuing their own endorsement opportunities, they may not seek endorsement by "any kind of company whose brand name is prominently associated with the production, manufacture, or distribution of a (banned substance) with respect to Anabolic Steroids and Related Substances.''

In *Gridiron.com, Inc. v. National Football League Player's Ass'n, Inc.*,[30] a court found that a website using more than six players' images without first obtaining a license violated the licensing agreement. Gridiron.com had aggregated individual player websites of over 150 NFL players on its website and ran a fantasy football game. To support itself, the website had sold space to third-party advertisers who were '' 'willing to pay top dollar for the opportunity to be affiliated with . . . a professional football player.' '' The Court noted that the 97 percent of NFL players were parties to the exclusive licensing agreement with the NFLPA, and the website's use violated the NFLPA's rights to the use of six or more player images. The Court went on to reject the plaintiff's first amendment claim on the grounds that plaintiff was using the players' attributes to attract advertising revenue, not to disseminate news about the players. Thus, the NFLPA was awarded a permanent injunction against Gridiron.com.

The validity of this ruling was not only been cast into doubt by *C.B.C.*, but was also undermined by a recent victory on summary judgment by CBS Interactive, Inc. against the NFLPA. CBS Interactive (''CBSI'') sued the NFLPA in Minnesota after refusing to renew its license agreement with NFLPA's Players, Inc., arguing that CBSI did not have to pay royalties to the NFLPA for use of ''the names and statistics of the individual players in connection with the fantasy football games that CBS Interactive provided to its customers . . .''[31] CBSI alleged that the NFLPA illegally monopolized the fantasy football market by requiring CBSI to purchase a license for NFL player statistics. The NFLPA responded that CBSI's use of the player information went beyond that which was protected in *C.B.C.* and that some uses constitute a violation of players' right of publicity. The court found that in light of *C.B.C.*, however, there were no issues of material fact as to whether CBSI's use of player information to operate its fantasy website was permissible, and granted summary judgment.

Though these antitrust issues—and the scope of the right of publicity in this context—remain to be fully resolved, the NFLPA did recently have to pay $28.1 million, including $21 million in punitive damages, to NFL retirees for failure to properly represent their interests when selling player rights to a video game designer, thereby violating its fiduciary duties to the players. The dispute arose out of the use of retired players' images in the popular ''Madden NFL'' games. Retiree Herb Adderley filed suit on behalf of 2,062 retired players, contending that the union cut them out of deals to give bigger royalty payments to active players. The most damaging evidence against the NFLPA was a letter from the union telling

---

30.   106 F. Supp. 2d 1309 (S.D.Fla. 2000).

31.   CBS Interactive, Inc. v. National Football League Players Association, Inc., No. 08–5097 (D. Minn. Apr. 28, 2009).

the video game designer to scramble images of the retired players so that the players would not have to be paid. Retired player Jim Brown also sued EA Sports and Sony for the creation of an "All Browns Team" in Madden. The game features a running back who is African–American and wears the same jersey number as Brown. Brown claims that he did not sign away his publicity rights.

C. NATIONAL BASKETBALL ASSOCIATION PUBLICITY RIGHTS

Under the terms of the NBA standard player contract, (see Appendix B) players grant to NBA Properties, Inc., the right to use "Player Attributes." Paragraph 14, "Group License," states:

> (a) The Player hereby grants to NBA Properties, Inc. (ant its related entities) the exclusive rights to use the Player's Player Attributes . . .

> (b) Notwithstanding anything to the contrary contained in the Group License or this Contract, NBA Properties (and its related entities) may use, in connection with League Promotions the Player's (i) name or nickname and/or (ii) the Player's Player Attributes (as defined in the Group License) as such Player Attributes may be captured in game action footage or photographs. NBA Properties (and its related entities) shall be entitled to use the Player's Player Attributes individually pursuant to the preceding sentence and shall not be required to use the Player's Player Attributes in a group or as one of multiple players. As used herein, League Promotion shall mean any advertising, marketing, or collateral materials or marketing programs conducted by the NBA, NBA Properties (and its related entities) or any NBA team that is intended to promote (A) any game in which an NBA team participates or game telecast, cablecast or broadcast . . . , (B) the NBA, its teams, or its players, or (C) the sport of basketball.

Note that unlike in the MLB and NFL, NBA Properties can use player attributes individually; there is no requirement that multiple players be featured. Recall that in MLB, two or more players are required to be present in the promotion, whereas in the NFL, six or more players are required to be present.

The NBA's relevant CBA provision circumscribes players' abilities to secure endorsement opportunities to the extent that the endorsement is not within the "reasonable interests of the Team or the NBA." The NBA's stance has been shaped by a 1986 arbitration decision, *Portland Trail Blazers v. Darnell Valentine and Jim Paxon*, which held that a team may not prohibit a "commercial endorsement by a Player that does not identify the Player or the Club." The NBA does, however, state that a player cannot endorse a product "on his body, on his hair, or otherwise" during a game.

SUMMARY QUESTIONS

1.   Consider *CBC Marketing and Distribution v. MLBPA/MLBAM* (8th Circuit) case. In particular, consider *Haelen Laboratories v. Topps Chewing Gum, Ventura v. Titan Sports, Palmer v. Schonhorn Enterprises, Gridiron.com v. NFLPA, Uhlaender v. Henricksen, Gionfriddo v. MLB*, etc., in connection with the foregoing. Based on these prior precedents, do you think that *CBC* was correctly decided?

2.   Do you agree with the *CBC* court that athletes' salaries are so high they do not need the economic incentive from their rights of publicity to play sports professionally? Should this matter in the court's analysis?

3.   Compare/contrast "fantasy rights" with other intellectual property rights regarding statistics. For example, should the "inventor" of the baseball box score format be able to "own" the rights to that form of statistical analysis? Should Bill James and/or the "inventor" of "Sabremetrics" be entitled to "own" the intellectual property rights to the statistical analyses that drives so much of the fantasy-related sports leagues?

Writing Exercise 1: Cease and Desist Letter from MLB to XYX Fantasy Sports and Response from XYX Fantasy Sports[32]

Assume that XYX Fantasy Sports has created a baseball fantasy online game, which XYX League players can access while the player's Team is "playing" its games. Assume further that the XYX fantasy baseball site provides asynchronous streaming of the real-time statistical performance of the Team's players. Assume further that as a Team's player "scores points" for the Team by, e.g., hitting a home run, the XYX website creates a digitally enhanced image of the player in question to highlight the player's performance, together with the player's updated statistics based thereon. (This "image" takes the form of a "parody" of the player's actual image, plus a creative "nickname" for the player, such as "Clammy Sosa.")

Finally, assume that on the XYX fantasy game website, the following two advertisements appear. (1.) One advertisement is for a XYX wholly-owned travel agency affiliate. The advertisement for this affiliate reads as follows: "XYX Fantasy Travel—the agency of choice for the fantasy players whose images appear on this XYX website." (2.) The second advertisement is for a wholly owned XYX technology company. The advertisement reads as follows: "XYX Technologies—the internet and multimedia provider of choice for the players whose images appear on this fantasy website."

With these Hypothetical facts in mind, imagine that MLBPA/MLBAM has asked you to draft a "cease and desist" letter to XYX. Consider which

---

32.   An "exemplar" student submission in response to this hypothetical can be found in the accompanying Teacher's Manual.

aspects of the website you find violate player rights. Next, imagine that XYX has enlisted you to respond to the letter. What arguments would you raise on behalf of XYX? Is there anything on the website you would be willing to change to appease MLBPA/MLBAM?

III.   LEAGUE VERSUS TEAM EXPLOITATION OF RIGHTS

Part III of this chapter introduced you to the disputes surrounding the use of player publicity rights. Part IV, by contrast, discusses disputes between teams and leagues regarding who can exploit intellectual property rights. Teams in larger markets are particularly concerned about sharing revenue earned from league-wide marketing efforts which are primarily attributable to sales from the big-market team's merchandise.

The Dallas Cowboys rebuffed the NFL's practice of aggregating each member clubs' marks for use in commercial purposes. At one point, the Cowboys' merchandise accounted for 25 percent of NFL Properties revenues, but the Cowboys only earned 3.3 percent of the proceeds. Eager to divert some of the revenue stream from the Cowboys' marks into its own coffers, the team made deals with Nike, Pepsi, American Express, Pizza hut, and Dr. Pepper. The NFL sued the team for circumventing the joint marketing plan, and the Cowboys responded with an antitrust suit against the NFL. Both parties settled the suits, and the Cowboys were permitted to retain its separate endorsement deals.

The New York Yankees similarly sued MLB regarding its merchandising and licensing practices in 1997. After the 1996 World Series, the Yankees signed a 10–year, $95 million merchandising agreement with Adidas. MLB responded by suspending George Steinbrenner from its executive council. The parties settled the suit before it was litigated, and the Yankees were permitted to continue the Adidas deal.

The Internet has proved to be a new frontier in sports marketing, and leagues and teams have clashed over who has the right to exploit the sport over the Internet. In September 2007, the New York Rangers sued the NHL after the NHL allegedly threatened to fine the Rangers $100,000 per day if the team did not stop independently operating its website. The team, owned by Madison Square Garden, was unsuccessful in its attempt to obtain a preliminary injunction against the NHL regarding the league's new media strategy. Pursuant to a 1994 agreement, NHL teams granted the NHL exclusive, worldwide rights to use or license team trademarks for marketing. Teams do so presumably to permit the League to promote itself and its member clubs. The NHL and member clubs integrate their websites on NHL.com, and the League reserved the right to control content on club pages. The Rangers did not want to migrate onto the NHL's central platform, and refused to provide the NHL with content for its centralized site. After failed attempts to resolve their differences, MSG finally used the NHL as an "illegal cartel". The District Court in the

Southern District of New York denied the claim, finding that "it is far from obvious that this restraint has no redeeming value." Rather, it accepted the NHL's argument that there are procompetitive effects from the media policy, such as minimum quality standards, increased interconnectivity, sharing team content, and reducing each team's operating costs. The integrated website could also "attract national sponsors and advertisers interested in uniform exposure across the NHL.com network," thereby increasing the NHL's competitiveness vis a vis other entertainment products.

In 2008, Major League Baseball Properties (MLBP), who controlled the licensing of MLB logos, sued Salvino for unauthorizedly using the logos on stuffed bears called "Bammers."[33] Salvino counterclaimed, alleging that MLBP's licensing scheme violated antitrust laws. The Second Circuit affirmed the district court's finding on summary judgment that Salvino could not formulate an successful claim. The Court declined to apply a per se or quick look analysis, stating that it was inappropriate given that the "the economic and competitive effects of the challenged practice are unclear." Applying a rule of reason analysis, the Court found that the joint venture at issue between MLB and MLBP actually increased the number of outstanding licenses, thereby making the market more competitive.

Most recently, the August 2009 *American Needle v. NFL* decision,[34] the Seventh Circuit ruled that the NFL teams act as a single entity "when promoting NFL football through licensing teams' intellectual property." Therefore, the antitrust challenges brought by the Cowboys and the Yankees may not pass muster in the Seventh Circuit if brought today. American Needle, an apparel manufacturer, lost its license to manufacture NFL clothing when the NFL—through the separate corporate entity NFL Properties formed by the member teams—signed a 10–year exclusive deal with Reebok. The Seventh Circuit reasoned that

> Certainly the NFL teams can function only as one source of economic power when collectively producing NFL Football. Asserting that a single football team could produce a football game is less of a legal argument then it is a Zen riddle: Who wins when a single football team plays itself? . . . It thus follows that only one source of economic power controls the promotion of NFL football; it makes little sense to assert that each individual team has the authority, if not the responsibility, to promote the jointly produced NFL football. Indeed, the NFL defendants introduced undisputed evidence that the NFL teams share a vital economic interest in collectively promoting NFL football. After all, the league competes with other forms of entertainment for an audience of finite (if extremely large) size, and the loss of audience members to alternative forms of entertainment necessarily impacts the individual team's success.

---

33. *Major League Baseball Props., LLC v. Salvino*, 542 F.3d 290 (2d Cir. 2008).

34. 538 F.3d 736 (7th Cir. 2008).

Thus, when the NFL is acting through NFL Properties, the court reasoned, it is acting as a single entity. Therefore, given that a single entity cannot illegally conspire, combine, or contract with itself to violate Section 1 of the Sherman Antitrust Act, the antitrust claims brought by American Needle lacked merit. The court rejected American Needle's Section 2 claim on the grounds that as the NFL is a single entity, its member teams are "free under § 2 to license their intellectual property on an exclusive basis." Importantly, the court also defined the relevant market as entertainment products, and not just professional football or professional sports. Both the NFL and American Needle have petitioned the Supreme Court to review the decision.[35]

The advent and popularity of sites with user-posted or user-generated content, such as Youtube.com and Twitter, are also presenting new methods of distributing sports materials while simultaneously presenting new legal challenges. The paramount challenge of such platforms is to ensure that content on the site does not infringe on the intellectual property rights of others, such as posting broadcast film from NFL games. An interesting question presented by Twitter is whether the "tweets" people post in live-time violate broadcast rights of leagues. The new technology has allowed players and coaches to connect with fans on a new level, though it can also get them into trouble. For instance, Tennesee football coach Lane Kiffin violated an NCAA rule when tweeting about a recruit who had not yet officially committed to the school. The NFL denied Chad Ocho Cinco's request to "tweet" during halftime at NFL games.

An additional challenge is presented to players, who are now vulnerable to having each and every move on and off the field embodied in cyberspace. Olympic swimmer Michael Phelps was infamously caught smoking marijuana in a picture posted when Phelps visited a college campus. Though Phelps was not prosecuted, he did lose his endorsement deal with Kellogg's and was suspended from swimming for three months. College players, such as Notre Dame's Jimmy Clausen, are often the targets of scrutiny when pictures appear of players at parties or engaging in other questionable conduct.

Summary Questions

1.   Recall the materials on antitrust law contained in Chapter 4. When, if ever, for the purposes of antitrust law, do you think that a sports league ought to be treated as a "single entity"? When is it more appropriate to think of the league as an association of competitors?

2.   Note that in 2009 the Arena Football League voted to suspend operations and reorganize itself as a single entity. In a single entity ownership structure,

---

35. Another important decision rendered in the summer of 2008 was that of the Deutscher Tennis Bund v. ATP Tour Inc., 07–cv–00178, U.S. District Court, Delaware (Wilmington) (2008). The ATP convinced a jury that when it reorganized its tournament calendar, pooled broadcast rights, and ranked players, it was acting as a single entity and not as a collection of tournaments and players.

the league would own and control each member team. Instead of owning a single team, investors would own a share in the league itself. This would, arguably, enable the Arena Football League to be more competitive with other sports and entertainment products, but would reduce competition among the teams. Do you think that this model is workable as compared with other professional sports leagues? Is it preferable? What problems might arise from organization as a single entity?

CHAPTER 8

FRANCHISE RELOCATION AND STADIUM "NAMING RIGHTS AGREEMENTS": THE MLB TERRITORIAL ANTITRUST EXEMPTION LIVES ON

■ ■ ■

Introduction

Professional sports teams, or franchises, are a scarce resource in high demand: very few entities can own and afford the limited number of teams, and very few cities can be home to the franchises. As you will read in the description of the important case law below, both actual and prospective owners, and cities often haggle over who can own a team, and where that team can reside.

Cities, who frequently use public monies to build stadia and attract professional teams, are often put in a precarious position when a team threatens to leave. While most leases are not subject to specific performance, given the readily quantifiable damages of lost lease payments, there is an argument that professional sports teams provide intangible benefits to cities, warranting more than just monetary damages in the event of a threat or actual breach. Teams might be interested in leaving a city for the promise of a more expensive, state-of-the-art stadium elsewhere, and the prospect of earning additional revenues through the "naming rights" agreement that would accompany the move.

As you read the materials below, consider what level of control you think the commissioner or owners ought to have over the movement of league franchises, what the proper relationship ought to be between cities and teams, and the legal issues associated with naming rights agreements upon the successful movement to a new venue.

I. FRANCHISE CONTRACTION AND RELOCATION

The ability of a league to constrain the movement of its franchises, or club teams, has been an important issue since the organization of the three leagues. Franchise relocations that are approved, such as the Baltimore Colts' move to Indianapolis, the St. Louis Cardinals' move to Phoenix, the Raiders' move back to Oakland, the Houston Oilers' move to Tennessee, and the Expos' move to Washington D.C. to become the Nationals, typically give rise to suits from those who have been left behind. Those that are disapproved have given rise to claims by the offended ownership party.

The first significant challenge to a league's authority in this respect arose when the NHL denied the San Francisco Seals' proposed relocation to Vancouver, a seemingly more hockey-friendly city. The Seals sued the NHL and all the other member teams. In *San Francisco Seals v. NHL*,[1] the court rejected the Seals' claim that the NHL's blockage violated antitrust laws, holding that the individual franchises were members of a single unit that competed with other professional sports leagues. The NHL constitution read, in relevant part,

> Section 4.2. Territorial Rights of League. The League shall have exclusive control of the playing of hockey games by member clubs in the home territory of each member, subject to the rights hereinafter granted to members. The members shall have the right to and agree to operate professional hockey clubs and play the League schedule in their respective cities or boroughs as indicated opposite their signatures hereto. No member shall transfer its club and franchise to a different city or borough. No additional cities or boroughs shall be added to the League circuit without the consent of three-fourths of all the members of the League. Any admission of new members with franchises to operate in any additional cities or boroughs shall be subject to the provisions of Section 4.3.'

> Section 4.3. Territorial Rights of Members. Each member shall have exclusive control of the playing of hockey games within its home territory including, but not being limited to, the playing in such home territory of hockey games by any teams owned or controlled by such member or by other members of the League. . . .

The court characterized the Seals complaint not as seeking a transfer of existing rights, but rather seeking to create a new franchise at a new location. The Court went on to conclude that the team was not competing with other NHL teams, but rather other entertainment products, given that the teams cooperate with the NHL "in pursuit of its main purpose, i.e. producing sporting events of uniformly high quality appropriately scheduled as to both time and location so as to assure all members of the league the best financial return." Therefore, the restrictions on relocation for each NHL member club imposed no restraint upon trade or commerce in the relevant economic market.

As you read the cases below, consider how subsequent courts have treated the leagues—either as a single entity competing with other entertainment products or as a collection of horizontal competitors—the indi-

---

1. 379 F.Supp. 966 (C.D.Cal. 1974)

vidual teams—competing against one another for fans of the same professional sport.

A. MAJOR LEAGUE BASEBALL

Recall from Chapter 2 that Major League Baseball benefits from a judicially created antitrust exemption. Though Curt Flood Act of 1998 removed relations with MLB players from the purview of the exemption, the exemption still applies with respect to territoriality. For expansion, the sale or transfer of control of a club, or the relocation of a club into another league's circuit, a three-fourths majority vote in the affected league, plus a simple majority vote in the other league is required. The Major League Rules describe specific regions that each team occupies. The territorial limits expanded between 1990 and 1994 to include not just a club's home city, but also surrounding counties. Below are some sample territories:

- The Orioles' territory includes Anne Arundel, Howard, Carroll and Harford Counties in Maryland;

- The Marlins' major league territory includes Palm Beach County;

- The Dodgers' and Angels' territory includes Orange, Ventura and Los Angeles Counties;

- The Yankees' and Mets' territory includes New York City, plus Nassau, Suffolk, Westchester and Rockland Counties in New York; Fairfield County south of I–84 and west of SR 58 in Connecticut; and Bergen, Hudson, Essex and Union Counties in New Jersey;

- The Athletics' territory includes Alameda and Contra Costa Counties;

- The Phillies' territory includes Gloucester, Camden and Burlington Counties in New Jersey;

- The Giants' territory includes San Francisco, San Mateo, Santa Cruz, Monterey and Marin Counties, plus Santa Clara County with respect to another major league team.

Under Rule 1(c), either league can move into a territory belonging to a club in the other league, so long as (a) 3/4 of the affected league's teams consent; (b) the two parks are at least five air miles apart unless the two clubs mutually agree otherwise; (c) the newcomer pays the existing club $100,000 plus half of any previous indemnification to invade the territory; and (d) the move leaves no more than two clubs in the territory. Rule 52 allows a major league club to block any other major or minor league clubs from playing within 15 miles of its territory without permission.

Before the passage of the Flood Act, at least one court was willing to entertain the possibility that the antitrust exemption applied only to the reserve system and not to territoriality. In *Piazza and Tirendi v. Major*

League Baseball,[2] the court narrowed the reading of the antitrust exemption and found that baseball's franchise relocation decisions could be subject to antitrust laws. San Francisco Giants owner, Robert Lurie, accepted an offer from Piazza and Tirendi's Tampa Bay ownership group to purchase the franchise for $115 million, with the intention of moving the team to St. Petersberg. The City of San Francisco and MLB put together a competing offer of $100 million that Lurie accepted after the National League owners rejected the relocation to St. Petersburg. Piazza and Tirendi challenged MLB's action in court as a violation of antitrust laws, to which MLB responded that its actions ought to be protected by the antitrust exemption.

The Court reasoned that in each of *Federal Baseball, Toolson,* and *Flood,* the facts giving rise to the litigation concerned the reserve system. After acknowledging that *Federal Baseball* relied on faulty commerce clause jurisprudence, and that *Toolson* discussed the exemption as applying to the business of professional baseball. Later, however, *Flood* narrowed the holdings of these earlier cases beyond the particular facts, given that the Supreme Court admitted the exemption was an anomaly preserved by congressional inaction and professional baseball's reliance. Given that antitrust exemption ought to be narrowly construed, the Court concluded that "the antitrust exemption created by *Federal Baseball* is limited to baseball's reserve system, and because the parties agree that the reserve system is not at issue in this case, I reject Baseball's argument that it is exempt from antitrust liability in this case." The court went on to engage in an antitrust analysis, and found that the relevant market is the sale of baseball teams by current owners to prospective owners. After the ruling, the parties settled the case for $6 million and an apology to Piazza and Tirendi.

At least two other courts were persuaded by the reasoning in *Piazza and Tirendi.* In *Butterworth v. National League of Professional Baseball Clubs,*[3] the Florida Supreme Court endorsed *Piazza and Tirendi*'s reading of *Flood* and permitted the state Attorney General to investigate the National League for refusing the Giants move to Florida. MLB subsequently granted expansion franchises to St. Petersburg and Phoenix. Marred by the earlier battles, however, a Florida group sued again in 1995 claiming that MLB had blocked the group's efforts to buy the Minnesota Twins in 1984. In *Morsani v. Major League Baseball,*[4] the court followed *Butterworth* and *Piazza* and declined to exempt MLB from antitrust law when addressing franchise relocation disputes.

This judicial rebellion regarding antitrust laws was short lived. In *McCoy v. Major League Baseball,*[5] a federal court in Seattle reaffirmed that the antitrust exemption applies to the business of baseball and

---

2.　1994 WL 385062 (E.D. Pa. 1994).

3.　644 So.2d 1021 (Fla. 1994).

4.　663 So.2d 653 (Fla.App.1995).

5.　911 F.Supp. 454 (W.D.Wash.1995).

rejected a class action lawsuit against the Mariners' owners when the players went on strike, thereby suspending all baseball games. When MLB announced its plans to contract two teams, the Florida attorney general issued civil investigative demands against MLB to gather information to determine if MLB was violating antitrust law. The District Court rejected *Piazza and Tirendi,* and found that the antitrust exemption does in fact immunize the league from liability stemming from threats of contraction.[6] The Eleventh Circuit upheld the broad exemption, and rejected the argument that state antitrust laws applies to franchise relocation and contraction decisions in *Major League Baseball v. Crist*.[7] The Circuit Court reasoned that the decision to contract is part of the business of baseball, given that the number and location of the clubs are the basic elements of production for MLB games. When Commissioner Bud Selig told the Minnesota governor that he would approve the Twins desired move to North Carolina and bar any new team from coming to the area unless the City constructed a publicly-financed ballpark, the Court similarly refused to enforce a civil investigative demand.[8]

Antitrust law is not the only way entities have tried to influence where teams are located. In *Metropolitan Sports Facilities Commission v. Minnesota Twins Partnership*,[9] the state of Minnesota sued and won an injunction to require the Twins to play the 2002 season in the Metrodome and preventing MLB form eliminating the franchise. The Twins did not pay rent for the use of the Hubert H. Humprey Metrodome; rather, the state of Minnesota (owner of the Metrodome) only received payments from concession sales and 25 percent of revenue from advertising during the games. Thus, the state's consideration was not the rent paid in the deal, but rather the Metrodome's "benefit of the bargain ... was the Twins' promise to play their home games at the Metrodome for the duration of their lease."

In 2002, the former minority owners of the now-relocated Montreal Expos adopted an innovative strategy to prevent the franchise from being contracted or relocated: the Racketeer Influenced and Corrupt Organizations (RICO) Act, which is designed to inflict criminal penalties on those in organized crime. The minority owners sued majority owner Jeff Loria and Commissioner Bud Selig for conspiring to devalue the team. The complaint alleged that Loria "attained this position [as a 24% interest owner] as a result of an effort by plaintiffs and various Canadian governmental entities to build a new baseball stadium in downtown Montreal, obtain additional equity financing for the franchise, and secure the future of the Expos in Montreal." Rather than fulfill these purposes, the complain alleged that Loria and his co-conspirators had "effectively destroyed the economic viability of baseball in Montreal included removing the Expos from local television, subverting well-developed plans for a new

---

6. Major League Baseball v. Butterworth, 181 F.Supp.2d 1316 (N.D. Fla. 2001).

7. 331 F.3d 1177 (11th Cir. 2003).

8. Minnesota Twins Partnership v. State ex rel. Hatch, 592 N.W.2d 847 (Minn. 1999).

9. 638 N.W.2d 214 (Minn. App. 2002), *rev. denied* (Minn., Feb. 4, 2002).

baseball stadium in downtown Montreal, purposefully alienating Expos sponsors and investors, abandoning agreed-upon financial plans for the franchise, and undermining a planned recapitalization of the franchise that would have added new Canadian partners." Simultaneous, Selig had withheld his "secret intention" to "eliminate major league baseball in Montreal" and instead "made false representations and material omissions" supporting the Expos. Specifically, the complaint alleged that Loria had the power to issue mandatory cash calls, which he abused to squeeze out the minority partners and offered to buy out the minority partners, dropping their ownership from 76% to 6%. The lawsuit ultimately went to arbitration and settled, and the team eventually moved to Washington, D.C.

B. NATIONAL FOOTBALL LEAGUE

Without MLB's antitrust exemption for the business of its sport, the NFL has been vulnerable to antitrust liability stemming from its handling of franchise relocations.

The most storied, and legally complicated, franchise relocation cases surround the Raiders' movements from Oakland to Los Angeles. The facts giving rise to the case began when the Rams moved from Los Angeles to Anaheim, thereby vacating the Los Angeles Coliseum. Raiders' owner Al Davis wanted to move the team from Oakland to Los Angeles. Pursuant to NFL Rule 4.3, a team's proposal to move into another team's home territory—a 75 mile radius around a team's home city—required unanimous approval. All other relocations required a three-fourths vote in favor. After Davis's proposed move was rejected by the owners, Davis filed suit.

The Ninth Circuit upheld the jury's verdict for the Raiders. Whether the NFL was a single entity was a question of fact for the jury to decide, and NFL's organization the "nature and extent of cooperation among the member clubs" was a matter of record. Therefore, the jury could reasonably have concluded that the NFL teams were sufficiently independent and competitive to find under a rule of reason analysis that the anticompetitive harms outweighed the procompetitive effects of the rule.[10] In support of the jury's finding the court noted that the teams are all independently owned, most are corporations, though some are partnerships and sole proprietorships, profit and losses are not shared, profits vary widely, clubs have independent management policies regarding "coaches, players, management personnel, ticket prices, concessions, [and] luxury box suites," and the teams compete with one another off the field to acquire players, coaches, and management personnel. The Court discussed the ancillary restraint doctrine, which protects agreements that restrain competition if they are subordinate and collateral to another legitimate transaction. Nevertheless, so long as there are less restrictive

---

10. *Los Angels Memorial Colisseum Com'n v. National Football League (Raiders I)*, 726 F.2d 1381 (9th Cir. 1984).

means, even if a restraint is ancillary, it will not be upheld. The Court noted that there are no standards or durational limits imposed on the voting requirement, and that the NFL would be well-served to include "an express recognition and consideration of those objective factors espoused by the NFL as important, such as population, economic projections, facilities, regional balance, etc. . . . "

The dissenting judge noted that the NFL ought to be treated as a single entity for the purpose at hand. Factors to consider in the single entity analysis include "formalistic aspects of operations such as ownership, overlapping directorates, joint marketing or manufacturing, legal identity, corporate law autonomy, and substantive aspects such as de facto autonomy of member clubs, chains of command over policy decisions, public perceptions and economic interdependency rendering otherwise independent member clubs subordinate to the integrated whole . . . the crucial criterion is whether the formally distinct member clubs compete in any economically meaningful sense in the marketplace." In answering this question in the negative regarding franchise location, the dissent distinguished between upstream flow—products such as players, coaches, and investors—and downstream output—the game of professional football. Though upstream aspects ought to remain challengeable, downstream output should not given that it is a joint product.

Raiders I did not end the dispute between the Raiders and the NFL. After the team moved to Los Angeles, the NFL sued alleging that the franchise had unilaterally appropriated the value of a location for a professional football team that the league as a whole had created and owned. In *Raiders II*,[11] the Ninth Circuit agreed with the NFL, reasoning that "the value of the league's expansion opportunity belonged to the league as a whole, or in other words, was owned in part by each franchise owner. Unquestionably, when the Raiders moved to Los Angeles, they appropriated for themselves the expansion value that had accumulated in Los Angeles." Given that the Los Angeles market was more valuable than the Oakland market the Raiders had vacated, the team owned something to the other member clubs.

The Raiders movement also gave rise to a state lawsuit regarding whether the City could condemn the franchise and acquire it by eminent domain.[12] The Court first reviewed the legal framework, establishing that a government can take property so long as it is for public use and just compensation is provided. Though franchises are not tangible property, "For eminent domain purposes, neither the federal nor the state constitution distinguishes between property which is real or personal, tangible or intangible." A use that promotes the recreation or pleasure of the public was within the sphere of public uses. Therefore, the Court reasoned, acquisition of a sports franchise may be a legitimate municipal function.

---

11.   791 F.2d 1356 (9th Cir. 1986).

12.   City of Oakland v. Oakland Raiders, 32 Cal.3d 60, 183 Cal.Rptr. 673, 646 P.2d 835 (1982).

Victor Kiam also used the NFL for Rule 4.3. After he had bought the New England Patriots in 1988, Kiam claimed he was forced to sell the team to James Orthwein just four years later. Kiam claimed he was coerced into selling because the NFL would not permit him to move the team to another location. The suit was dismissed on the grounds that Kiam had signed a valid waiver of the right to sue when he sold the Patriots to Orthwein, and the antitrust issue was not resolved.[13] Nevertheless, the Court reaffirmed that "While some restraints on trade are illegal per se, others, such as trade restrictions on sports leagues, are analyzed to determine whether the restriction's 'harm to competition outweighs any procompetitive effects.' "

After the Mid–South Grizzlies were denied entry to be an NFL team, they sued the NFL on the grounds that they ought to have the right to join the league. The Court rejected the antitrust argument, finding that the merger between the AFL and the NFL had been Congressionally approved, and the exclusion of the team was procompetitive, because it kept the Memphis area open for expansion of an NFL team to compete with the Grizzlies.[14]

C. NATIONAL BASKETBALL ASSOCIATION

A rule of reason analysis is also appropriate in litigation regarding NBA franchise restrictions.[15] When the Clippers sued the NBA for a rule similar to Rule 4.3, the Ninth Circuit reversed summary judgment for the team, and found that a number of genuine issues of fact existed, including "(1) the purpose of the restraint as demonstrated by the NBA's use of a variety of criteria in evaluating franchise movement, (2) the market created by professional basketball, which the NBA alleges is different from professional football, and (3) the actual effect the NBA's limitations on movement might have on trade." The litigation settled, and the Clippers paid the NBA to remain in Los Angeles.

Similar to the challenge brought by the Mid–South Grizzlies regarding entry into the NFL, Levin sued the NBA after the league rejected his bid to buy the Celtics. The Court rejected the claim that the act violated antitrust laws, nothing that the plaintiff "wanted to join with those unwilling to accept him, not to compete with them, but to be partners in the operation of a sports league for plaintiffs profit."[16]

The NBA has faced the most recent franchise relocation fight. After several unsuccessful attempts to get a new arena built in Seattle, on July 17, 2006, the Seattle-based owners of the SuperSonics announced the NBA team's sale to Clay Bennett and his partnership from Oklahoma City, Oklahoma. The taxpayers were presumably fed up from building new

---

13. VKK Corp. v. NFL, 55 F. Supp. 2d 196 (S.D.N.Y. 1999), *aff'd*, 244 F.3d 114 (2d Cir. 2001).

14. Mid–South Grizzlies v. NFL, 720 F.2d 772 (3d Cir. 1983).

15. *See* NBA v. San Diego Clippers Basketball Club, 815 F.2d 562 (9th Cir. 1987).

16. Levin v. NBA, 385 F.Supp. 149 (S.D.N.Y. 1974).

venues for MLB's Mariners and the NFL's Seahawks, and staunchly refused to give the NBA team a new home as well. From the moment the sale was revealed, Seattle commentators and fans feared that the new owners would take the team away from Seattle in favor of the owners' home town; these fears turned out to be well-founded By the fall of 2007, despite a lease with the City of Seattle for KeyArena through 2010, the new owners were attempting to find a way out of the lease and were negotiating with Oklahoma City to relocate the team. Soon thereafter, Bennett and his partners filed a demand for arbitration to determine the team's right to leave KeyArena before the end of the lease. Bennett's arbitration demand was denied, however, because the lease's arbitration clause did not include claims arising out of the specific performance clause. The City of Seattle, in response, filed a lawsuit demanding specific performance of the lease.

The trial that took place in the courtroom was a fairly straightforward commercial lease bench trial. The case tried in the media, however, added much public attention, and may have been part of the driving force behind he last minute settlement. The key legal issue at trial was whether or not the City could obtain specific performance of the lease, forcing the Sonics to remain in Seattle through the 2009–2010 NBA season, or whether monetary damages were sufficient to remedy the club's breach of the lease. In most commercial landlord-tenant disputes, regardless of the contractual provisions to the contrary, specific performance is unavailable because damages can be readily monetized, i.e. the damages are the lost lease payments. Seattle argued, however, that the Sonics provided the City with numerous intangible benefits distinct from the lease payments. Therefore, the court could not fashion appropriate monetary damages; rather, the court should order specific performance and require the Sonics to play KeyArena until the termination of the lease's term. Since Seattle and the Sonics reached a monetary settlement after trial but before the verdict was announced, we do not know whether the Seattle would have prevailed on this theory. Nevertheless, given that Seattle received between $3.5 and $6 million annually, the lease looked like a traditional landlord-tenant relationship in which monetary damages were appropriate. The deal did not resemble the deal in *Minnesota Twins*, discussed in Part IA above.

In an attempt to prove that monetary damages were impossible to derive from a breach, the City called Andrew Zimbalist, a sports economist, as an expert witness. Zimbalist readily testified that sports franchises provide intangible benefits to cities, including public morale, increase rents around the stadium, and other factors that make quantifying the benefits impossible. The City may have made a mistake in choosing Zimbalist, however, because the economist had testified in 2005 for the Anaheim Angels that the team enhanced the quality of life for Los Angeles residents by $7.75 million. In fact, despite Zimbalist's deposition testimony that the Seattle report was new research specific to the Sonics' case, a few sections of Zimbalist's report were copied verbatim from the Anaheim research. Thus, on cross-examination, Zimbalist unpersuasively attempted to explain that, on the one hand, when the Angels needed an expert to testify that the team's benefits could be quantified, he was able to do so, but on the other hand, when Seattle's case required an expert to testify that the Sonics provided unquantifiable benefits to the City, his study did reach that conclusion.

The Sonics' attorneys were also able to seize upon a document discussing a plan by a group of Seattle businessmen to ride in as white knights and save Seattle from this terrible situation. The group discussing the plan included the City's attorney, and former United States Senator, Slade Gorton. The group's plan was to increase the financial exposure to the NBA and the new owners, divide their loyalties, make it too costly to move the team, and show the NBA that the new owners would be a better fit than Bennett's group. The presentation had the unfortunate title, "The Sonics Challenge: Why a Poisoned Well Offers a Unique Opportunity." The poisoned well plan states, among other things, "Gorton, et al., increase pain of staying, financial and reputation ..." Additionally, the presentation describes the plan as, "a pincer movement: increasing the Oklahomans costs in an unpleasant environment while increasing the league's belief that an alternative solution gains it a good new owner to keep it in a desirable market." When this plan hit the media, it made the case seem more about a power struggle to keep the team in Seattle than a case of incalculable damages to KeyArena and the City. The lawyers arguably ought to have been more careful in keeping those discussion private, and Gorton should not have been involved in sabotage discussions with Seattle businessmen that could have become public during trial.

Alongside Seattle's lawsuit against the Sonics, and part of the poisoned well plan, former owner Howard Schultz sued Bennett's ownership group for breach of contract. When Schultz's partnership sold the team, the contract included a provision requiring the new owners to use their "best efforts" to keep the Sonics in Seattle. E-mails later revealed that less than one year after the sale, the owners were already trying to move the team to Oklahoma City. For instance, Tom Ward, a member of Bennett's ownership group, wrote to Bennett in April 2007, "Is there any way to move here [Oklahoma City] for next season or are we doomed to have another lame duck season in Seattle?" Bennett responded to Ward, "I am a man possessed! Will do everything we can." Based on these comments and others, Schultz sued to unwind the transaction. He dropped the lawsuit in late August 2008, almost two months after Seattle had settled with the Sonics owners, once it became clear nothing could be done to keep the team in Seattle. The combination of a $45 million settlement to pay the debt remaining on KeyArena and Schultz dropping his lawsuit permitted the team to move to Oklahoma City, where the team renamed itself the Oklahoma City Thunder. The Oklahoma City ownership will have to pay an additional $30 million if Seattle does not get a new team within five years.

As the worldwide economy took a severe downtown in late 2007, many teams began struggling to remain financially viable. The NHL's Phoenix Coyotes declaration of bankruptcy in 2008 was just the beginning of a long process through which potential buyers would be carefully scrutinized and an easy movement of the team to Canada would be thwarted by the bankruptcy judge. The founder and CEO of the company who produces the Blackberry, Jim Balsillie, was eager to take the team back to Canada, but the NHL refused to agree with the move. In addition to the price of the team, per the NHL's agreement, Balsillie would have to pay a relocation fee and taxes, Balsillie would have to pay an indemnity fee for entering the Toronto Maple Leafs and Buffalo Sabres territory, a total cost of about $200 million. Moreover, officials from Glendale, Arizona, promised to force the team to pay a hefty fee if it broke its stadium lease by departing prior to the end of the term. As of the writing of this book, the NHL owners had unanimously voted to deny Balsillie's application to buy the team, given his professed desire to relocate.

SUMMARY QUESTIONS

1. Focus on Raiders-related cases, and distinguish between two types of relocation cases: (a.) cases in which a franchise, like the Raiders (or Seattle Supersonics/Oklahoma Thunder), very much wants to "move," and third-parties are trying to "stop them" from moving; vs. (b.) "contraction cases," like the Montreal Expos cases, where the League is "forcing" a team to cease operations and "be relocated."

2. What role does the MLB "territorial antitrust exemption," which continued to exist after the 1998 Flood Act, play in this in area of "sports and the law," versus the NFL and NBA "franchise relocation cases," where no such "antitrust exemption" exists?

3. Of Raiders I (majority or dissenting opinion?) and Raiders II, which is the better legally-reasoned opinion, and why, in light of our prior Syllabus readings referenced therein.

4. Rule 4.3 of the NFL Rules, as amended, provides for a ¾ vote re: relocation into a "home territory." Why was (or was not) that "amendment" sufficient to pass the "rule of reason" test, etc.?

5. What explains the difference in the treatment accorded Victor Kiam/Patriots antitrust litigation, and the Rams/St. Louis Convention and Visitors Commission dispute (p. 596 of Weiler). How does the "single entity" defense factor in here? Does it matter if NFL football is moving into (or out of) a "home territory" already occupied by an NFL franchise (or not)?

Writing Exercise 1: Confidential and Privileged Memorandum on Franchise Relocation and Contraction[17]

There are many moving parts to this Hypothetical. Be sure to read and organize the facts in a simple and clear way so that your client can understand the various issues that arise from his decisions.

MLB "Voluntary Relocations." Assume the Pittsburgh Pirates want to relocate to Charlotte, North Carolina because their favorable lease in Pittsburgh is expiring, and the team's tax advantages are ending, while attendance has decreased significantly. Charlotte and Pittsburgh have reached an "agreement in principle" for the relocation. Charlotte will build a new "baseball only" stadium for an MLB team, so that all favorable tax advantages to the new MLB owner will be available, plus an owner-friendly lease agreement and all rights to a new team-controlled regional cable television station that will be owned by the new MLB team in Charlotte.

Las Vegas learns of Charlotte's offer and agrees to match it, to lure an MLB franchise to Las Vegas. Assume further that the Las Vegas group offers a one-time payment of $X million to MLB if it relocates an MLB team to Las Vegas.

The Milwaukee Brewers learn of these pending offers and decides to relocate to Las Vegas, while still being owned by Commissioner Selig's "blind trust"—even though Milwaukee's attendance in a relatively recently built stadium has allowed the Brewers to "break even" for the last few years.

The Florida Marlins' owner also wants to relocate his franchise, as does the owner of the Tampa Bay franchise, due to many years of losing money in their respective Florida markets. In particular, the Marlins' owner has repeatedly been denied public funding for a new Miami regional baseball only stadium, while the University of Miami has received public funding for a new football stadium.

MiLB "Dislocation." Assume Minor League Baseball (MiLB) will be required to vacate the Charlotte and Las Vegas territories, and that the MiLB teams playing there will need to be "compensated" for vacating the territories and for being relocated to another available MiLB territory. The Charlotte MiLB owner, however, also owns an "independent" league team, which violates MLB's (unwritten) rule against affiliated MiLB team owners also owning an independent league team.

Given the foregoing facts, Commissioner Selig makes a decision "in the best interests of baseball," in consultation with his hand-picked "Relocation Committee" of MLB owners, within the "ultimate" powers reserved to him by the MLB Constitution and By–Laws.

MLB's Affirmative Relocation Decision. Assume that the final MLB Owners' decision is as follows: the Milwaukee Brewers will be relocated to Las

---

17. An "exemplar" student submission in response to this hypothetical can be found in the accompanying Teacher's Manual.

Vegas, and the Las Vegas MiLB owner will be "rewarded" by being paid a "relocation fee," and being relocated to Reno, Nevada—a most favorable MiLB market which has been trying to attract a AAA team for many years. Additionally, Reno has promised to build a new MiLB stadium for the relocated MiLB owners. In return, the MLB owners receive the extra $X million payment promised by the City of Las Vegas for such relocation, and that the fee is split equally among all MLB owners.

The Charlotte territory is awarded to the Florida Marlins franchise, leaving no MLB team in the Miami, Florida area. To "punish" the Charlotte MiLB owner for violating the MLB rule against owning an independent league team, the Charlotte MiLB owner is relocated to the baseball-unfriendly Hickory, NC market, where many prior MiLB teams have failed.

MLB's Denials of Relocation Requests. Assume Tampa is not permitted to relocate to Las Vegas because its ownership group wanted to affiliate with a local Las Vegas group that owns a hotel attached to, but which is not a part of, a casino complex. The Pirates are not permitted to relocate to Charlotte, because they have not used their revenue-sharing monies from other MLB teams' "luxury tax" and "revenue-sharing" payments to reinvest in the Pirates' player development system. Instead, the Pirates' owners have used the other MLB owners' monies to declare a healthy annual profit, given their extremely friendly lease arrangement in Pittsburgh.

Commissioner Selig and his Relocation Committee will therefore not permit the Pirates to relocate to Charlotte. They also condition Charlotte's admission into the MLB ownership ranks upon Charlotte voiding its "agreement in principle" with the Pirates, and upon Charlotte's paying "liquidated damages" to the Pirates to make them "whole."

Threatened litigation. In light of these facts, the Pirates are considering filing an antitrust suit against Selig/the MLB owners, challenging the MLB "antitrust exemption." Similarly, the "Milwaukee Loves Its Brewers" Citizens Group (the "MCG") is considering filing an antitrust suit to prevent Selig/MLB from "contracting" the Brewers and forcing them to relocate to Las Vegas, in return for the Owners getting their "big payday" from the Las Vegas-based ownership group.

Imagine that you represent MLB owners and Commissioner Selig. You have received a memorandum from the General Counsel to the Pirates' ownership group, with the "best arguments" for challenging Commissioner Selig's decision prohibiting the clients from relocating to Charlotte, per the "agreement in principle" that they had reached with the Charlotte ownership group.

You have also received a memorandum from the General Counsel to the MCG which contains the "best arguments" against the "contraction" and "relocation" of the Brewers' franchise, based on the *Minnesota Twins* and other precedents in the readings. In particular, the memorandum attacks the MLB "antitrust exemption" in this context, by also citing the "awarding" of the potentially valuable Reno territory, plus cash compensation, to the displaced Las Vegas MiLB ownership group.

Be prepared to conclude which alleged "antitrust violation" is the most obvious or abusive so as to justify revoking MLB's antitrust exemption in the context of an antitrust suit filing by the Pirates or by the MCG.

Prepare a "confidential/privileged" bullet-point memo to your clients, responding to the Pirates and MCG's General Counsels' "best arguments." In your memorandum, explain who gets the better of the arguments, and recommend to Selig/the Owners if the "antitrust exemption" is in jeopardy, given the Pirates and MCG's "best arguments," if (a) antitrust litigation is filed by the Pirates and the MCG; or (b) if the Congressional Committees responsible for investigating antitrust violations were to launch an investigation into the above-described facts, given the relevant case precedents that have thus far avoided decisive Congressional scrutiny. In particular, alert your clients to their most vulnerable actions taken in the Hypothetical. Based on same, recommend what remedial action, if any, Selig should take to prevent the Pirates or MCG from filing an antitrust lawsuit.

"Exemplar" student responses are, as usual, set forth in the accompanying Teacher's Manual.

II. NAMING RIGHTS AGREEMENTS

Teams seek to relocate not only to move to better markets or better multi-purpose facilities and venue-related inventory streams (including, *e.g.*, parking; concessions; club seats and/or PSL-related revenues, etc.), but also to ink lucrative naming rights deals. Naming Rights Agreements—generally speaking, an agreement that grants an entity the right to give a sport's stadium a name (and, to receive many related and integrated benefits) in exchange for monetary payments over a period of time—have become quite a lucrative revenue source for teams and a method of relatively inexpensive advertising for companies. If a company's name is already in an NFL stadium, it need not dole out huge sums of money for Super Bowl advertising. Rather, it benefits from consistent visual and auditory exposure during the "big game" at no additional charge. Naming Rights Agreements, as alluded to above, are typically accompanied by a slew of other benefits for the company, such as pouring rights for PepsiCo. at the Pepsi Center in Denver or the now-famously defunct Enron's exclusive agreement to be the energy provider for the Astros' Enron field.

A. DRAFTING A NAMING RIGHTS AGREEMENT[18]

After the preamble, recitals, and definitions that typically begin all agreements, Naming Rights Agreements (NRA) begin with a grant of the

---

18. For more information, see Martin J. Greenberg, The Stadium Game (2001).

naming rights from the franchise to the company and a description of what the grant includes. This grant also typically states if the grant is exclusive or categorically exclusive, the naming sponsor's right to approve or veto other potential sponsors, and the right to approve the advertising plan including media/multimedia "tie-ins" to the Naming Rights Agreement. NFL and MLB franchises usually have their own venues, while NHL and NBA teams usually share venues, and consequently, split the revenues and other rights from the grant of naming rights. If, as is normally done nowadays, the agreement also confers other benefits on the company—luxury suites, playoff tickets, etc.—the parties may enumerate these benefits here or in a separate exhibit. (Read the portion of the brief submitted by the City against the Oakland Raiders, included in the reading materials, for potentially litigable issues that might arise with respect to the grant and the scope thereof.)

The agreement will next go on to describe the term of the agreement, and any options for renewal or rights of first refusal. The description of the options may be accompanied by a description of how either party can renew the term, e.g. in writing by a specified date.

Of course, a critical term of the agreement will outline the payment or fees. The payments might be a lump sum, installments, installments that increase uniformly or fluctuate, or some other permutation. The agreement might provide for the amount, timing, and method of payments.

Depending on the parties' preferences, the NRAs might warrant the creation of a new, joint logo. Regardless, the parties will want the right to use one another's logos. The agreement will likely provide the team with the right to use the company's trademarks for advertising and promotion, subject to the company's approval. The agreement should also provide for granting similar rights to the team's logo to the company. This provision of the agreement might read:

> **Development of Arena Mark and Arena Graphic Logo.** The parties agree that the Franchise shall develop, at the Franchise's expense, the Arena Mark and the Arena Graphic Logo, provided that the final design of the Arena Mark and Arena Graphic Logo shall be subject to the approval of Naming Rights Holder, which approval shall not be unreasonably withheld, delayed or conditioned.

Since the parties are using one another's marks, and the use of the mark reflects on the reputation of the parties, they might also demand that such use be of a certain quality. For instance, the company might require that all team-related merchandise with its logo or the joint stadium logo be of high quality and free from all defects. Or, the team may require that the company not use the mark in a manner that "is contrary to public morals or which has been found to be deceptive or misleading, or which reflects unfavorably on the good name, goodwill, reputation or image of the Team." The agreement may also give the company the right in connection with the promotion of games or other events to produce its own event-related merchandise bearing its trademark, the trademark of the event, and the logo of the stadium. In the interest of preserving the quality of the mark, the parties may specify the ability of each party to license the logo as well. This, of course, will be related to who "owns" the mark.

If there is a change of control at either party, the parties will likely have to modify the contractual terms. Naming Rights Agreements will provide for the time period within which such amendments must be made, the attendant approval rights, and who is responsible for launching and funding the changes. The parties might also consider changing the exclusivity / category exclusivity provision in the event that the company's business changes. For example, assume that Gillette expands the scope of its business from razors and other shaving related products to bath soaps, body washes, lotions, and other grooming products from men. In this case, a company like Axe may become a competitor. The naming company may want to preserve the right to modify the definition of "Competitor" or "Direct Competitor" in the event of such a change.

At this point in the agreement, the parties should include a section on representations and warranties. The "reps and warranties" might certify that:

- the entity operating the team has the right, power and authority to enter into the agreement,
- that the entity is duly organized and in good standing,
- that no additional consents are required,
- that the team has a valid lease for the stadium, and
- that there are no league rules that would impair the company's rights under the agreement.

The scope and import of reps and warranties will be covered in greater detail later in this chapter.

The indemnification provision will typically contain cross-indemnification provisions that effectively make each party responsible for claims or liabilities incurred by that party (and its affiliates, heirs, assigns, etc.) as a result of breaching conduct under the agreement or its breach. The company might require indemnity for any claims for infringement by a third party, any breaches of the team's obligations, any claims raised by event attendees, or any claims by people who argue that are not paid for services in relation to game day productions. The team, by contrast, might require indemnity for breach of obligations under the agreement and the company's use of the intellectual property.

To pay at least part of the indemnity, the parties might also require one another to carry insurance. The parties should be required to carry insurance covering personal injury, death, property damage, contractual obligations, product liability protection, worker's compensation, and any other insurance necessary to protect the parties.

As with stadium leases, the "force majeure," or other events that limit the company's anticipated exposure, might also be addressed in the agreement. Parties should also negotiate what happens in the event of a strike / lockout, or any other event that effects the value of the agreement in a material manner.

Naming Rights Agreements should also explicitly state that the parties are not joint venturers, and therefore, neither part has the authority or right to incur obligations for the other or to commit or bind the other.[19]

Finally, as in any other agreement, the Naming Rights Agreement will explain the parties rights and remedies upon termination, including what happens to any trademarks or service marks produced. The Agreement might also have a dispute resolution section and a limitation of liability. The parties may also want to include a "Confidentiality" provision, that prohibits each party from disclosing the terms and conditions of the agreement.

B. INTELLECTUAL PROPERTY: TRADEMARKS, TRADE NAMES, SERVICE MARKS AND LOGOS

Naming Rights Agreements, obviously, involve the negotiation of significant intellectual property right transfers. Below is a brief overview of broad classifications of such intellectual property, and how each plays a role in the Naming Rights Agreement.

Trademarks. A trademark, as defined in the Lanham Act, is ". . . any word, name, symbol, or device, or any combination thereof adopted and used by a manufacturer or merchant to identify his goods and distinguish them from those of others."[20] Unlike copyrights—which after a specified period[21] become part of the public domain—a trademark may be in the public domain before it is selected by a person / business to represent that business or product, or rather, before it becomes a trademark. The trademark owner gets a property right in the trademark.

The Lanham Act protects trademark owners from unauthorized uses that are likely to cause confusion, to cause mistake, or to deceive.[22] The robustness of the trademark—and the level of protection afforded to it— varies depending upon the uniqueness of the mark. A mark that is very unique will get greater protection, while a mark that is weaker, also known as a "suggestive mark," will get narrower protection.

---

19. This might be especially important for state-owned entities. In 1995, the Georgia state attorney general claimed that the sponsorship agreement between McDonald's and Georgia Tech University violated the state Constitution, which prohibited the state becoming a joint owner with a private organization.

20. Lanham Trademark Act, 15 U.S.C. § 1127.

21. The time period of a copyright differs depending upon whether the work was published or unpublished, with or without notice, renewed or not, and the prevailing copyright law at the time of publication. For works created today, the copyright lasts for 70 years from the death of the author or 95 years from creation if the author is a corporate entity.

22. 15 U.S.C. § 1114(1)(a).

Some trademarks may have difficulty even getting narrow protection. "Generic terms" that fail to distinguish one product or brand from another are never granted trademark status because they only generally describe the class of product, and do not identify the specific product.[23] Similarly, descriptive marks, such as geographic terms (e.g. Pitt) or terms of a general nature (e.g. Musicfest), will not be protected unless there is a secondary meaning that distinguishes the product. Secondary meaning can be proven by showing the following elements: (1.) the amount and type of advertising; (2.) the volume of sales; (3.) the length and manner of use; (4.) direct consumer testimony, or (5.) consumer surveys.[24] Whichever party bears the responsibility for creating the trademark should expect to spend time and money not only filing the trademark application, but also ensuring that the trademark is robust enough to qualify for protection.

If a party has to pursue a potential trademark infringer, the court will apply the "likelihood of confusion" test, an eight-factor test designed to determine if the allegedly infringing mark will create consumer confusion as to the origin of the product. The eight elements of the test are: (1.) the strength of the mark, (2.) the degree of similarity between the two marks, (3.) the proximity of the products, (4.) the likelihood that the prior owner will bridge the gap, (5.) actual confusion, (6.) the defendant's good faith in adopting its own mark, (7.) the quality of the defendant's mark, and (8.) the sophistication of the buyers. ETW Corp. v. Jireh Publishing, Inc.

Trade Names. A trade name is the name a business uses for commercial purposes. The trade name may be, but need not be, registered as a trademark. Trade names are protected to the extent that another business in the same jurisdiction cannot use the same trade name in particular circumstances. To prevent such conflicting uses, trade names must be registered with the state. But, don't assume that the protections afforded to trademarks apply to trade names upon registration of a trade name—they are often considered two different types of registrations.

Service marks. While trademarks apply to products, the term "service mark" is used to distinguish marks that apply to services. According to the Lanham Act, a service mark is "any word, name, symbol or device, or any combination thereof (1.) used by a person, or (2.) which a person has a bona fide intention to use in commerce and applies to register on the principal register established by this Chapter, to identify and distinguish the services of one person, including a unique service, from the services of others and to indicate the source of the services, even if that source is unknown." For example, a company like 1–800–Flowers might put their mark on their trucks, but not on the flowers themselves. Service marks are also registered with the USPTO and are protectible to the extent of trademarks. Whereas trademarks need to be used in goods to count as in

23. University of Georgia Athletic Ass'n v. Laite, 756 F.2d 1535, 1540 (11th Cir. 1985).

24. For an example of cases involving "secondary meaning" disputes, see University of Pittsburgh v. Champion Products, Inc., 566 F.Supp. 711 (D. Pa. 1983), American Basketball Association v. AMF Voit, Inc., 358 F.Supp. 981 (D. N.Y. 1973).

commerce, service marks need only be used in advertising to warrant protection. Corporate naming rights sponsors register their service under the class "education and entertainment."

The registered service marks of corporate naming rights sponsors characteristically consist of their previously established marks plus the term "Field," "Stadium," "Park," or "Center." Some examples are: Gillette Stadium, Busch Stadium, Enron Field, United Center, Minute Maid Park, Citi Field, the Staples Center, and the TD Bank Garden.

Logos. A logotype, or logo, is a graphical symbol created for an individual company or product. Logos are designed to communicate quickly by virtue of being a distinctive and easily recognizable symbol. Logos often include a special typeface or font used to spell out the company name or initials. They also tend to include specific colors and graphical shapes. Perhaps the simplest logo is the Nike "swoosh," that is immediately associated with the sports apparel company's brand. Logos can be protected as trademarks / service marks, and all of the above rules regarding trademarks / service marks will apply to logos.

Naming Rights Agreements should specify who is responsible for creating and preserving all of the above-described IP, the permissible uses of the IP, and who is the owner of the rights during and after the term of the agreement.

Writing Exercise 2: Drafting a Naming Rights Agreement[25]

In light of the foregoing considerations, consider the following negotiating and drafting points for a Naming Rights sponsor in the "auto sales, new and used cars" category.

Define "Available Inventory." In attempting to negotiate the parameters of the Naming Rights Agreement, describe how you will define the Available Inventory for negotiation purposes.

Describe the list of benefits to be offered to the Naming Rights Sponsor, and how it relates to preserving certain other rights for the presenting and other category sponsors that will be required to be sold to maximize the revenue from the available inventory both inside and outside park. Pay particular attention to the "grant of rights" in the benefits description in the relevant Naming Rights Agreement clauses and any appendices relating thereto.

Track the buying and selling of the naming rights from the City/landlord to the team owner to the Naming Rights Sponsor. How would you negotiate the conditionality of the grant of rights from the owner to the Sponsor? What "outs" would you reserve for the owner, e.g. obtaining all necessary (state of federal) approvals from the City/State to erect signage in public spaces and over public roads?

---

25. An "exemplar" student submission in response to this hypothetical can be found in the accompanying Teacher's Manual.

Define the intellectual property issues raised thereby, (e.g. the ownership of the logo developed in connection with the Naming Rights Agreement). Consider a separate grant of rights for any intellectual property-related agreements within the Naming Rights Agreement, including, for example, use of the logo/trademarks of the Naming Rights Sponsor and of the Owner. Attempt to achieve reciprocity, depending upon leverage, while also providing for rights/duties to pursue any alleged infringement of the relevant marks.

Negotiate insurance and indemnification clauses. Address the Owner's use of the Sponsor's products in promotions and the Sponsor's use of the Owner's premises for special events or promotions. Consider, for example, the use of a Sponsor Car during the game, a tee shirt toss in connection with the Car, as well as a Sponsor Dance Team dancing on the Team's dugout between innings. Who should be responsible for which potential liabilities in each of those settings.

Consider the termination provisions for any material breaches of any of the foregoing clauses. Consider limitation of liability clauses in connection with the same. Also consider assignment and successor in interest clauses. Further consider a dispute resolution clause that will keep any disputes confidential via mediation/arbitration, unless injunctive relief might be required.

Provide for disposition of any unused inventory, post-termination, plus the phasing out of the use of the Naming Rights Sponsor's advertising and promotional materials.

Negotiate and draft and right of first negotiation or refusal language that actuates at the end of the initial term of the agreement, assuming that the initial term has been satisfactory to both parties.

Consider what rights would likely have been sold to the Presenting Sponsor and other product-category sponsors during the initial term of the Naming Rights Agreement, which might limit the Owner's ability to expand the benefits to the Naming Rights Sponsor upon renewal of the initial term.

A particularly effectively negotiated "exemplar" Naming Rights Agreement is set forth below, with the permission of the Harvard Law School students who prepared it while taking Professor Peter Carfagna's 2009 spring semester course "Advanced Contract Drafting in Sports Law".

NAMING RIGHTS AGREEMENT

between

ANHEUSER-BUSCH INBEV, INC.

as Naming Sponsor

and

BOSTON RED SOX LLC,

as Team

Dated as of February 25, 2009

TABLE OF CONTENTS

DEFINITIONS

"Agreement" shall mean the entirety of the understanding reached between Team and Naming Sponsor, as written and signed below.

"Arena Graphic Logo" shall mean the jointly developed logo between Team and Naming Sponsor pertaining to the Stadium.

"Arena Mark" shall mean the jointly developed trademark and service mark between Team and Naming Sponsor pertaining to the Stadium.

"Club Level" shall mean the 300 level of the Stadium.

"Concession Stands" shall mean stations located in the Concourse Areas of the Stadium at which food and beverages are sold. "Concession Stands" shall not mean any areas located in the Stadium Suites or Club Level areas of the ballpark where food and beverages are sold or dispensed.

"Concourse Areas" shall mean the areas located within the Stadium but outside of the 100 and 500 level seating areas of the Stadium.

"Joint Logo" shall mean all jointly developed logos, trademarks, and service marks between Team and Naming Sponsor, including, but not limited to, the Arena Mark and Arena Graphic Logo.

"Naming Sponsor" shall mean Anheuser-Busch InBev, Inc.

"Stadium" shall mean the facility owned by the City of Boston and leased by the Boston Red Sox located at 1000 Municipal Stadium Drive, Boston, Massachusetts.

"Stadium Suites" shall mean the exclusive boxes sold on a yearly basis located on the 200 and 400 levels of the Stadium.

"Team" shall mean the Boston Red Sox LLC.

1. Grant of Naming Rights

   (a)   Subject to the conditions set forth in Section 2 hereof Team thereby grants to Naming Sponsor the Naming Rights for the Ballpark during the Term as described in Section 4 unless terminated pursuant to Section 6 hereof. Accordingly, the name of the structure located at 1000 Municipal Stadium Drive, Boston, Massachusetts at which the Team plays its home baseball games (the "Ballpark") for the term of this Agreement shall be "Bud Field." Notwithstanding the above, the Team reserves all right and interest in sponsorship and advertising revenue related to areas and aspects of the Premises pursuant to the Lease dated February 25, 2009 between the City of Boston as Landlord and the Team as Tenant (the "Lease"), the term "Premises" having the same meaning as defined in the Lease, including but not limited to the advertising rights in Section 8 of the Lease, the playing field, concert stages, exterior of the Ballpark, areas on or near the Facility (as defined in the Lease) and parking areas, provided that at all times the Ballpark and its location shall be designated Bud Field.

   (b)   Naming Sponsor has granted to the Team the right to use Naming Sponsor's name in connection with the Ballpark and Ballpark related events. The Service Mark and Trademark Grant of Rights Agreement is attached hereto as Exhibit B and is made a part of this Agreement. The Team agrees that all advertising and promotional uses of Naming Sponsor's name, logo, and trademark are subject to the approval of Naming Sponsor. Naming Sponsor agrees that any material submitted by the Team shall not be unreasonably disapproved and, if it is disapproved, that the Team shall be advised in writing of the grounds of the disapproval.

   (c)   In furtherance of the grant set forth in Section 1(a) above, but subject always to Section 3 hereof, Naming Sponsor grants to the Team the right to use the name of the Ballpark (i.e. "Bud Field") and any logos or emblems directly related to the name of the Ballpark.

   (d)   During the term of this Agreement, Naming Sponsor agrees that it will inform the Team in writing at least six months before entering into an agreement to become the naming sponsor of any other ballpark.

   (e)   During the term of this Agreement the Team shall have the exclusive right to install any and all necessary equipment to provide for ticket sales to all Ballpark events at all Team business locations together with an appropriate window and interior signage indicating the availability of tickets to all Ballpark events, for which the Team shall provide at its sole cost high speed internet access and a connection. The Team shall provide at its sole cost all necessary computer hardware and software.

5. Payment

128

(a) For the Naming Rights herein granted, Naming Sponsor agrees to pay the Team a fee (the "Fee") of Ten Million Dollars in annual payments. In each of the first 3 years under this Agreement the annual payment shall be 1 Million Dollars per annum, due in its entirety on the First of January of each year. Thereafter, such annual payments shall be in the sum of 500,000 Dollars per year payable on the First of January of each year. Payments shall be adjusted annually to account for inflation.

(b) Naming Sponsor further agrees to pay on or before January 1 of the first year of this Agreement a sum of 3 Million Dollars pursuant to an agreement relating to an advertisement located on the lower right corner of the Ballpark scoreboard. The Team agrees to keep such advertisement in place from the beginning of the Baseball season through the All-Star Break of each season throughout the duration of this agreement. At all other times the Team shall own all rights and privileges to such advertisement space. Naming Sponsor agrees that the Team retains approval rights over the contents of this advertisement. The Team agrees that any material submitted by Naming Sponsor shall not be unreasonably disapproved and, if it is disapproved, that Naming Sponsor shall be advised in writing of the grounds of the disapproval.

(c) All payments due to the Team hereunder shall be paid to the order of "The Boston Red Sox, LLC." Past due payments hereunder shall bear interest at the rate of (i) the Prime Rate for the nation's largest banks as reported in the Wall Street Journal on the business day next preceding the payment due date, plus 2.0% or (ii) the maximum interest rate permissible under law, whichever is less.

9. Change of Logo

(a) During the Term, the parties agree that Team shall develop, at the equally shared expense of Team and Naming Sponsor, the Arena Mark and the Arena Graphic Logo, provided that the final design of the Arena Mark and Arena Graphic Logo shall be subject to the approval of Naming Sponsor, whose approval shall not be unreasonably withheld, delayed, or conditioned. Team shall be the sole and exclusive owner of the Arena Mark, Arena Graphic Logo, and all other jointly developed logos, trademarks, and service marks.

(b) During the Term, Team shall have the exclusive right to use the Arena Mark, Arena Graphic Logo, and all other jointly developed logos, trademarks, and service marks. Team shall have the right to use Naming Sponsor's logos, trademarks, and service marks in promotion of the relationship between Team and Naming Sponsor, subject at all times to Naming Sponsor's approval. Team shall have the right, in connection with the promotion of games or other events, to produce its own event-related merchandise bearing its logos, trademarks, and service marks, the logos, trademarks, or service marks of the event, and jointly developed logos, trademarks, and service marks (including, but not limited to Arena Mark and Arena Graphic Logo). All merchandise produced by Team bearing Naming Sponsor's logos, trademarks, or service marks or jointly developed logos, trademarks, or service marks, shall be of high qualify and free from defects. Team shall have the ability to license the jointly developed logos, trademarks, and service marks, in order to promote the Team and/or Naming Sponsor.

(c)   During the Term, Naming Sponsor shall have the right to use the Arena Mark, Arena Graphic Logo, and all other jointly developed logos, trademarks, and service marks, subject at all times to Team's approval, not to be unreasonably withheld. Naming Sponsor shall have the right to use Team's logos, trademarks, and service marks in promotion of the relationship between Naming Sponsor and Team, subject at all times to Team's approval. Naming Sponsor shall have the right, subject at all times to the Team's approval, not to be unreasonably withheld, in connection with the promotion of games or other events, to produce its own event-related merchandise bearing its logos, trademarks, and service marks, the logos, trademarks, or service marks of the event, and jointly developed logos, trademarks, and service marks (including, but not limited to Arena Mark and Arena Graphic Logo). Naming Sponsor shall not use Team's logos, trademarks, or service marks or jointly developed logos, trademarks, or service marks in a manner that is contrary to public morals or which has been found to be deceptive or misleading, or which reflects unfavorably on the good name, goodwill, reputation, or image of Team. Naming Sponsor shall have the ability to license the jointly developed logos, trademarks and service marks, in order to promote Naming Sponsor and/or Team, subject at all times to Team's approval, not to be unreasonably withheld.

(d)   During the Term, if there is a change of control at either Team or Naming Sponsor, such that the name of the Stadium or jointly developed logos, trademarks, or service marks are not materially affected, each party shall continue to maintain the same rights and obligations as it held prior to the change of control. If there is a change of control at either Team or Naming Sponsor, such that the name of the Stadium or jointly developed logos, trademarks, or service marks are materially affected, the party who has not undergone a change of control shall have thirty (30) days to request the development of a new Arena Mark and Arena Graphic Logo, and other appropriate jointly developed logos, trademarks, and service marks. The party who has undergone a change of control shall be solely responsible for the costs associated with developing these new logos, trademarks, and service marks. The party who has not undergone a change of control shall have exclusive approval rights over the newly created logos, trademarks, and service marks, such approval not to be unreasonably withheld, delayed, or conditioned. In the event that Naming Sponsor undergoes a change in control or substantially changes its core business areas, both parties agree to negotiate in good faith regarding modifying the exclusivity and category exclusivity provisions in this Agreement to reflect such changes. Nothing in this paragraph shall be construed to conflict with the rights and obligations of the parties under paragraph 13 regarding Assignment.

(e)   The Team shall retain all ownership interest in the service mark and/or trademark rights in the Joint Logo, to be designed by Team and Naming Sponsor pursuant to this paragraph. The Team must promptly register the Joint Logo upon its completion with the United States Patent and Trademark Office at its own expense.

(f)   The Team shall also own the goodwill in the Joint Logo.

(g)   The Team grants to the Naming Sponsor the unlimited use of the Joint Logo for:

    (1)   Written and visual advertising, including traditional, Internet, and new media advertising;

    (2)   Printed materials, including signs and posters displayed to the public;

    (3)   Any other purpose expressly provided for in this Agreement.

(h)   All uses of the logo not listed in paragraph 9(g) require express approval from the Team. The Team shall respond to any requests for use of the Joint Logo within thirty (30) days. The Team retains the right to disapprove the proposed use of the Joint Logo for any reason deemed in the best interest of the Team and/or the sport of baseball.

(i)   All uses of the Joint Logo by the Naming Sponsor are subject to quality restrictions. Use of the Joint Logo in advertising, printed materials, or in any other medium shall be of the highest quality and shall not feature the logo of any other professional sports franchise.

(j)   In the event of alleged service mark and/or trademark infringement, the Team and the Naming Sponsor shall jointly bear the cost of pursuing the alleged infringers. The Naming Sponsor's legal fees shall be reimbursed, but the Team shall retain all other proceeds from service mark and/or trademark litigation as the owner of these rights.

(k)   Upon the expiration or termination of this Agreement, Team and Naming Sponsor shall cease use of the Joint Logo for any purposes, besides those merely historical or commemorative, within three (3) months. The Team shall select a new service mark for identification of the Ballpark within six (6) months.

(l)   In the event of any alleged breach of this paragraph, the party alleging breach must notify the allegedly breaching party of its complaint within thirty (30) days. After the allegedly breaching party is put on notice by receipt of the complaint, the parties must meet within fourteen (14) days. If unable to arrive at an agreement within fourteen (14) days of meeting, the parties shall engage in Dispute Resolutions pursuant to Article 17.

20.   Exhibits

The exhibits listed below are attached to this Agreement and are incorporated herein by reference and made a part thereof. In the event of a conflict between the terms of an exhibit and the terms of this Agreement, the terms of this Agreement will govern.

Exhibit A: Naming Rights Benefits

IN WITNESS WHEREOF, the parties hereto have executed this Agreement as of the date first written above.

By: _____   By: _____
     Boston Red Sox, LLC   Anheuser-Busch InBev, Inc.

Date: _____   Date: _____

EXHIBIT A

Naming Rights Benefits

A. Official Sponsor. Naming Sponsor shall have the right to refer to itself as the "Official Malt Beverage Provider of the Boston Red Sox," or as the "Official Beer Provider of the Boston Red Sox." Naming Sponsor can use these designations in any advertisements provided that all such advertisements contain a disclosure stating: "You must be 21 or older to purchase InBev products. Please drink responsibly."

B. Signage. Naming Sponsor shall have the right to have the Stadium Name and/or Stadium Marks displayed on the following signage located within the Stadium:
  (i) All signage identifying the Stadium.
  (ii) A "Welcome to Bud Field" sign located on the outside of the Stadium behind the home-plate entrance. Such sign will be no smaller than twenty (20) feet horizontally and no smaller than five (5) feet vertically.
  (iii) A sign, of dimensions determined by Team, on the clock located on the center-field scoreboard.
  (iv) A sign no larger than fifteen (15) feet horizontally and no larger than three (3) feet vertically to be painted on the top of the visitor's dugout.

B. Additional Signage. Naming Sponsor may purchase additional signage at prices specified by Team.

C. Tickets. Team shall place the Stadium Name and/or the Stadium Marks on every admissions ticket to Major League Baseball games and non-baseball events hosted by the Team. [Team shall have the right to determine the size and location of the Stadium Name and/or the Stadium Marks on all such inventory.]

D. Publications / Stationary. Team shall place the Stadium Name and/or the Stadium Marks on all Team stationary and on the front or back cover of every Program guide and Media guide sold during Major League Baseball games and non-baseball events hosted by the Team. [Team shall have the right to determine the size and location of the Stadium Name and/or the Stadium Marks on all such inventory.]

E. Napkins / Beer Cups. Team shall place the Stadium Name and/or the Stadium Marks on all napkins made available at Stadium Concession Stands. Team shall also place the Stadium Name and/or the Stadium Marks on all cups in which beer is served at Stadium Concession Stands. [Team shall have the right to determine the size and location of the Stadium Name and/or the Stadium Marks on all such inventory. Nothing herein shall limit Team's right to use alternative napkins or beer cups in its Stadium Suites and Club Areas.]

F. Media. Team shall make a good-faith effort to encourage all radio, TV, and print media to refer to the stadium by its full name.

G. Giveaway Day. Naming Sponsor shall have the right to giveaway merchandise bearing its name to attendees twenty-one (21) years old or older at one Major League Baseball game during each season of the term of the Agreement. At such event, Naming Sponsor may designate one (1) person to throw out a ceremonial first pitch. Team shall have the right to determine the date of Naming Sponsor's giveaway each year.

H. Stadium Suite. Subject to the signing of a separate skybox suite agreement, Naming Sponsor shall receive the use of one (1) skybox suite for its use during each Major League Baseball Season throughout the term of this Agreement. The skybox shall be provided to Naming Sponsor at no additional cost. The skybox suite shall be located between first-base and third-base, but its precise location shall be determined by Team.

I. Club Seats. Naming Sponsor shall not receive any club seats as part of this Agreement, but may purchase club seats at prices specified by Team.

*

Appendix A

Player Contracts

■ ■ ■

A. MLB Uniform Player Contract

MAJOR LEAGUE UNIFORM PLAYER'S CONTRACT

Parties

Between, herein called the Club, and of, herein called the Player.

Recital

The Club is, along with other Major League Clubs, signatory to the Major League Constitution and has subscribed to the Major League Rules.

Agreement

In consideration of the facts above recited and of the promises of each to the other, the parties agree as follows:

Employment

1. The Club hereby employs the Player to render, and the Player agrees to render, skilled services as a baseball player during the year(s) including the Club's training season, the Club's exhibition games, the Club's playing season, the Division Series, the League Championship Series and the World Series (or any other official series in which the Club may participate and in any receipts of which the Player may be entitled to share).

Payment

2. For performance of the Player's services and promises hereunder the Club will pay the Player the sum of $in semimonthly installments after the commencement of the championship season(s) covered by this contract except as the schedule of payments may be modified by a special covenant. Payment shall be made on the day the amount becomes due, regardless of whether the Club is "home" or "abroad." If a monthly rate of payment is stipulated above, it shall begin with the commencement of the championship season (or such subsequent date as the Player's services may commence) and end with the termination of the championship season and shall be payable in semi-monthly installments as above provided.

Nothing herein shall interfere with the right of the Club and the Player by special covenant herein to mutually agree upon a method of payment whereby part of the Player's salary for the above year can be deferred to subsequent years.

If the Player is in the service of the Club for part of the championship season only, he shall receive such proportion of the sum above mentioned, as the number of days of his actual employment in the championship season bears to the number of days in the championship season.

Notwithstanding the rate of payment stipulated above, the minimum rate of payment to the Player for each day of service on a Major League Club shall be at the applicable rate set forth in Article VI(B)(1) of the Basic Agreement between the Thirty Major League Clubs and the Major League Baseball Players Association, effective December 20, 2006 ("Basic Agreement"). The minimum rate of payment for Minor League service for all Players (a) signing a second Major League contract (not covering the same season as any such Player's initial Major League contract) or a subsequent Major League contract, or (b) having at least one day of Major League service, shall be at the applicable rate set forth in Article VI(B)(2) of the Basic Agreement. The minimum rate of payment for Minor League service for all Players signing a first Major League contract who are not covered by Article VI(B)(2) of the Basic Agreement shall be at the applicable rate set forth in Article VI(B)(3) of the Basic Agreement.

Payment to the Player at the rate stipulated above shall be continued throughout any period in which a Player is required to attend a regularly scheduled military encampment of the Reserve of the Armed Forces or of the National Guard during the championship season.

Loyalty

3.   (a) The Player agrees to perform his services hereunder diligently and faithfully, to keep himself in first-class physical condition and to obey the Club's training rules, and pledges himself to the American public and to the Club to conform to high standards of personal conduct, fair play and good sportsmanship.

Baseball Promotion

3.   (b) In addition to his services in connection with the actual playing of baseball, the Player agrees to cooperate with the Club and participate in any and all reasonable promotional activities of the Club and Major League Baseball, which, in the opinion of the Club, will promote the welfare of the Club or professional baseball, and to observe and comply with all reasonable requirements of the Club respecting conduct and service of its team and its players, at all times whether on or off the field.

Pictures and Public Appearances

3.   (c) The Player agrees that his picture may be taken for still photo-graphs, motion pictures or television at such times as the Club may

designate and agrees that all rights in such pictures shall belong to the Club and may be used by the Club for publicity purposes in any manner it desires. The Player further agrees that during the playing season he will not make public appearances, participate in radio or television programs or permit his picture to be taken or write or sponsor newspaper or magazine articles or sponsor commercial products without the written consent of the Club, which shall not be withheld except in the reasonable interests of the Club or professional baseball.

PLAYER REPRESENTATIONS

Ability

4.   (a) The Player represents and agrees that he has exceptional and unique skill and ability as a baseball player; that his services to be rendered hereunder are of a special, unusual and extraordinary character which gives them peculiar value which cannot be reasonably or adequately compensated for in damages at law, and that the Player's breach of this contract will cause the Club great and irreparable injury and damage. The Player agrees that, in addition to other remedies, the Club shall be entitled to injunctive and other equitable relief to prevent a breach of this contract by the Player, including, among others, the right to enjoin the Player from playing baseball for any other person or organization during the term of his contract.

Condition

4.   (b) The Player represents that he has no physical or mental defects known to him and unknown to the appropriate representative of the Club which would prevent or impair performance of his services.

Interest in Club

4.   (c) The Player represents that he does not, directly or indirectly, own stock or have any financial interest in the ownership or earnings of any Major League Club, except as hereinafter expressly set forth, and covenants that he will not hereafter, while connected with any Major League Club, acquire or hold any such stock or interest except in accordance with Major League Rule 20(e).

Service

5.   (a) The Player agrees that, while under contract, and prior to expiration of the Club's right to renew this contract, he will not play baseball otherwise than for the Club, except that the Player may participate in post-season games under the conditions prescribed in the Major League Rules. Major League Rule 18(b) is set forth herein.

Other Sports

5.   (b) The Player and the Club recognize and agree that the Player's participation in certain other sports may impair or destroy his ability and skill as a baseball player. Accordingly, the Player agrees that he will not

engage in professional boxing or wrestling; and that, except with the written consent of the Club, he will not engage in skiing, auto racing, motorcycle racing, sky diving, or in any game or exhibition of football, soccer, professional league basketball, ice hockey or other sport involving a substantial risk of personal injury.

Assignment

6. (a) The Player agrees that his contract may be assigned by the Club (and reassigned by any assignee Club) to any other Club in accordance with the Major League Rules. The Club and the Player may, without obtaining special approval, agree by special covenant to limit or eliminate the right of the Club to assign this contract.

Medical Information

6. (b) The Player agrees:

(1) that the Club's physician and any other physician or medical professional consulted by the Player pursuant to Regulation 2 of this contract or Article XIII(D) of the Basic Agreement may furnish to the Club all relevant medical information relating to the Player. Except as permitted by Article XIII(G) of the Basic Agreement, which is incorporated herein by reference, the Club is prohibited from re-disclosing any such information without the express written consent of the Player. The Club's physician shall be the custodian of the medical records furnished to a Club pursuant to this Paragraph 6(b). The Club's trainers shall have access to all such records provided to the Club.

(2) that, should the Club contemplate an assignment of this contract to another Club or Clubs, the Club's physician may furnish to the physicians and officials of such other Club or Clubs all relevant medical information relating to the Player; provided, however, that said physicians and officials are prohibited from re-disclosing any such information without the express written consent of the Player. In addition, within thirty (30) days from the receipt of the Player's medical information, the physicians and officials of the Club which requested the medical information will return any and all documents received to the Player's Club, and will not keep copies of any documents it received or any other records indicating the substance of the medical information transmitted. If the Player's UPC is assigned before the information is returned in accordance with this subparagraph (2), the assignee Club may retain the information. A Player may, at the time that he is no longer under reserve to the Club or on December 1 or every other year, whichever is earlier, request that the Club notify him of the Clubs to which his medical information was provided pursuant to this Paragraph 6(b)(2).

No Salary Reduction

6. (c) The amount stated in paragraph 2 and in special covenants hereof which is payable to the Player for the period stated in paragraph 1 hereof

shall not be diminished by any such assignment, except for failure to report as provided in the next subparagraph (d).

Reporting

6.   (d) The Player shall report to the assignee Club promptly (as provided in the Regulations) upon receipt of written notice from the Club of the assignment of this contract. If the Player fails to so report, he shall not be entitled to any payment for the period from the date he receives written notice of assignment until he reports to the assignee Club.

Obligations of Assignor and Assignee Clubs

6.   (e) Upon and after such assignment, all rights and obligations of the assignor Club hereunder shall become the rights and obligations of the assignee Club; provided, however, that

(1) The assignee Club shall be liable to the Player for payments accruing only from the date of assignment and shall not be liable (but the assignor Club shall remain liable) for payments accrued prior to that date.

(2) If at any time the assignee is a Major League Club, it shall be liable to pay the Player at the full rate stipulated in paragraph 2 hereof for the remainder of the period stated in paragraph 1 hereof and all prior assignors and assignees shall be relieved of liability for any payment for such period.

(3) Unless the assignor and assignee Clubs agree otherwise, if the assignee Club is a Minor League Baseball Club, the assignee Club shall be liable only to pay the Player at the rate usually paid by said assignee Club to other Players of similar skill and ability in its classification and the assignor Club shall be liable to pay the difference for the remainder of the period stated in paragraph 1 hereof between an amount computed at the rate stipulated in paragraph 2 hereof and the amount so payable by the assignee Club.

(4) If performance and/or award bonuses are included as Special Covenants hereunder and an assignment is made during the championship season, the responsibility for such bonuses shall be as follows:

(i) All performance and/or award bonuses earned prior to the assignment shall be the responsibility of the assignor Club;

(ii) The responsibility for any and all performance bonuses earned after the assignment shall be prorated between the assignor and assignee Clubs in proportion to the total number of relevant events attained during the season with each Club involved; and

(iii) The responsibility for any and all award bonuses earned after the assignment shall be the full and exclusive responsibility of the Club for whom the Player was performing services at the end of the championship season. For purposes of this paragraph, an award bonus for election or selection to the All–Star Game shall be deemed to be earned on the day of the announcement of the election or selection, an award bonus for performance over the championship season shall be deemed earned on the last day of the championship season and an award bonus for performance in the post-season shall be deemed earned on the day of the announcement of the award.

Moving Allowances

6. (f) The Player shall be entitled to moving allowances under the circumstances and in the amounts set forth in Articles VII(F) and VIII of the Basic Agreement.

"Club"

6. (g) All references in other paragraphs of this contract to "the Club" shall be deemed to mean and include any assignee of this contract.

TERMINATION

By Player

7. (a) The Player may terminate this contract, upon written notice to the Club, if the Club shall default in the payments to the Player provided for in paragraph 2 hereof or shall fail to perform any other obligation agreed to be performed by the Club hereunder and if the Club shall fail to remedy such default within ten (10) days after the receipt by the Club of written notice of such default. The Player may also terminate this contract as provided in subparagraph (d)(4) of this paragraph 7. (See Article XV(I) of the Basic Agreement.)

By Club

7. (b) The Club may terminate this contract upon written notice to the Player (but only after requesting and obtaining waivers of this contract from all other Major League Clubs) if the Player shall at any time:

(1) fail, refuse or neglect to conform his personal conduct to the standards of good citizenship and good sportsmanship or to keep himself in first-class physical condition or to obey the Club's training rules; or

(2) fail, in the opinion of the Club's management, to exhibit sufficient skill or competitive ability to qualify or continue as a member of the Club's team; or

(3) fail, refuse or neglect to render his services hereunder or in any other manner materially breach this contract.

7. (c) If this contract is terminated by the Club, the Player shall be entitled to termination pay under the circumstances and in the amounts set forth in Article IX of the Basic Agreement. In addition, the Player shall be entitled to receive an amount equal to the reasonable traveling expenses of the Player, including first-class jet air fare and meals en route, to his home city.

Procedure

7.   (d) If the Club proposes to terminate this contract in accordance with subparagraph (b) of this paragraph 7, the procedure shall be as follows:

(1) The Club shall request waivers from all other Major League Clubs. Such waivers shall be good for two (2) business days only. Such waiver request must state that it is for the purpose of terminating this contract and it may not be withdrawn.

(2) Upon receipt of waiver request, any other Major League Club may claim assignment of this contract at a waiver price of $1.00, the priority of claims to be determined in accordance with the Major League Rules.

(3) If this contract is so claimed, the Club shall, promptly and before any assignment, notify the Player that it had requested waivers for the purpose of terminating this contract and that the contract had been claimed.

(4) Within five (5) days after receipt of notice of such claim, the Player shall be entitled, by written notice to the Club, to terminate this contract on the date of his notice of termination. If the Player fails to so notify the Club, this contract shall be assigned to the claiming Club.

(5) If the contract is not claimed, the Club shall promptly deliver written notice of termination to the Player at the expiration of the waiver period.

7.   (e) Upon any termination of this contract by the Player, all obligations of both Parties hereunder shall cease on the date of termination, except the obligation of the Club to pay the Player's compensation to said date.

Regulations

8.   The Player accepts as part of this contract the Regulations set forth herein.

Rules

9.   (a) The Club and the Player agree to accept, abide by and comply with all provisions of the Major League Constitution, and the Major League Rules, or other rules or regulations in effect on the date of this Uniform Player's Contract, which are not inconsistent with the provisions of this contract or the provisions of any agreement between the Major League Clubs and the Major League Baseball Players Association, provided that the Club, together with the other Major League Clubs and Minor League Baseball, reserves the right to modify, supplement or repeal any provision of said Constitution, Major League Rules or other rules and regulations in a manner not inconsistent with this contract or the provisions of any then existing agreement between the Major League Clubs and the Major League Baseball Players Association.

Disputes

9.   (b) All disputes between the Player and the Club which are covered by the Grievance Procedure as set forth in the Basic Agreement shall be resolved in accordance with such Grievance Procedure.

Publication

9. (c) The Club, the Vice President, On–Field Operations and the Commissioner, or any of them, may make public the findings, decision and record of any inquiry, investigation or hearing held or conducted, including in such record all evidence or information given, received, or obtained in connection therewith.

Renewal

10. (a) Unless the Player has exercised his right to become a free agent as set forth in the Basic Agreement, the Club may retain reservation rights over the Player by instructing the Office of the Commissioner to tender to the Player a contract for the term of the next year by including the Player on the Central Tender Letter that the Office of the Commissioner submits to the Players Association on or before December 12 (or if a Sunday, then on or before December 11) in the year of the last playing season covered by this contract. (See Article XX(A) of and Attachments 9 and 12 to the Basic Agreement.) If prior to the March 1 next succeeding said December 12, the Player and the Club have not agreed upon the terms of such contract, then on or before ten (10) days after said March 1, the Club shall have the right by written notice to the Player at his address following his signature hereto, or if none be given, then at his last address of record with the Club, to renew this contract for the period of one year on the same terms, except that the amount payable to the Player shall be such as the Club shall fix in said notice; provided, however, that said amount, if fixed by a Major League Club, shall be in an amount payable at a rate not less than as specified in Article VI, Section D, of the Basic Agreement. Subject to the Player's rights as set forth in the Basic Agreement, the Club may renew this contract from year to year.

10. (b) The Club's right to renew this contract, as provided in subparagraph (a) of this paragraph 10, and the promise of the Player not to play otherwise than with the Club have been taken into consideration in determining the amount payable under paragraph 2 hereof.

Governmental Regulation–National Emergency

11. This contract is subject to federal or state legislation, regulations, executive or other official orders or other governmental action, now or hereafter in effect respecting military, naval, air or other governmental service, which may directly or indirectly affect the Player, Club or the League and subject also to the right of the Commissioner to suspend the operation of this contract during any national emergency during which Major League Baseball is not played.

Commissioner

12. The term "Commissioner" wherever used in this contract shall be deemed to mean the Commissioner designated under the Major League Constitution, or in the case of a vacancy in the office of Commissioner, the Executive Council or such other body or person or persons as shall be

designated in the Major League Constitution to exercise the powers and duties of the Commissioner during such vacancy.

Supplemental Agreements

The Club and the Player covenant that this contract, the Basic Agreement, the Agreement Re Major League Baseball Players Benefit Plan effective April 1, 2007 and Major League Baseball's Joint Drug Prevention and Treatment Program and applicable supplements thereto fully set forth all understandings and agreements between them, and agree that no other understandings or agreements, whether heretofore or hereafter made, shall be valid, recognizable, or of any effect whatsoever, unless expressly set forth in a new or supplemental contract executed by the Player and the Club (acting by its President or such other officer as shall have been thereunto duly authorized by the President or Board of Directors as evidenced by a certificate filed of record with the Commissioner) and complying with the Major League Rules.

Approval

This contract or any supplement hereto shall not be valid or effective unless and until approved by the Commissioner.

Signed in duplicate this day of, A.D.
(Player) (Club)
By
(Home address of Player) (Authorized
Signature)
Social Security No.
Approved,
Commissioner

REGULATIONS

1.　The Club's playing season for each year covered by this contract and all renewals hereof shall be as fixed by the Office of the Commissioner.

2.　The Player, when requested by the Club, must submit to a complete physical examination at the expense of the Club, and if necessary to treatment by a regular physician or dentist in good standing. Upon refusal of the Player to submit to a complete medical or dental examination, the Club may consider such refusal a violation of this regulation and may take such action as it deems advisable under Regulation 5 of this contract. Disability directly resulting from injury sustained in the course and within the scope of his employment under this contract shall not impair the right of the Player to receive his full salary for the period of such disability or for the season in which the injury was sustained (whichever period is shorter), together with the reasonable medical and hospital expenses incurred by reason of the injury and during the term of this contract or for a period of up to two years from the date of initial treatment for such injury, whichever period is longer, but only upon the express prerequisite conditions that (a) written notice of such injury, including the time, place, cause and nature of the injury, is served upon and received by the Club within twenty days of the sustaining of said injury and (b) the Club shall have the right to designate the doctors and hospitals furnishing such medical and hospital services. Failure to give such notice shall not impair the rights of the Player, as herein set forth, if the Club has actual knowledge of such injury. All workmen's compensation payments received by the Player as compensation for loss of income for a specific period during which the Club is paying him in full, shall be paid over by the Player to the Club. Any other disability may be ground for suspending or terminating this contract.

3.   The Club will furnish the Player with two complete uniforms, exclusive of shoes, unless the Club requires the Player to wear nonstandard shoes in which case the Club will furnish the shoes. The uniforms will be surrendered by the Player to the Club at the end of the season or upon termination of this contract.

4.   The Player shall be entitled to expense allowances under the circumstances and in the amounts set forth in Article VII of the Basic Agreement.

5.   For violation by the Player of any regulation or other provision of this contract, the Club may impose a reasonable fine and deduct the amount thereof from the Player's salary or may suspend the Player without salary for a period not exceeding thirty days or both. Written notice of the fine or suspension or both and the reason therefor shall in every case be given to the Player and the Players Association. (See Article XII of the Basic Agreement.)

6.   In order to enable the Player to fit himself for his duties under this contract, the Club may require the Player to report for practice at such places as the Club may designate and to participate in such exhibition contests as may be arranged by the Club, without any other compensation than that herein elsewhere provided, for a period beginning not earlier than thirty-three (33) days prior to the start of the championship season; provided, however, that the Club may invite players to report at an earlier date on a voluntary basis in accordance with Article XIV of the Basic Agreement. The Club will pay the necessary traveling expenses, including the first-class jet air fare and meals en route of the Player from his home city to the training place of the Club, whether he be ordered to go there directly or by way of the home city of the Club. In the event of the failure of the Player to report for practice or to participate in the exhibition games, as required and provided for, he shall be required to get into playing condition to the satisfaction of the Club's team manager, and at the Player's own expense, before his salary shall commence.

7.   In case of assignment of this contract, the Player shall report promptly to the assignee Club within 72 hours from the date he receives written notice from the Club of such assignment, if the Player is then not more

than 1,600 miles by most direct available railroad route from the assignee Club, plus an additional 24 hours for each additional 800 miles.

Post–Season Exhibition Games. Major League Rule 18(b) provides:

(b) EXHIBITION GAMES. No player shall participate in any exhibition game during the period between the close of the Major League championship season and the following training season, except that, with the consent of the player's Club and permission of the Commissioner, a player may participate in exhibition games for a period of not less than 30 days, such period to be designated annually by the Commissioner. Players who participate in barnstorming during this period cannot engage in any Winter League activities. Player conduct, on and off the field, in connection with such postseason exhibition games shall be subject to the discipline of the Commissioner. The Commissioner shall not approve of more than three players of any one Club on the same team. The Commissioner shall not approve of more than three players from the joint membership of the World Series participants playing in the same game. No player shall participate in any exhibition game with or against any team which, during the current season or within one year, has had any ineligible player or which is or has been during the current season or within one year, managed and controlled by an ineligible player or by any person who has listed an ineligible player under an assumed name or who otherwise has violated, or attempted to violate, any exhibition game contract; or with or against any team which, during said season or within one year, has played against teams containing such ineligible players, or so managed or controlled. Any player who participates in such a game in violation of this Rule 18 shall be fined not less than $50 nor more than $500, except that in no event shall such fine be less than the consideration received by such player for participating in such game.

B. NFL Standard Player Contract

NFL PLAYER CONTRACT

THIS   CONTRACT   is   between
_____, hereinafter   "Player,"   and
_____, a
_____ corporation (limited partnership) (partnership), hereinafter "Club," operating under the name of the _____ as a member of the National Football League, hereinafter "League." In consideration of the promises made by each to the other, Player and Club agree as follows:

1.   TERM. This contract covers _____ football season(s), and will begin on the date of execution or March 1, _____, whichever is later, and end on February 28 or 29, _____, unless extended, terminated, or renewed as specified elsewhere in this contract.

2.   EMPLOYMENT AND SERVICES. Club employs Player as a skilled football player. Player accepts such employment. He agrees to give his

best efforts and loyalty to the Club, and to conduct himself on and off the field with appropriate recognition of the fact that the success of professional football depends largely on public respect for and approval of those associated with the game. Player will report promptly for and participate fully in Club's official mandatory minicamp(s), official preseason training camp, all Club meetings and practice sessions, and all preseason, regular season and postseason football games scheduled for or by Club. If invited, Player will practice for and play in any all-star football game sponsored by the League. Player will not participate in any football game not sponsored by the League unless the game is first approved by the League.

3. OTHER ACTIVITIES. Without prior written consent of the Club, Player will not play football or engage in activities related to football otherwise than for Club or engage in any activity other than football which may involve a significant risk of personal injury. Player represents that he has special, exceptional and unique knowledge, skill, ability, and experience as a football player, the loss of which cannot be estimated with any certainty and cannot be fairly or adequately compensated by damages. Player therefore agrees that Club will have the right, in addition to any other right which Club may possess, to enjoin Player by appropriate proceedings from playing football or engaging in football-related activities other than for Club or from engaging in any activity other than football which may involve a significant risk of personal injury.

4. PUBLICITY AND NFLPA GROUP LICENSING PROGRAM.

(a) Player grants to Club and the League, separately and together, the authority to use his name and picture for publicity and the promotion of NFL Football, the League or any of its member clubs in newspapers, magazines, motion pictures, game programs and roster manuals, broadcasts and telecasts, and all other publicity and advertising media, provided such publicity and promotion does not constitute an endorsement by Player of a commercial product. Player will cooperate with the news media, and will participate upon request in reasonable activities to promote the Club and the League. Player and National Football League Players Association, hereinafter "NFLPA," will not contest the rights of the League and its member clubs to telecast, broadcast, or otherwise transmit NFL Football or the right of NFL Films to produce, sell, market, or distribute football game film footage, except insofar as such broadcast, telecast, or transmission of footage is used in any commercially marketable game or interactive use. The League and its member clubs, and Player and the NFLPA, reserve their respective rights as to the use of such broadcasts, telecasts or transmissions of footage in such games or interactive uses, which shall be unaffected by this subparagraph.

(b) Player hereby assigns to the NFLPA and its licensing affiliates, if any, the exclusive right to use and to grant to persons, firms, or corporations (collectively "licensees") the right to use his name, signature facsimile, voice, picture, photograph, likeness, and/or biographical information (collectively "image") in group licensing programs. Group licensing programs are defined as those licensing programs in which a licensee utilizes a total of six (6) or more NFL player images on or in conjunction with products (including, but not limited to, trading cards, clothing, videogames, computer games, collectibles, internet sites, fantasy games, etc.) that are sold at retail or used as promotional or premium items. Player retains the right to grant permission to a licensee to utilize his image if that licensee is not concurrently utilizing the images of five (5) or more other NFL players on products that are sold at retail or are used as promotional or premium items. If Player's inclusion in a particular NFLPA program is precluded by an individual exclusive endorsement agreement, and Player provides the NFLPA with timely written notice of that preclusion, the NFLPA will exclude Player from that particular program. In consideration for this assignment of rights, the NFLPA will use the revenues it receives from group licensing programs to support the objectives as set forth in the Bylaws of the NFLPA. The NFLPA will use its best efforts to promote the use of NFL player images in group licensing programs, to provide group licensing opportunities to all NFL players, and to ensure that no entity utilizes the group licensing rights granted to the NFLPA without first obtaining a license from the NFLPA. This paragraph shall be construed under New York law without reference to conflicts of law principles. The assignment in this paragraph shall expire on December 31 of the later of (a) the third year following the execution of this contract, or (b) the year in which this contract expires. Neither Club nor the League is a party to the terms of this paragraph, which is included herein solely for the administrative convenience and benefit of Player and the NFLPA. The terms of this subparagraph apply unless, at the time of execution of this contract, Player indicates by striking out this subparagraph (b) and marking his initials adjacent to the stricken language his intention to not participate in the NFLPA Group Licensing Program. Nothing in this subparagraph shall be construed to supersede or any way broaden, expand, detract from, or otherwise alter in any way whatsoever, the rights of NFL Properties, Inc. as permitted under Article V (Union Security), Section 4 of the 1993 Collective Bargaining Agreement ("CBA").

5.　COMPENSATION. For performance of Player's services and all other promises of Player, Club will pay Player a yearly salary as follows:

$_____for the 20_____season;
$_____for the 20_____season;
$_____for the 20_____season;
$_____for the 20_____season;
$_____for the 20_____season.

In addition, Club will pay Player such earned performance bonuses as may be called for in this contract; Player's necessary traveling expenses from his residence to training camp; Player's reasonable board and lodging expenses during preseason training and in connection with playing preseason, regular season, and postseason football games outside Club's home city; Player's necessary traveling expenses to and from preseason, regular season, and postseason football games outside Club's home city; Player's necessary traveling expenses to his residence if this contract is terminated by Club; and such additional compensation, benefits and reimbursement of expenses as may be called for in any collective bargaining agreement in existence during the term of this contract. (For purposes of this contract, a collective bargaining agreement will be deemed to be "in existence" during its stated term or during any period for which the parties to that agreement agree to extend it.)

6.　PAYMENT. Unless this contract or any collective bargaining agreement in existence during the term of this contract specifically provides otherwise, Player will be paid 100% of his yearly salary under this contract in equal weekly or biweekly installments over the course of the applicable regular season period, commencing with the first regular season game played by Club in each season. Unless this contract specifically provides otherwise, if this contract is executed or Player is activated after the beginning of the regular season, the yearly salary payable to Player will be reduced proportionately and Player will be paid the weekly or biweekly portions of his yearly salary becoming due and payable after he is activated. Unless this contract specifically provides otherwise, if this contract is terminated after the beginning of the regular season, the yearly salary payable to Player will be reduced proportionately and Player will be paid the weekly or bi weekly portions of his yearly salary having become due and payable up to the time of termination.

7.　DEDUCTIONS. Any advance made to Player will be repaid to Club, and any properly levied Club fine or Commissioner fine against Player will be paid, in cash on demand or by means of deductions from payments coming due to the Player under this contract, the amount of such deductions to be determined by Club unless this contract or any collective bargaining agreement in existence during the term of this contract specifically provides otherwise. physical condition. Player will undergo a complete physical examination by the Club physician upon Club request, during which physical examination Player agrees to make full and complete disclosure of any physical or mental condition known to him which might impair his performance under this contract and to respond fully and in good faith when questioned by the Club physician about such condition. If Player fails to establish or maintain his excellent physical condition to the satisfaction of the Club physician, or make the required full and complete disclosure and good faith responses to the Club physician, then Club may terminate this contract.

9.　INJURY. Unless this contract specifically provides otherwise, if Player is injured in the performance of his services under this contract and promptly reports such injury to the Club physician or trainer, then Player will receive such medical and hospital care during the term of this contract as the Club physician may deem necessary, and will continue to receive his yearly salary for so long, during the season of injury only and for no subsequent period covered by this contract, as Player is physically unable to perform the services required of him by this contract because of such injury. If Player's injury in the performance of his services under this contract results in his death, the unpaid balance of his yearly salary for the season of injury will be paid to his stated beneficiary, or in the absence of a stated beneficiary, to his estate.

10. WORKERS' COMPENSATION. Any compensation paid to Player under this contract or under any collective bargaining agreement in existence during the term of this contract for a period during which he is entitled to workers' compensation benefits by reason of temporary total, permanent total, temporary partial, or permanent partial disability will be deemed an advance payment of workers' compensation benefits due Player, and Club will be entitled to be reimbursed the amount of such payment out of any award of workers' compensation.

11. SKILL, PERFORMANCE AND CONDUCT. Player understands that he is competing with other players for a position on Club's roster within the applicable player limits. If at any time, in the sole judgment of Club, Player's skill or performance has been unsatisfactory as compared with that of other players competing for positions on Club's roster, or if Player has engaged in personal conduct reasonably judged by Club to adversely affect or reflect on Club, then Club may terminate this contract. In addition, during the period any salary cap is legally in effect, this contract may be terminated if, in Club's opinion, Player is anticipated to make less of a contribution to Club's ability to compete on the playing field than another player or players whom Club intends to sign or attempts to sign, or another player or players who is or are already on Club's roster, and for whom Club needs room.

12. TERMINATION. The rights of termination set forth in this contract will be in addition to any other rights of termination allowed either party by law. Termination will be effective upon the giving of written notice, except that Player's death, other than as a result of injury incurred in the performance of his services under this contract, will automatically terminate this contract. If this contract is terminated by Club and either Player or Club so requests, Player will promptly undergo a complete physical examination by the Club physician.

13. INJURY GRIEVANCE. Unless a collective bargaining agreement in existence at the time of termination of this contract by Club provides otherwise, the following injury grievance procedure will apply: If Player believes that at the time of termination of this contract by Club he was physically unable to perform the services required of him by this contract because of an injury incurred in the performance of his services under this contract, Player may, within 60 days after examination by the Club physician, submit at his own expense to examination by a physician of his choice. If the opinion of Player's physician with respect to his physical ability to perform the services required of him by this contract is contrary to that of the Club's physician, the dispute will be submitted within a reasonable time to final and binding arbitration by an arbitrator selected

by Club and Player or, if they are unable to agree, one selected in accordance with the procedures of the American Arbitration Association on application by either party.

14. RULES. Player will comply with and be bound by all reasonable Club rules and regulations in effect during the term of this contract which are not inconsistent with the provisions of this contract or of any collective bargaining agreement in existence during the term of this contract. Player's attention is also called to the fact that the League functions with certain rules and procedures expressive of its operation as a joint venture among its member clubs and that these rules and practices may affect Player's relationship to the League and its member clubs independently of the provisions of this contract.

15. INTEGRITY OF GAME. Player recognizes the detriment to the League and professional football that would result from impairment of public confidence in the honest and orderly conduct of NFL games or the integrity and good character of NFL players. Player therefore acknowledges his awareness that if he accepts a bribe or agrees to throw or fix an NFL game; fails to promptly report a bribe offer or an attempt to throw or fix an NFL game; bets on an NFL game; knowingly associates with gamblers or gambling activity; uses or provides other players with stimulants or other drugs for the purpose of attempting to enhance on-field performance; or is guilty of any other form of conduct reasonably judged by the League Commissioner to be detrimental to the League or professional football, the Commissioner will have the right, but only after giving Player the opportunity for a hearing at which he may be represented by counsel of his choice, to fine Player in a reasonable amount; to suspend Player for a period certain or indefinitely; and/or to terminate this contract.

16. EXTENSION. Unless this contract specifically provides otherwise, if Player becomes a member of the Armed Forces of the United States or any other country, or retires from professional football as an active player, or otherwise fails or refuses to perform his services under this contract, then this contract will be tolled between the date of Player's induction into the Armed Forces, or his retirement, or his failure or refusal to perform, and the later date of his return to professional football. During the period this contract is tolled, Player will not be entitled to any compensation or benefits. On Player's return to professional football, the term of this contract will be extended for a period of time equal to the number of seasons (to the nearest multiple of one) remaining at the time the contract was tolled. The right of renewal, if any, contained in this contract will remain in effect until the end of any such extended term.

17. ASSIGNMENT. Unless this contract specifically provides otherwise, Club may assign this contract and Player's services under this contract to any successor to Club's franchise or to any other Club in the League. Player will report to the assignee Club promptly upon being informed of the assignment of his contract and will faithfully perform his services

under this contract. The assignee club will pay Player's necessary traveling expenses in reporting to it and will faithfully perform this contract with Player.

18.   FILING. This contract will be valid and binding upon Player and Club immediately upon execution. A copy of this contract, including any attachment to it, will be filed by Club with the League Commissioner within 10 days after execution. The Commissioner will have the right to disapprove this contract on reasonable grounds, including but not limited to an attempt by the parties to abridge or impair the rights of any other club, uncertainty or incompleteness in expression of the parties' respective rights and obligations, or conflict between the terms of this contract and any collective bargaining agreement then in existence. Approval will be automatic unless, within 10 days after receipt of this contract in his office, the Commissioner notifies the parties either of disapproval or of extension of this 10–day period for purposes of investigation or clarification pending his decision. On the receipt of notice of disapproval and termination, both parties will be relieved of their respective rights and obligations under this contract.

19.   DISPUTES. During the term of any collective bargaining agreement, any dispute between Player and Club involving the interpretation or application of any provision of this contract will be submitted to final and binding arbitration in accordance with the procedure called for in any collective bargaining agreement in existence at the time the event giving rise to any such dispute occurs.

20.   NOTICE. Any notice, request, approval or consent under this contract will be sufficiently given if in writing and delivered in person or mailed (certified or first class) by one party to the other at the address set forth in this contract or to such other address as the recipient may subsequently have furnished in writing to the sender.

21.   OTHER AGREEMENTS. This contract, including any attachment to it, sets forth the entire agreement between Player and Club and cannot be modified or supplemented orally. Player and Club represent that no other agreement, oral or written, except as attached to or specifically incorporated in this contract, exists are conflicting provisions in any collective bargaining agreement in existence during the term of this contract, in which case the provisions of the collective bargaining agreement will take precedence over conflicting provisions of this contract relating to the rights or obligations of either party.

22.   LAW. This contract is made under and shall be governed by the laws of the State of ————————————————.

23.   WAIVER AND RELEASE. Player waives and releases any claims that he may have arising out of, related to, or asserted in the lawsuit entitled White v. National Football League, including, but not limited to, any such claim regarding past NFL Rules, the College Draft, Plan B, the first refusal/compensation system, the NFL Player Contract, preseason compensation, or any other term or condition of employment, except any

claims asserted in Brown v. Pro Football, Inc. This waiver and release also extends to any conduct engaged in pursuant to the Stipulation and Settlement Agreement in White ("Settlement Agreement") during the express term of that Settlement Agreement or any portion thereof. This waiver and release shall not limit any rights Player may have to performance by the Club under this Contract or Player's rights as a member of the White class to object to the Settlement Agreement during its review by the court in Minnesota. This waiver and release is subject to Article XIV (NFL Player Contract), Section 3(c) of the CBA.

24. OTHER PROVISIONS.

(a) Each of the undersigned hereby confirms that (i) this contract, renegotiation, extension or amendment sets forth all components of the player's remuneration for playing professional football (whether such compensation is being furnished directly by the Club or by a related or affiliated entity); and (ii) there are not undisclosed agreements of any kind, whether express or implied, oral or written, and there are no promises, undertakings, representations, commitments, inducements, assurances of intent, or understandings of any kind that have not been disclosed to the NFL involving consideration of any kind to be paid, furnished or made available to Player or any entity or person owned or controlled by, affiliated with, or related to Player, either during the term of this contract or thereafter. (b) Each of the undersigned further confirms that, except insofar as any of the undersigned may describe in an addendum to this contract, to the best of their knowledge, no conduct in violation of the Anti–Collusion rules of the Settlement Agreement took place with respect to this contract. Each of the undersigned further confirms that nothing in this contract is designed or intended to defeat or circumvent any provisions of the Settlement Agreement, including but not limited to the Rookie Pool and Salary Cap provisions; however, any conduct permitted by the CBA and/or the Settlement Agreement shall not be considered a violation of this confirmation. (c) The Club further confirms that any information regarding the negotiation of this contract that it provided to the Neutral Verifier was, at the time the information was provided, true and correct in all material respects.

25. SPECIAL PROVISIONS.

THIS CONTRACT is executed in six (6) copies. Player acknowledges that before signing this contract he was given the opportunity to seek advice from or be represented by persons of his own selection.

---------------------------------   ---------------------------------
PLAYER   CLUB

---------------------------------   ---------------------------------
Home Address   By

---------------------------------   ---------------------------------
Telephone Number   Club Address

_____   _____
Date   Date

_____
PLAYER'S CERTIFIED AGENT

_____
Address

_____
Telephone Number

_____
Date

Copy Distribution: White–League Office Yellow–Player

Green–Member Club Blue–Management Council

Gold–NFLPA Pink–Player Agent

C. NBA Uniform Player Contract

NATIONAL BASKETBALL ASSOCIATION UNIFORM PLAYER CON-
   TRACT

THIS AGREEMENT made this _____ day of _____, is by and
between (hereinafter called the "Team"), a member of the National
Basketball Association (hereinafter called the "NBA" or "League") and
_____, an individual whose address is shown below (here-
inafter called the "Player"). In consideration of the mutual promises
hereinafter contained, the parties hereto promise and agree as follows:

1. TERM.

The Team hereby employs the Player as a skilled basketball player for a
term of _____ year(s) from the 1st day of September_____.

2. SERVICES.

The services to be rendered by the Player pursuant to this Contract shall
include: (a) training camp, (b) practices, meetings, workouts, and skill or
conditioning sessions conducted by the Team during the Season, (c) games
scheduled for the Team during any Regular Season, (d) Exhibition games
scheduled by the Team or the League during and prior to any Regular
Season, (e) if the Player is invited to participate, the NBA's All–Star Game
(including the Rookie–Sophomore Game) and every event conducted in
association with such All–Star Game, but only in accordance with Article
XXI of the Collective Bargaining Agreement currently in effect between
the NBA and the National Basketball Players Association (hereinafter the
"CBA"), (f) Playoff games scheduled by the League subsequent to any
Regular Season, (g) promotional and commercial activities of the Team

and the League as set forth in this Contract and the CBA, and (h) any NBADL Work Assignment in accordance with Article XLII of the CBA.

3.   COMPENSATION.

(a) Subject to paragraph 3(b) below, the Team agrees to pay the Player for rendering the services and performing the obligations described herein the Compensation described in Exhibit 1 or Exhibit 1A hereto (less all amounts required to be withheld by any governmental authority, and exclusive of any amount(s) which the Player shall be entitled to receive from the Player Playoff Pool). Unless otherwise provided in Exhibit 1, such Compensation shall be paid in twelve (12) equal semi-monthly payments beginning with the first of said payments on November 15th of each year covered by the Contract and continuing with such payments on the first and fifteenth of each month until said Compensation is paid in full.

(b) The Team agrees to pay the Player $1,500 per week, pro rata, less all amounts required to be withheld by any governmental authority, for each week (up to a maximum of four (4) weeks for Veterans and up to a maximum of five (5) weeks for Rookies) prior to the Team's first Regular Season game that the Player is in attendance at training camp or Exhibition games; provided, however, that no such payments shall be made if, prior to the date on which he is required to attend training camp, the Player has been paid $10,000 or more in Compensation with respect to the NBA Season scheduled to commence immediately following such training camp. Any Compensation paid by the Team pursuant to this subparagraph shall be considered an advance against any Compensation owed to the Player pursuant to paragraph 3(a) above, and the first scheduled payment of such Compensation (or such subsequent payments, if the first scheduled payment is not sufficient) shall be reduced by the amount of such advance.

(c) The Team will not pay and the Player will not accept any bonus or anything of value on account of the Team's winning any particular NBA game or series of games or attaining a certain position in the standings of the League as of a certain date, other than the final standing of the Team.

4.   EXPENSES.

The Team agrees to pay all proper and necessary expenses of the Player, including the reasonable lodging expenses of the Player while playing for the Team "on the road" and during the training camp period (defined for this paragraph only to mean the period from the first day of training camp through the day of the Team's first Exhibition game) for as long as the Player is not then living at home. The Player, while "on the road" (and during the training camp period, only if the Player is not then living at home and the Team does not pay for meals directly), shall be paid a meal expense allowance as set forth in the CBA. No deductions from such meal expense allowance shall be made for meals served on an airplane. During the training camp period (and only if the Player is not then living at home and the Team does not pay for meals directly), the meal expense allowance shall be paid in weekly installments commencing with the first week of training camp. For the purposes of this paragraph, the Player shall be considered to be "on the road" from the time the Team leaves its home city until the time the Team arrives back at its home city.

5. CONDUCT.

(a) The Player agrees to observe and comply with all Team rules, as maintained or promulgated in accordance with the CBA, at all times whether on or off the playing floor. Subject to the provisions of the CBA, such rules shall be part of this Contract as fully as if herein written and shall be binding upon the Player.

(b) The Player agrees: (i) to give his best services, as well as his loyalty, to the Team, and to play basketball only for the Team and its assignees; (ii) to be neatly and fully attired in public; (iii) to conduct himself on and off the court according to the highest standards of honesty, citizenship, and sportsmanship; and (iv) not to do anything that is materially detrimental or materially prejudicial to the best interests of the Team or the League.

(c) For any violation of Team rules, any breach of any provision of this Contract, or for any conduct impairing the faithful and thorough discharge of the duties incumbent upon the Player, the Team may reasonably impose fines and/or suspensions on the Player in accordance with the terms of the CBA.

(d) The Player agrees to be bound by Article 35 of the NBA Constitution, a copy of which, as in effect on the date of this Contract, is attached hereto. The Player acknowledges that the Commissioner is empowered to impose fines upon and/or suspend the Player for causes and in the manner provided in such Article, provided that such fines and/or suspensions are consistent with the terms of the CBA.

(e) The Player agrees that if the Commissioner, in his sole judgment, shall find that the Player has bet, or has offered or attempted to bet, money or anything of value on the outcome of any game participated in by any team which is a member of the NBA, the Commissioner shall have the power in his sole discretion to suspend the Player indefinitely or to expel him as a player for any member of the NBA, and the Commissioner's finding and decision shall be final, binding, conclusive, and unappealable.

(f) The Player agrees that he will not, during the term of this Contract, directly or indirectly, entice, induce, or persuade, or attempt to entice, induce, or persuade, any player or coach who is under contract to any NBA team to enter into negotiations for or relating to his services as a basketball player or coach, nor shall he negotiate for or contract for such services, except with the prior written consent of such team. Breach of this subparagraph, in addition to the remedies available to the Team, shall be punishable by fine and/or suspension to be imposed by the Commissioner.

(g) When the Player is fined and/or suspended by the Team or the NBA, he shall be given notice in writing (with a copy to the Players Association), stating the amount of the fine or the duration of the suspension and the reasons therefor.

6. WITHHOLDING.

(a) In the event the Player is fined and/or suspended by the Team or the NBA, the Team shall withhold the amount of the fine or, in the case of a suspension, the amount provided in Article VI of the CBA from any Current Base Compensation due or to become due to the Player with respect to the contract year in which the conduct resulting in the fine and/or the suspension occurred (or a subsequent contract year if the Player has received all Current Base Compensation due to him for the then current contract year). If, at the time the Player is fined and/or suspended, the Current Base Compensation remaining to be paid to the Player under this Contract is not sufficient to cover such fine and/or suspension, then the Player agrees promptly to pay the amount directly to the Team. In no case shall the Player permit any such fine and/or suspension to be paid on his behalf by anyone other than himself.

(b) Any Current Base Compensation withheld from or paid by the Player pursuant to this paragraph 6 shall be retained by the Team or the League, as the case may be, unless the Player contests the fine and/or suspension by initiating a timely Grievance in accordance with the provisions of the CBA. If such Grievance is initiated and it satisfies Article XXXI, Section 13 of the CBA, the amount withheld from the Player shall be placed in an interest-bearing account, pursuant to Article XXXI, Section 9 of such Agreement, pending the resolution of the Grievance.

7. PHYSICAL CONDITION.

(a) The Player agrees to report at the time and place fixed by the Team in good physical condition and to keep himself throughout each NBA Season in good physical condition.

(b) If the Player, in the judgment of the Team's physician, is not in good physical condition at the date of his first scheduled game for the Team, or if, at the beginning of or during any Season, he fails to remain in good physical condition (unless such condition results directly from an injury sustained by the Player as a direct result of participating in any basketball practice or game played for the Team during such Season), so as to render the Player, in the judgment of the Team's physician, unfit to play skilled basketball, the Team shall have the right to suspend such Player until such time as, in the judgment of the Team's physician, the Player is in sufficiently good physical condition to play skilled basketball. In the event of such suspension, the Base Compensation payable to the Player for any Season during such suspension shall be reduced in the same proportion as the length of the period during which, in the judgment of the Team's physician, the Player is unfit to play skilled basketball, bears to the length of such Season. Nothing in this subparagraph shall authorize the Team to suspend the Player solely because the Player is injured or ill.

(c) If, during the term of this Contract, the Player is injured as a direct result of participating in any basketball practice or game played for the Team, the Team will pay the Player's reasonable hospitalization and medical expenses (including doctor's bills), provided that the hospital and doctor are selected by the Team, and provided further that the Team shall be obligated to pay only those expenses incurred as a direct result of medical treatment caused solely by and relating directly to the injury sustained by the Player. Subject to the provisions set forth in Exhibit 3, if in the judgment of the Team's physician, the Player's injuries resulted directly from playing for the Team and render him unfit to play skilled basketball, then, so long as such unfitness continues, but in no event after the Player has received his full Base Compensation for the Season in which the injury was sustained, the Team shall pay to the Player the Base Compensation prescribed in Exhibit 1 to this Contract for such Season. The Team's obligations hereunder shall be reduced by (i) any workers' compensation benefits, which, to the extent permitted by law, the Player hereby assigns to the Team, and (ii) any insurance provided for by the Team whether paid or payable to the Player.

(d) The Player agrees to provide to the Team's coach, trainer, or physician prompt notice of any injury, illness, or medical condition suffered by him that is likely to affect adversely the Player's ability to render the services required under this Contract, including the time, place, cause, and nature of such injury, illness, or condition.

(e) Should the Player suffer an injury, illness, or medical condition, he will submit himself to a medical examination, appropriate medical treatment by a physician designated by the Team, and such rehabilitation activities as such physician may specify. Such examination when made at the request of the Team shall be at its expense, unless made necessary by some act or conduct of the Player contrary to the terms of this Contract.

(f) The Player agrees (i) to submit to a physical examination at the commencement and conclusion of each Contract year hereunder, and at such other times as reasonably determined by the Team to be medically necessary, and (ii) at the commencement of this Contract, and upon the request of the Team, to provide a complete prior medical history.

(g) The Player agrees to supply complete and truthful information in connection with any medical examinations or requests for medical information authorized by this Contract.

(h) A Player who consults a physician other than a physician designated by the Team shall give notice of such consultation to the Team and shall authorize and direct such other physician to provide the Team with all information it may request concerning any condition that in the judgment of the Team's physician may affect the Player's ability to play skilled basketball.

(i) If and to the extent necessary to enable or facilitate the disclosure of medical information as provided for by this Contract or Article XXII of the CBA, the Player shall execute such individual authorization(s) as may be requested by the Team or as may be required by health care providers who examine or treat the Player.

8.   PROHIBITED SUBSTANCES.

The Player acknowledges that this Contract may be terminated in accordance with the express provisions of Article XXXIII (Anti–Drug Program) of the CBA, and that any such termination will result in the Player's immediate dismissal and disqualification from any employment by the NBA and any of its teams. Notwithstanding any terms or provisions of this Contract (including any amendments hereto), in the event of such termination, all obligations of the Team, including obligations to pay Compensation, shall cease, except the obligation of the Team to pay the Player's earned Compensation (whether Current or Deferred) to the date of termination.

9.   UNIQUE SKILLS.

The Player represents and agrees that he has extraordinary and unique skill and ability as a basketball player, that the services to be rendered by him hereunder cannot be replaced or the loss thereof adequately compensated for in money damages, and that any breach by the Player of this Contract will cause irreparable injury to the Team, and to its assignees. Therefore, it is agreed that in the event it is alleged by the Team that the Player is playing, attempting or threatening to play, or negotiating for the purpose of playing, during the term of this Contract, for any other person, firm, entity, or organization, the Team and its assignees (in addition to any other remedies that may be available to them judicially or by way of arbitration) shall have the right to obtain from any court or arbitrator having jurisdiction such equitable relief as may be appropriate, including a decree enjoining the Player from any further such breach of this Contract, and enjoining the Player from playing basketball for any other person, firm, entity, or organization during the term of this Contract. The Player agrees that this right may be enforced by the Team or the NBA. In any suit, action, or arbitration proceeding brought to obtain such equitable relief, the Player does hereby waive his right, if any, to trial by jury, and does hereby waive his right, if any, to interpose any counterclaim or set-off for any cause whatever.

10.   ASSIGNMENT.

(a) The Team shall have the right to assign this Contract to any other NBA team and the Player agrees to accept such assignment and to faithfully perform and carry out this Contract with the same force and effect as if it had been entered into by the Player with the assignee team instead of with the Team.

(b) In the event that this Contract is assigned to any other NBA team, all reasonable expenses incurred by the Player in moving himself and his family to the home territory of the team to which such assignment is made, as a result thereof, shall be paid by the assignee team.

(c) In the event that this Contract is assigned to another NBA team, the Player shall forthwith be provided notice orally or in writing, delivered to the Player personally or delivered or mailed to his last known address, and the Player shall report to the assignee team within forty-eight (48) hours after said notice has been received (if the assignment is made during a Season), within one (1) week after said notice has been received (if the assignment is made between Seasons), or within such longer time for reporting as may be specified in said notice. The NBA shall also promptly notify the Players Association of any such assignment. The Player further agrees that, immediately upon reporting to the assignee team, he will submit upon request to a physical examination conducted by a physician designated by the assignee team.

(d) If the Player, without a reasonable excuse, does not report to the team to which this Contract has been assigned within the time provided in subsection (c) above, then (i) upon consummation of the assignment, the Player may be disciplined by the assignee team or, if the assignment is not consummated or is voided as a result of the Player's failure to so report, by the assignor Team, and (ii) such conduct shall constitute conduct prejudicial to the NBA under Article 35(d) of the NBA Constitution, and shall therefore subject the Player to discipline from the NBA in accordance with such Article.

11.   VALIDITY AND FILING.

(a) This Contract shall be valid and binding upon the Team and the Player immediately upon its execution.

(b) The Team agrees to file a copy of this Contract, and/or any amendment(s) thereto, with the Commissioner of the NBA as soon as practicable by facsimile and overnight mail, but in no event may such filing be made more than forty-eight (48) hours after the execution of this Contract and/or amendment(s).

(c) If pursuant to the NBA Constitution and By–Laws or the CBA, the Commissioner disapproves this Contract (or amendment) within ten (10) days after the receipt thereof in his office by overnight mail, this Contract (or amendment) shall thereupon terminate and be of no further force or effect and the Team and the Player shall thereupon be relieved of their respective rights and liabilities thereunder. If the Commissioner's disapproval is subsequently overturned in any proceeding brought under the arbitration provisions of the CBA (including any appeals), the Contract shall again be valid and binding upon the Team and the Player, and the Commissioner shall be afforded another ten-day period to disapprove the Contract (based on the Team's Room at the time the Commissioner's disapproval is overturned) as set forth in the foregoing sentence. The NBA will promptly inform the Players Association if the Commissioner disapproves this Contract.

12.   OTHER ATHLETIC ACTIVITIES.

The Player and the Team acknowledge and agree that the Player's participation in certain other activities may impair or destroy his ability and skill as a basketball player, and the Player's participation in any game or exhibition of basketball other than at the request of the Team may result in injury to him. Accordingly, the Player agrees that he will not, without the written consent of the Team, engage in any activity that a reasonable person would recognize as involving or exposing the participant to a substantial risk of bodily injury including, but not limited to: (i) sky-diving, hang gliding, snow skiing, rock or mountain climbing (as distinguished from hiking), rappelling, and bungee jumping; (ii) any fighting, boxing, or wrestling; (iii) driving or riding on a motorcycle or moped; (iv) riding in or on any motorized vehicle in any kind of race or racing contest; (v) operating an aircraft of any kind; (vi) engaging in any other activity excluded or prohibited by or under any insurance policy which the Team procures against the injury, illness or disability to or of the Player, or death of the Player, for which the Player has received written notice from the Team prior to the execution of this Contract; or (vii) participating in any game or exhibition of basketball, football, baseball, hockey, lacrosse, or other team sport or competition. If the Player violates this Paragraph 12, he shall be subject to discipline imposed by the Team and/or the Commissioner of the NBA. Nothing contained herein shall be intended to require the Player to obtain the written consent of the Team in order to enable the Player to participate in, as an amateur, the sports of golf, tennis, handball, swimming, hiking, softball, volleyball, and other similar sports that a reasonable person would not recognize as involving or exposing the participant to a substantial risk of bodily injury.

13.   PROMOTIONAL ACTIVITIES.

(a) The Player agrees to allow the Team, the NBA, or a League-related entity to take pictures of the Player, alone or together with others, for still photographs, motion pictures, or television, at such reasonable times as the Team, the NBA or the League-related entity may designate. No matter by whom taken, such pictures may be used in any manner desired by either the Team, the NBA, or the League-related entity for publicity or promotional purposes. The rights in any such pictures taken by the Team, the NBA, or the League-related entity shall belong to the Team, the NBA, or the League-related entity, as their interests may appear.

(b) The Player agrees that, during any year of this Contract, he will not make public appearances, participate in radio or television programs, permit his picture to be taken, write or sponsor newspaper or magazine articles, or sponsor commercial products without the written consent of the Team, which shall not be withheld except in the reasonable interests of the Team or the NBA. The foregoing shall be interpreted in accordance with the decision in Portland Trail Blazers v. Darnell Valentine and Jim Paxson, Decision 86–2 (August 13, 1986).

(c) Upon request, the Player shall consent to and make himself available for interviews by representatives of the media conducted at reasonable times.

(d) In addition to the foregoing, and subject to the conditions and limitations set forth in Article II, Section 8 of the CBA, the Player agrees to participate, upon request, in all other reasonable promotional activities of the Team, the NBA, and any League-related entity. For each such promotional appearance made on behalf of a commercial sponsor of the Team, the Team agrees to pay the Player $2,500 or, if the Team agrees, such higher amount that is consistent with the Team's past practice and not otherwise unreasonable.

14. GROUP LICENSE.

(a) The Player hereby grants to NBA Properties, Inc. (and its related entities) the exclusive rights to use the Player's Player Attributes as such term is defined and for such group licensing purposes as are set forth in the Agreement between NBA Properties, Inc. and the National Basketball Players Association, made as of September 18, 1995 and amended January 20, 1999 and July 29, 2005 (the "Group License"), a copy of which will, upon his request, be furnished to the Player; and the Player agrees to make the appearances called for by such Agreement.

(b) Notwithstanding anything to the contrary contained in the Group License or this Contract, NBA Properties (and its related entities) may use, in connection with League Promotions, the Player's (i) name or nickname and/or (ii) the Player's Player Attributes (as defined in the Group License) as such Player Attributes may be captured in game action footage or photographs. NBA Properties (and its related entities) shall be entitled to use the Player's Player Attributes individually pursuant to the preceding sentence and shall not be required to use the Player's Player Attributes in a group or as one of multiple players. As used herein, League Promotion shall mean any advertising, marketing, or collateral materials or marketing programs conducted by the NBA, NBA Properties (and its related entities) or any NBA team that is intended to promote (A) any game in which an NBA team participates or game telecast, cablecast or broadcast (including Pre–Season, Exhibition, Regular Season, and Playoff games), (B) the NBA, its teams, or its players, or (C) the sport of basketball.

15. TEAM DEFAULT.

In the event of an alleged default by the Team in the payments to the Player provided for by this Contract, or in the event of an alleged failure by the Team to perform any other material obligation that it has agreed to perform hereunder, the Player shall notify both the Team and the League in writing of the facts constituting such alleged default or alleged failure.

If neither the Team nor the League shall cause such alleged default or alleged failure to be remedied within five (5) days after receipt of such written notice, the National Basketball Players Association shall, on behalf of the Player, have the right to request that the dispute concerning such alleged default or alleged failure be referred immediately to the Grievance Arbitrator in accordance with the provisions of the CBA. If, as a result of such arbitration, an award issues in favor of the Player, and if neither the Team nor the League complies with such award within ten (10) days after the service thereof, the Player shall have the right, by a further written notice to the Team and the League, to terminate this Contract.

16.   TERMINATION.

(a) The Team may terminate this Contract upon written notice to the Player if the Player shall:

    (i) at any time, fail, refuse, or neglect to conform his personal conduct to standards of good citizenship, good moral character (defined here to mean not engaging in acts of moral turpitude, whether or not such acts would constitute a crime), and good sportsmanship, to keep himself in first class physical condition, or to obey the Team's training rules;

    (ii) at any time commit a significant and inexcusable physical attack against any official or employee of the Team or the NBA (other than another player), or any person in attendance at any NBA game or event, considering the totality of the circumstances, including (but not limited to) the degree of provocation (if any) that may have led to the attack, the nature and scope of the attack, the Player's state of mind at the time of the attack, and the extent of any injury resulting from the attack;

    (iii) at any time, fail, in the sole opinion of the Team's management, to exhibit sufficient skill or competitive ability to qualify to continue as a member of the Team; provided, however, (A) that if this Contract is terminated by the Team, in accordance with the provisions of this subparagraph, prior to January 10 of any Season, and the Player, at the time of such termination, is unfit to play skilled basketball as the result of an injury resulting directly from his playing for the Team, the Player shall (subject to the provisions set forth in Exhibit 3) continue to receive his full Base Compensation, less all workers' compensation benefits (which, to the extent permitted by law, and if not deducted from the Player's Compensation by the Team, the Player hereby assigns to the Team) and any insurance provided for by the Team paid or payable to the Player by reason of said injury, until such time as the Player is fit to play skilled basketball, but not beyond the Season during which such termination occurred; and provided, further, (B) that if this Contract is terminated by the Team, in accordance with the provisions of this subparagraph, during the period from the January 10 of any Season through the end of such Season, the Player shall be entitled to receive his full Base Compensation for said Season; or

(iv) at any time, fail, refuse, or neglect to render his services hereunder or in any other manner materially breach this Contract.

(b) If this Contract is terminated by the Team by reason of the Player's failure to render his services hereunder due to disability caused by an injury to the Player resulting directly from his playing for the Team and rendering him unfit to play skilled basketball, and notice of such injury is given by the Player as provided herein, the Player shall (subject to the provisions set forth in Exhibit 3) be entitled to receive his full Base Compensation for the Season in which the injury was sustained, less all workers' compensation benefits (which, to the extent permitted by law, and if not deducted from the Player's Compensation by the Team, the Player hereby assigns to the Team) and any insurance provided for by the Team paid or payable to the Player by reason of said injury.

(c) Notwithstanding the provisions of paragraph 16(b) above, if this Contract is terminated by the Team prior to the first game of a Regular Season by reason of the Player's failure to render his services hereunder due to an injury or condition sustained or suffered during a preceding Season, or after such Season but prior to the Player's participation in any basketball practice or game played for the Team, payment by the Team of any Compensation earned through the date of termination under paragraph 3(b) above, payment of the Player's board, lodging, and expense allowance during the training camp period, payment of the reasonable traveling expenses of the Player to his home city, and the expert training and coaching provided by the Team to the Player during the training season shall be full payment to the Player.

(d) If this Contract is terminated by the Team during the period designated by the Team for attendance at training camp, payment by the Team of any Compensation earned through the date of termination under paragraph 3(b) above, payment of the Player's board, lodging, and expense allowance during such period to the date of termination, payment of the reasonable traveling expenses of the Player to his home city, and the expert training and coaching provided by the Team to the Player during the training season shall be full payment to the Player.

(e) If this Contract is terminated by the Team after the first game of a Regular Season, except in the case provided for in subparagraphs (a)(iii) and (b) of this paragraph 16, the Player shall be entitled to receive as full payment hereunder a sum of money which, when added to the salary which he has already received during such Season, will represent the same proportionate amount of the annual sum set forth in Exhibit 1 hereto as the number of days of such Regular Season then past bears to the total number of days of such Regular Season, plus the reasonable traveling expenses of the Player to his home.

(f) If the Team proposes to terminate this Contract in accordance with subparagraph (a) of this paragraph 16, it must first comply with the following waiver procedure:

(i) The Team shall request the NBA Commissioner to request waivers from all other clubs. Such waiver request may not be withdrawn.

(ii) Upon receipt of the waiver request, any other team may claim assignment of this Contract at such waiver price as may be fixed by the League, the priority of claims to be determined in accordance with the NBA Constitution and By–Laws.

(iii) If this Contract is so claimed, the Team agrees that it shall, upon the assignment of this Contract to the claiming team, notify the Player of such assignment as provided in paragraph 10(c) hereof, and the Player agrees he shall report to the assignee team as provided in said paragraph 10(c).

(iv) If the Contract is not claimed prior to the expiration of the waiver period, it shall terminate and the Team shall promptly deliver written notice of termination to the Player.

(v) The NBA shall promptly notify the Players Association of the disposition of any waiver request.

(vi) To the extent not inconsistent with the foregoing provisions of this subparagraph (f), the waiver procedures set forth in the NBA Constitution and By–Laws, a copy of which, as in effect on the date of this Contract, is attached hereto, shall govern.

(g) Upon any termination of this Contract by the Player, all obligations of the Team to pay Compensation shall cease on the date of termination, except the obligation of the Team to pay the Player's Compensation to said date.

17. DISPUTES.

In the event of any dispute arising between the Player and the Team relating to any matter arising under this Contract, or concerning the performance or interpretation thereof (except for a dispute arising under paragraph 9 hereof), such dispute shall be resolved in accordance with the Grievance and Arbitration Procedure set forth in Article XXXI of the CBA.

18. PLAYER NOT A MEMBER.

Nothing contained in this Contract or in any provision of the NBA Constitution and By–Laws shall be construed to constitute the Player a member of the NBA or to confer upon him any of the rights or privileges of a member thereof.

19. RELEASE.

The Player hereby releases and waives any and all claims he may have, or that may arise during the term of this Contract, against (a) the NBA and its related entities, the NBADL and its related entities, and every member of the NBA or the NBADL, and every director, officer, owner, stockholder, trustee, partner, and employee of the NBA, NBADL and their respective related entities and/or any member of the NBA or NBADL and their related entities (excluding persons employed as players by any such member), and (b) any person retained by the NBA and/or the Players

Association in connection with the NBA/NBPA Anti–Drug Program, the Grievance Arbitrator, the System Arbitrator, and any other arbitrator or expert retained by the NBA and/or the Players Association under the terms of the CBA, in both cases (a) and (b) above, arising out of, or in connection with, and whether or not by negligence, (i) any injury that is subject to the provisions of paragraph 7 hereof, (ii) any fighting or other form of violent and/or unsportsmanlike conduct occurring during the course of any practice, any NBADL game, and/or any NBA Exhibition, Regular Season, and/or Playoff game (in all cases on or adjacent to the playing floor or in or adjacent to any facility used for such practices or games), (iii) the testing procedures or the imposition of any penalties set forth in paragraph 8 hereof and in the NBA/NBPA Anti–Drug Program, or (iv) any injury suffered in the course of his employment as to which he has or would have a claim for workers' compensation benefits. The foregoing shall not apply to any claim of medical malpractice against a Team-affiliated physician or other medical personnel.

20.   ENTIRE AGREEMENT.

This Contract (including any Exhibits hereto) contains the entire agreement between the parties and, except as provided in the CBA, sets forth all components of the Player's Compensation from the Team or any Team Affiliate, and there are no other agreements or transactions of any kind (whether disclosed or undisclosed to the NBA), express or implied, oral or written, or promises, undertakings, representations, commitments, inducements, assurances of intent, or understandings of any kind (whether disclosed or undisclosed to the NBA) (a) concerning any future Renegotiation, Extension, or other amendment of this Contract or the entry into any new Player Contract, or (b) involving compensation or consideration of any kind (including, without limitation, an investment or business opportunity) to be paid, furnished, or made available to the Player, or any person or entity controlled by, related to, or acting with authority on behalf of the Player, by the Team or any Team Affiliate.

EXAMINE THIS CONTRACT CAREFULLY BEFORE SIGNING IT.

THIS CONTRACT INCLUDES EXHIBITS _____, WHICH ARE ATTACHED HERETO AND MADE A PART HEREOF.

IN WITNESS WHEREOF the Player has hereunto signed his name and the Team has caused this Contract to be executed by its duly authorized officer.

Dated:

By: _____
Title: _____
Team: _____

Dated:

Player: _____
Player's Address: _____

APPENDIX B

SAMPLE COURSE STUDY GUIDE

■ ■ ■

Sample Course Study Guide

Most legally-significant cases which shifted the course of each of the three major sports:

- Baseball:
  - Flood v. Kuhn—limits antitrust exemption to the reserve clause.
  - Messersmith v. McNally—fatal blow to the reserve system.
  - Finley v. Kuhn—articulated commissioner's best interest power; enables commissioner to veto trades in game's best interest.
- Basketball:
  - Haywood—overruled age eligibility requirement in NBA; stated that basketball is not exempt from antitrust laws.
  - Wood—court rules against Woods; allowing him to challenge the NBA salary cap and draft would destroy fundamental principles of collective bargaining
  - Williams—non-statutory labor exemption precluded antitrust challenge to various terms and conditions of employment.
- Football:
  - Clarett—upholds age eligibility requirement.
  - Mackey—3–prong test for non-statutory exemption articulated; strikes down Rozelle Rule.
  - Goodell and the PCP—defining factor going forward in the evolution of the NFL.

Most poorly-reasoned cases:

- Baseball:
  - Toolson—upheld a flawed ruling; didn't take into account changes in baseball over time.

- Football:
  - Brown—unilateral imposition of last pre-impasse proposal by employers is contrary to principles of fair negotiation.
- Basketball:
  - Sprewell—court intervening and limiting commissioner's punishment was overstepping court's bounds.

	MLB	NFL	NBA	Other

I) Moral Integrity of the Sport: The Role of the Commissioner and the Law
 	
Number of cases: 30
	Models for a Professional Sports League:
	1. NFL Model:
	    a. NFL commissioner wields vast power to discipline/fine/suspend without being challenged by players' union or **2nd** guessed by arbitrator (see Clayton Holmes case)
	        i. Commissioner has power to 1) fine player a reasonable amount; 2) suspend for period certain or indefinitely; 3) terminate contract
	    b. Appeals of punishments are made only to commissioner; there is no arbitration procedure
	    c. Article VII of the NFL Constitution: Commissioner has authority to withdraw from arbitration any action taken against a player by the Commissioner for conduct detrimental to public confidence
	    d. Goodell imposed a new Personal Conduct Policy (PCP) in April of 2007:
	        i. PacMan Jones suspended without pay for entire 2007 season
	2. NBA Model:
	    a. This is a compromise between the strong union/strong commissioner model; NBPA wields influence in matters of player discipline, but gives commissioner significant leeway
	    b. NBA has sweeping authority to enact rules without prior consent from the NBPA
	    c. NBA commissioner has the greatest authority to control matters within the game
	    d. § 35 of the NBA Constitution: The commissioner can "expel, suspend, or fine any club official, employee or player for detrimental conduct," but such executive decisions are subject to review by NBA Board of Governors
	    e. NBA grievance process under Article XXXI of the CBA involves a neutral arbitrator; reviews disciplinary action to determine whether there is just cause for punishment
	    f. NBA has adopted several regulations of players including dress code, prohibiting players from attending nightclubs.
	3. MLB Model:
	    a. Article I, § 5 of the Major League Constitution: Limits the powers of the commissioner to act in the game's best interests only to matters outside the CBA
	    b. MLB commissioner benefited historically from antitrust immunity, and waiver of recourse to courts largely insulated the Commissioner's decisions from reversal upon judicial review
	        i. Waiver of recourse to courts was eliminated
	        ii. CBA established a grievance procedure which originally had the Commissioner as arbitrator, then replaced by neutral arbitrator (see Seitz's role in the Messersmith case)
	        iii. Flood v. Kuhn, which held that baseball was interstate commerce and limited the antitrust exemption to the reserve system, chipped away at power of commissioner
	    c. Standard of review of commissioner's power is just cause standard
	    d. Best interests power first evolved in baseball; important to remember that baseball has been shielded by antitrust exemption, while football and basketball have been subject to antitrust.
	    e. Larry Walker case: team discipline cannot be added on top of league action or would be double punishment (same result in Vida Blue/Willie Wilson)
	
	Best Interests Power of the MLB Commissioner:
	  • Article I,§ 2 of the Baseball Agreement: "Best Interests" power—Functions of the Commissioner include:
	    ○ To investigate, either upon complaint or upon own initiative, any act, transaction, or practice charged, alleged or suspected to be not in the best interests of the national game of baseball, with authority to summon persons and to order production of documents...
	    ○ To determine, after investigation, what preventive, remedial or punitive action is appropriate in the premises.			

- Article I, § 5 of the Major League Constitution:
  - ○ Limits the power of the Commissioner to act in bests interests only to matters outside the CBA.
- Article § 1, § 4:
  - ○ The Commissioner shall take no action in the best interests of baseball that requires the clubs to take, or refrain from taking, joint league action on any of the matters requiring a vote of the clubs that are set forth in [various articles] or relating to any matter pursuant to League Constitution
- Article XI, A(1)(b): gives commissioner the power to remove a disciplinary case from arbitration, and make decision in the matter final and binding on player under best interest power
  - ○ Commissioner has never once invoked this power because it gives union the right to reopen the bargaining agreement with respect to this article if union finds action unsatisfactory

Our posited rule for where courts should step in to limit the best interests power of the commissioner:
- 1) where a party is not adequately represented in collective bargaining (such as the female reporter in the Ludtke case)
- 2) when the commissioner has overstepped his bounds and exceeded limitations on commissioner's authority

Yankees v. Johnson (1919): Player was suspended by Commissioner Ban Johnson after walking off mound; Yankees sued Holding: Judge holds that commissioner's authority is limited to acts taking place on field ***Milwaukee Ass'n v. Landis:*** Commissioner finds out that Bennett was transferred several times between minor league clubs controlled by Phil Ball; refuses to approve transaction Court rules that commissioner has power of paterfamilias ***Charles Finley v. Bowie Kuhn*** (1978): Finley of A's doesn't want to re-sign Joe Rudi, Rollie Fingers or Vida Blue; wants to sell them in order to build through draft; sells rights to Rudi and Fingers to Sox for $2 m, and Vida Blue to Yankees for $1.5 mm Court holds that Major Leagues and constituent clubs agree to be bound by the decisions of the commissioner and by the discipline imposed by him; further agree to waive	***NFL Management Council v. NFLPA (Arb. 1979)*** 2 Dolphins players (Randy Crowder, Don Reese) arrested for distribution of cocaine, plead nolo contendere Commissioner allowed return conditional on mandatory 5k contribution to drug rehab facility. Grievance filed by PA. Arbitrator upholds commissioner power to withdraw from general grievance procedure any disciplinary action taken by commissioner for any conduct detrimental to the NFL. ***Holmes v. NFL*** District Court upheld Commissioner's authority to reject appeal of player from his involuntary enrollment in league's drug treatment program and four-game suspension without pay. League had suspended after testing positive, player appealed to commissioner who is the arbitrator under CBA for such appeals. Court holds Commissioner does not need to give full constitutional due process protection Further held that Commissioner con-	***Riko Enterprises (76ers) v. Seattle Supersonics (SDNY 1973)*** Court held that only NBA board of governors, not Commissioner, had power to award Supersonics' first-round draft pick to 76ers when Seattle had signed a player, Brisker, who had remained on the 76ers reserve player list while played in the ABA. ***Sprewell:*** Court intervened; overruled commissioner's penalty for Sprewell's choking coach ***Molinas v. NBA*** Molinas drafted by Pistons; bet on own team and was indefinitely suspended Court says rule banning betting on own team is not only reasonable but necessary; holds that there is no antitrust violation; league should be able to effectuate policies, restore and maintain confidence ***Ortiz–Del Valle v. NBA*** Held League liable for gender discrimination. ***Connie Hawkins v. NBA*** While Hawkins was initially suspected of being involved with the	***Dambrot v. Central Michigan Univ.*** Dambrot, coach of men's basketball team, used racial slur to pump his team up during half-time of a game. Fired by school. Sues on grounds termination violated his 1st Amendment rights Court finds in favor of the school ***Marge Schott:*** Schott used various racial epithets; agreed to accept $25k fine and one-year suspension from management of the Reds ***Marty McSorley v. Donald Brashear*** Commissioner gave McSorley a record-setting suspension, and there was no right to appeal because it was on-ice conduct (under NHL collective agreement) ***Martha Burk v. Hootie Johnson*** Controversy about the lack of female members at Augusta National Golf Course, home of the Masters Tournament Augusta National was comfortable giving up its sponsorships, in order to protect its right as a private club to control its

the right of recourse to courts as would otherwise have existed; court says that commissioner acted in good faith, in manner which he determined to be in best interests of game

Atlanta Braves/ Ted Turner v. Bowie Kuhn:
Turner tampers with Gary Matthews in violation of limits on re-entry draft Kuhn allows Matthew's contract with Braves but suspends Turner for 1 year and deprives Atlanta of pick Court says that Commissioner has authority to issue and enforce directives that bar any owner from dealing with another teams players before the draft; says it's strange that Matthews signing allowed while Turner suspended, but it's not abuse of discretion; prevents penalty of pick, however, because is NOT one of the commissioner's enumerated powers

Chicago National League Ball Club v. Francis Vincent, Jr.
Fay Vincent orders that Cubs and Cardinals be shifted to National League's Western Division; court says that Commissioner's general authority is preempted by specific language providing that no member club be transferred without consent

MLBPA (Larry Walker) v. MLB Player Relations Committee (Expos) (arbitration 1994)
Walker sparked bench-clearing brawl when he charged mound af-

duct/discretion should not be disturbed if it draws its essence from the CBA

Paul Hornung case: Rozelle suspended Hornung of Packers and Alex Karras of Lions for betting on own teams to win

Commissioner Goodell's handling of Spygate and implementation of the Player Conduct Policy
Broad exercise of "best interests" power

Molinas *controversy, he eventually* settled his suit, allowing him to play in the NBA

John "Hot Rod" Williams v. NBA
Williams was not permitted to play pending trial for point shaving, but once he was acquitted, he was permitted to play

Mahmoud Abdul–Rauf v. NBA NBA argued that its suspension of Mahmoud Abdul–Rauf for not standing for the national anthem was under the "conduct prejudicial or detrimental to the NBA" clause, but many others thought that the suspension constituted discrimination on the basis of religion under Title VII of the Civil Rights Case was resolved amicably when Abdul–Rauf complied with NBA policy

membership

Bob Knight:
Knight choked player; Indiana president suspended him and fined him; Knight then fired after confrontation with Indiana freshman

ter being hit by pitch Walker suspended by league and Expos tried to not pay him his salary during suspension Arbitrator held that club was bound by consistent longstanding owner practice of not withholding salary for suspensions by league for on-field conduct.

Willie Wilson:
Vida Blue, Willie Wilson, Jerry Martin and Willie Aikens were arrested and convicted in 1983 for possession of cocaine and sentenced to 3 months in jail; Kuhn imposed 1–year suspension covering entire 1984 baseball season. The issue was that while 1–year suspension rule was posted in all clubhouses, the players could challenge it under just cause standard, which was part of basic agreement Neutral arbitrator ruled that commissioner had just cause for suspension, given the negative impact of drugs upon society and the game

Tony Phillips:
Phillips arrested in motel after buying cocaine from undercover agent Phillips won unanimous arbitration award reinstating him as long as he would undergo treatment

Ludtke v. Kuhn:
Ludtke is woman banned from Yankee Locker Room based on Gender. Court finds this is an equal protection issue (action is state action because of lease structure on Yankee Stadium) There are less sweeping ways to protect concerns of commissioner, and

family values/decen-
cy are not sufficient
concerns to out-
weigh violations of
equal protection and
harmful effects of
policy

***Messersmith and
McNally Arbitra-
tions:***
Commissioner Kuhn
claimed he had the
authority to remove
the grievance from
arbitration, but
didn't do so Com-
missioner also had
power to remove Ar-
bitrator Seitz before
the decision, but
didn't do so

Rose v. Giamatti:
Commissioner
Giamatti banned
Rose for life for bet-
ting on baseball
games while manag-
er of the Cincinnati
Reds Rose had sued
to prevent Giamatti
from acting; Rose
and Giamatti settled
and Rose accepted
lifetime ban

***Steinbrenner v.
Vincent:***
Steinbrenner given
lifetime ban by com-
missioner Vincent
for paying gambler
Spira for informa-
tion on Dave Win-
field; lifted two
years later

Alomar Case:
Alomar spit in face
of umpire; suspen-
sion held in abey-
ance while Alomar
exercise right to ap-
peal

***MLBPA and MLB
Commissioner
(Steve Howe
Case):***
Howe was suspend-
ed 6x from baseball
for drugs Court
states that burden
for establishing just
cause for discipline
is imposed on those
imposing it Court
holds that commis-
sioner didn't pro-
vide requisite condi-
tions for Howe to
adhere to suspen-
sion requirements;

	fundamental fairness required that punishment be set aside ***Frick case:*** Minor league team sues Commissioner Frick for failing to act, alleging that MLB teams encroached on MILB territory Court steps in and says commish CAN be held liable for failure to act			
II) **Constructing a Player's Market from Contract to Antitrust Law** **Number of Cases: 15**	***Toronto Blue Jays v. Boston Celtics and Danny Ainge*** • While under contract with the Toronto Blue Jays to play baseball, Ainge wanted to sign instead with the Boston Celtics and play basketball. • Standard player contract included an affirmative promise by Ainge to play baseball and an undertaking that he would refrain from playing for other professional teams and any other sport involving a substantial risk of personal injury. ***Philadelphia Ball Club v. Lajoie*** • While Lajoie was under contract to one club, he chose to disregard his his contract and arranged to play for organization. • Where one person agrees to render personal services to another, which require and presuppose a special knowledge, skill, and ability in the	***Winnipeg Rugby Football Club v. Freeman*** • Two players wanted to play for the NFL's Cleveland Browns, in breach of an ongoing contract with a CFL team. • Court found that players had a unique skill and ability, and were much more valuable to the CFL team because of the lower caliber of play in that league. ***New York Football Giants, Inc. v. Los Angeles Chargers Football Club, Inc. (Flowers)*** • Giants kept their contract with Flowers a secret to preserve his eligibility, but then Flowers chose to sign with the Chargers after they offered more money. • Court establishes "clean hands" doctrine: he who comes into equity must come with clean hands, thus denying Giants any relief.	***Central New York Basketball, Inc. (Syracuse Nationals) v. Barnett*** • While Barnett had agreed to play for Syracuse, he subsequently signed a contract with a rival team from Cleveland. • Barnett's contract acknowledged his exceptional and unique skill and ability as a basketball player whose peculiar value to the club could only be remedied by injunctive relief not just damages for breach of contract • Court issued injunction to prohibit Barnett from switching; used same logic as Lajoie case; injunctions ensures that employer not deprived of services of unique player • NBA has reached an agreement with FIBA under which neither will allow teams under its jurisdiction to sign players under contract to a	***Yashin v. NHL (Ont.Sup.Court)*** • Yashin was player who had 1 year left on his K at 3 million/yr. Player told team (Senators) unless they extended K for two more years at significant salary increase, he would not play. • Team did not cooperate, Yashin went home to Russia. • Court upheld arbitrator's ruling finding team allowed to require that before Yashin could play for any other NHL team, he had to play another year for the Senators before becoming a free agent (read K term as years of service, not years expired since signing of K) • Reasoning: only player's union, not individual player, had right to challenge an arbitrator's interpretation of the collective agreement. Also, court not persuaded the arbitrator's

employee, so that in case of a default the same service could not easily be obtained from others, although specific performance is beyond the power of the court, its performance will be negatively enforced by enjoining its breach.

Houston Oilers v. Neely

- After Neely agreed to a deal with Houston of the AFL, which he wanted kept secret, his representatives began negotiating with Dallas of the NFL, and Neely eventually returned Houston's money and signed with Dallas.
- Clean hands doctrine does not exclude all wrongdoers from a court of equity nor should it be applied in every case where the conduct of a party may be considered unconscionable or inequitable.
- Houston was not under any legal duty publicize the contract or to keep it secret. Its agreement to keep secret that which it had a legal right to keep secret cannot be considered inequitable or unconscionable.

Mike Keenan case:

- Keenan signed a new deal then tried to get out of it; violated a key contract provision
- NFL commissioner fined virtually every party, including Keenan for trying to get out of contract, as well as tampering parties

Morris v. NY Football Giants (NY Sup)

- Union had decertified as players bar-

team under the jurisdiction of the other.

Boston Celtics v. Brian Shaw

- Shaw was under contract to an Italian team and chose to exercise his option to terminate that contract and signed a new deal with the Boston Celtics for future seasons, but was later concerned that he signed for below market value.
- Court found that there was nothing improper, unclean, or unfair about the Celtics' convincing Shaw to exercise his contractual right in their favor; issued injunction to prevent their losing his services

Munchak Corp v. Cunningham

- Standard "no assignment" clause merely meant that the player could not be traded to a different club, not that he could not be traded to a different owner of the same club.

Washington Capitals Basketball Club v. Barry

- There was no actionable wrong in an athlete signing a new contract during the period of his existing contract, as long as performance and consideration under the

decision subjected Yashin to "perpetual servitude"

Vanderbilt University v. Dinardo

- Contract "buyout" provision says that if coach leaves during the term to go work at any other institution, he would pay the university an amount equal to the net salary that the university had agreed to pay him during the remainder of his contract gaining rep and there was no CBA in effect.

- Court held provision in player contracts requiring contract disputes be resolved by NFL commissioner non-enforceable because the commissioner was not an unbiased neutral since he was hired and fired by the owners.

Alexander v. Minnesota Vikings (Minn.App)

- Assistant coach fired, claimed he was shorted on compensation. Contract called for Commissioner as arbitrator.
- Coach sought order from court replacing commissioner as arbitrator.
- Court held it could not enforce the clause but replace commissioner. Did not rule whether the clause was enforceable.

Cincinnati Bengals v. Bergey

- While under contract with the Bengals, Bergey signed a contract for future services with a team in the newly formed WFL, to begin after his contract with the Bengals expired.
- Court concludes that it is not illegal for either the player or the sports organization, at the time when the player is under a

new contract were to begin after expiry of the existing agreement, and there was no encouragement to terminate the latter contract early.

	valid contract to one team to negotiate and enter into a contract with a different, competing, team and league, under the terms of which the player agrees to render his services at the expiration of his current contract.		

III) The Baseball "Trilogy" —Flood v. Kuhn and the Creation of the Baseball "Antitrust Exemption" **Number of Cases: 17**	Background on the MLB Reserve System: • Each team listed players with whom it had a contractual relationship; all other teams respected the reserve list and did not pursue those players ○ Even if the team didn't sign the player, no other team could sign him • All teams agreed to sign players to a form contract, which provided the team the option to renew the contract for another season, for the same terms Sherman Act: • § 1: Every contract, combination in the form of trust or otherwise, or conspiracy, in restraint of trade or commerce among the several states, or with foreign nations, is declared to be illegal. • § 2: Every person who shall monopolize, or attempt to monopolize, or combine or conspire with any other person or persons, to monopolize any part of the trade or commerce among the several states, or with foreign nations, shall be deemed guilty of a felony.

Metro Exhibition v. Ward:	*Radovich v. NFL*	*Haywood v. NBA*	*US v. Intl Boxing Club (SCOTUS)*
• NY Supreme Court refused to grant NY Ball Club an injunction preventing Ward for playing for another club during 1890 season ***American League Baseball Club of Chicago v. Chase*** • Chase signed a contract with the White Sox for the upcoming season, but soon after terminated the contract and signed with a team in the new Federal Baseball League. • Court will not assist in enforcing an agreement which is a part of a general plan having for its object the maintenance of a monopoly, interference with the personal liberty of a citi-	• Court held that football, unlike baseball, was not exempt from federal antitrust laws. ***Partee v. San Diego Chargers Football Co.*** • Partee tried to strike down NFL's version of reserve system under California antitrust law. • Court relied on Dormant Commerce Clause analysis to say that state business regulation is judged to have imposed an unreasonable burden on interstate commerce where it governs those phases of the national commerce which, because of the need for national uniformity, demand their regulation be prescribed by a	• Court said that basketball, unlike baseball, does not enjoy exemption from federal antitrust laws.	• Refuses to extend antitrust exemption to boxing. ***Amateur Softball Assn of America v. US (10th Cir)*** • Holding amateur sports like softball are not exempt from antitrust laws

zen, and the control of his free right to labor wherever and for whom he pleases, and will not extend its aid to further the purposes and practices of an unlawful combination, by restraining the defendant from working for any one but the plaintiff.

Flood v. Kuhn (1972)
- After Flood was traded to the Phillies, he rejected the trade and declared himself a free agent, and filed suit to establish these rights under antitrust law; argued that his being prevented from contracting with chosen team was antitrust violation
- Baseball's antitrust exemption is an aberration, but it is a long-standing aberration that has been recognized by several cases and Congress has done nothing to change it, thus is entitled to stare decisis.
- Dissent emphasizes that precedent should not be lightly overruled, but when court errors deny substantial federal rights, like the right to compete freely and effectively to the best of one's ability as guaranteed by the antitrust laws, the court must admit its error and correct it.

single authority.

Hebert v. Los Angeles Raiders
- Hebert wanted to use California's Labor Code to move from the Saints to the Raiders.
- Court said that the Dormant Commerce Clause precluded application of California's Labor Code to this case.

Matuszak v. Houston Oilers
- Under Dormant Commerce Clause, the court refused to apply Texas antitrust law to NFL restraints on player movement.

Dutton (NFLPA v. NFL Management Council:
- Dutton tests the NFL reserve system by playing out option year and seeking a ruling
- Arbitrator says that neither side explicitly addressed whether renewal was perpetual; rules that term was perpetual given other language in the contract.

- There is no argument that the reserve clause falls within CBA, because it was prevalent before formation of MLBPA

Federal Baseball Club of Baltimore v. National League of Professional Baseball Clubs
- Federal League sued American and National League on antitrust grounds.
- Court held that the business of providing public baseball games for profit between clubs of professional baseball players was not within the scope of the federal antitrust laws (not interstate commerce).

Toolson v. New York Yankees (1953)
- Upheld reasoning of _Federal Baseball_ on stare decisis grounds.

State of Wisconsin v. Milwaukee Braves
- Under Dormant Commerce Clause, the court refused to apply Wisconsin antitrust law to block the move of the Braves from Milwaukee to Atlanta.

Salerno v. American League
- Court applied baseball's antitrust exemption to MLB's dealings with umpires; went the same way as Flood v. Kuhn

	Portland Baseball Club v. Kuhn • Court applied baseball's antitrust exemption to MLB's dealings with minor leagues. *Catfish Hunter:* • Hunter brought dispute regarding payment term in his contract; case went to grievance arbitration • Hunter won in arbitration and was granted free agent status			

Statutory Exemption from Antitrust Law:
- Statutory Exemption: Clayton Act, § 6: Nothing contained in the antitrust laws shall be construed to forbid the existence or labor . . . organizations, or to forbid or restrain individual members from lawfully carrying out the legitimate objects thereof . . .

IV) The Football Trilogy: Smith, Brown, Mackey and the creation of the non-statutory labor exemption
Number of Cases: 10

Non–Statutory Exemption from Antitrust Law:

- Non-statutory exemption protects collectively-bargained agreements from reach of antitrust law, subject to conditions developed by courts (see Mackey Test, Brown)

		Brown v. Pro Football I	*Wood v. NBA:*	*Meat Cutters v. Jewel Tea:*
		• NFL owners unilaterally imposed provision to pay development players a fixed salary to avoid stashing; Brown sued alleging that the fixed salary violated antitrust laws • Court holds that price-fixing through fixed salary is illegal restraint of trade; Clayton Act provides broad latitude to prevent price-fixing. *Brown v. Pro Football II (Supreme Court):* • Breyer holds that unilaterally imposed, last pre-impasse owner proposal is protected by non-statutory exemption • New test is articulated for unilateral implementation of last pre-impasse proposal:	• Wood filed suit alleging that salary cap, college draft, and prohibition of player corporations violate § 1 of the Sherman act and are not exempt from antitrust scrutiny through the non-statutory exemption • Court stated that draft and salary cap are product of collective agreement reached through procedures mandated by federal labor legislation; to allow Wood to individually invalidate them because of unique ability would be to destroy the nature of	• Union insists on restricted working hours for meat counters; Jewel accepts under duress and then brings suit. • Alleged violations are exempt from reach of antitrust; hours and days of week are mandatory subjects set out by NLRA; marketing-hours restriction is so intimately related to wages, hours and working conditions provision falls within protection of national labor policy. *Pennington:* • Small coal mine operator

○ 1) new terms included in employers' last pre-impasse proposal:
○ 2) employers cannot have bargained in bad faith
○ 3) implemented terms concern only parties to the collective bargaining agreement
○ 4) terms must involve a matter on which parties required to negotiate

Mackey v. NFL I:
- Rozelle Rule required team acquiring free agent to pay compensation payment to old club in form of draft picks; Mackey challenged it
- We hold that the Rule unreasonably restrains trade in violation of § 1 of the Sherman Act; we need not decide whether system of compensation itself is essential; Rule is plainly more restrictive than necessary.

Smith v. Pro Football
- Yazoo Smith signed a 1–year contract under mandatory NFL pay scale; had career-ending neck injury; filed suit attacking rookie draft pay scale
- Court declines to adopt per se rule but states that balancing test must be applied, comparing pro-competitive ad-

collective agreements

claimed that miners union violated anti-trust laws by agreeing with large coal mine companies that union would demand higher wage scale from small operators
- Court holds that while union may make wage agreements with multi-employer bargaining unit, and may in pursuance of own interests seek to obtain same terms from other employers without incurring anti-trust liability, forfeits exemption when it is clearly shown that it favors one set of employers

McCourt v. California Sports:
- Case focused on equalization payments; young star was exchanged as an equalization payment for signing a free agent and sued to prevent the exchange.
- All of the Mackey prongs were satisfied; NHLPA used every form of negotiating pressure it could muster; union got the league to yield significantly on other issues; this is good-faith, arms' length bargaining.

Allen Bradley:
- NY electrical workers union negotiated a series of agreements in which local manufacturers agreed to deal only

| | | vantages of draft effects; states that there are no pro-competitive effects because NFL teams are not competitors in economic sense; holds that NFL draft violates § 1 of Sherman Act | | with other manufacturers employing union labor
• Court refuses to apply the non-statutory exemption where agreement between employers and union prejudices one set of employers

Frasor v. MLS (2002):
• Payers challenged single-entity system in MLS, which caps max salary and pays all players from a central pot
• Single entity determination precludes § 1 scrutiny
• Court sides with MLS; not conclusive that less restrictive salary system would have increased salaries |
| **V) NFL and NBA Age Eligibility and Related CBA Issues**

Number of Cases: 18 | **MLB and MILB Eligibility Rule:**
• Eligibility post-high school for American players
• Antitrust exemption lives on here

Silverman v. MLBPRC:
• Court recognized that a mix of free agency and reserve clauses combined with other provisions such as rookie draft and salary caps is the universal method by which leagues and players unions set individual salaries in professional sports | **NFL Rule: At least 3 seasons after high school graduation must have passed before player is eligible**

Clarett I (District Court):
• Court holds that NFL eligibility rule is not protected under non-statutory exemption; Clarett is not a party to the agreement and rule is not a mandatory subject

Clarett v. NFL (II)
(2d Cir 2004) P challenged age eligibility rule. Circuit held non-statutory labor exemption applied. Found *Mackey* did not define limits of exemption. Held: eligibility rules mandatory subject of bargaining (define literal condition for initial | **NBA Rule: At least 1 year after high school graduation must have passed before player is eligible**

Denver Rockets v. All–Pro Management (D.Cal 1971) (Haywood)—Held non-collectively bargained age eligibility requirement that contained no exceptions illegal boycott was a per se antitrust violation.

Robertson v. NBA:
• Plaintiffs alleged that the reserve clause, uniform player contract, and college draft violated the antitrust laws, and sought to enjoin the league in which they played and a rival league from merging or en- | ***NCAA v. Board of Regents***—SCOTUS—recognized some industries have unique characteristics requiring the use of trade restraints in order to maintain the industry's existence. Found NCAA is industry where horizontal restraints are necessary for the product to exist. Contributed to emergence of "quick look" analysis.

Linseman v. World Hockey Assn—(D.Conn 1977) P challenged age requirement, court held rule to be completely arbitrary and struck it down as per se violation of Sherman Act.

Boris v. USFL
(C.D.Cal 1984)—Court struck down eligibility requirement as an illegal group boycott, de- |

employment, affect job security for veteran players, both mandatory subjects), eligibility rule was tied into the CBA, CBA validly negotiated between employer and legal worker rep (NFLPA). Fact that rule affects players outside union irrelevant, fact that rule bars Clarett despite his qualifications to play/work irrelevant (no different than ordinary prospective worker who feels qualified but doesn't meet established minimum requirements). Fact NFL clubs agreed to impose this rule irrelevant, clubs may function as multi-employer bargaining unit. Non-statutory exemption prevents nonmembers of union from filing antitrust suit.

McNeil v. NFL:
- Players were able to avoid application of the labor exemption defense after the NFLPA successfully renounced its status as a union bargaining agent
- Court found that Plan B harmed players by diminishing competition among NFL clubs for their services, that nonetheless the system contributed significantly to competitive balance among NFL teams, but that the system was unreasonable because it was more restrictive than necessary for that purpose
- Settlement was reached in 1993 with the

tering into a non-competition agreement
- Court held that the challenged items were not mandatory subjects of collective bargaining; that leagues were not entitled to advantage of labor exemption from antitrust laws; that player draft, uniform player contract, and reserve clause were analogous to devices that were *per se* violative of the antitrust laws
- Court says that the non-statutory labor exemption extends only to labor or union activities, and not to the activities of employers

NBA v. Williams:
- Court agreed with Eighth Circuit's holding that the non-statutory labor exemption precluded an antitrust challenge to various terms and conditions of employment implemented after impasse in a collective bargaining session following expiration of a previous agreement

Caldwell v. ABA:
- Caldwell had represented players in labor negotiations; was blacklisted by owners and never returned to game
- Court concluded that his claims concerned a mandatory subject under the CBA

clared rule per se illegal.

Blalock v. LPGA (N.D.Ga 1973)—court threw out one-year suspension levied upon the P by LPGA, held to be per se illegal.

Deesen v. PGA (9th cir 1966)—Player sued for being barred from tour for poor play. Court applied rule of reason test, held PGA's performance requirement to be reasonable mandate.

Neeld v. NHL (D.C.Cir 1978)
- Player with one eye sued, claiming rule barring players with sight in one eye was antitrust violation. Court applied rule of reason, held any anticompetitive affect was de minimis at most, and agreed with justification of NHL that rule was meant to promote player safety

Philadelphia World Hockey Club v. Philadelphia Hockey Club:
- Operation of a collectively-bargained lifetime reserve clause denies a new league access to the available supply of top-flight athletes whom the new league needs to survive as a serious competitor to the established league

		NFL paying $195 million to satisfy the claims of the players who had been restricted by Plan B **_Powell v. NFL:_** • Court held that antitrust laws are inapplicable under the circumstances of this case because the nonstatutory labor exemption extends not just beyond termination but also beyond impasse **_Zimmerman v. NFL:_** • _Mackey_ test was applied and Court found that the exemption protected the supplemental draft because it had been agreed to by the union through good faith, arm's-length bargaining	• Court presumed that the conduct in question was illegal absent the presence of a collective bargaining relationship, but that in this case, the claims were barred by the exemption; this should be negotiated through labor union	
VI) CBA Issues **Number of Cases: 10**	**_Ntl & Am. League Professional Baseball Clubs v. MLBPA:_** • Messersmith and McNally refused to sign new K's at the end of the '74 season and played '75 season under UPC 10(c), the team's renewal option. When they claimed the new contract did not contain the renewal option, an arbiter was asked: (1) if an arbiter could hear the case despite the CBA's prohibition on challenges to the reserve system (2) If renewed K's contain a team option for	**_NFLPA v. NFL Management Council:_** • After Dutton's K ended he had no offers so he took his teams option. After this year he still had no offers and sued declaring that he should be a true free agent because the "right of first refusal/compensation" provisions don't renew with the contract. • The arbiter ruled for the league holding that it doesn't appear the two parties considered this and from where the rule (Article XV § 17) ap-	**_Central New York Basketball v. Barnett:_** • The renewal clause in basketball's standard player K was for one year only, not perpetual **_Lemat Corp. v. Barry:_** • Following _Barnett_, the court stated that the renewal clause in basketball's standard player contract was for one year only, not perpetual	**_Steelworker's Trilogy:_** Created a strong set of presumptions in favor of arbitration including: 1. The court should strongly presume the matter to be arbitrable unless the K language creating the grievance procedure makes it unmistakable that no such claim was meant to be arbitrated 2. Once an arbitrator has rendered a decision the court must enforce the decision if it draws its essence form the CBA. • Applied in: Davis v. Pro Basketball, Erving v. Virginia Squires Basketball Club, KC Royals v. MLBPA.

the next sea-
son. (3) If a
club can re-
serve a player
they do not
have under
contract

- The arbiter
decided the
following: (1)
The question
didn't chal-
lenge the re-
serve system
only dealt with
an issue relat-
ing to the re-
serve clause.
(2) The re-
newed K
doesn't contain
a team option
only includes
all of the
agreements re-
lating to the
terms of em-
ployment be-
cause the
clause deals
with IF a K ex-
ists, it is not a
term of the
contract. (3)
Baseball can-
not reserve a
player that is
not under con-
tract because
from the begin-
ning, the re-
serve system
assumes a
player under
contract as evi-
denced by the
fact that the
Cincinnati
Compact states
*"reserve
players
under
contract."*

**Kansas City
Royals v. MLBPA:**
- After Messers-
mith, the Roy-
als appealed on
behalf of base-
ball challeng-
ing (1) arbiters
ability to hear
the case under
Article XV of
the 1973 agree-
ment and (2)
whether the
arbiter's ruling
"drew its es-
sence from the
agreement".
- The court held
(1) the arbiter

pears it seems
as if it applies
to all veteran
free agents,
thus the re-
strictions re-
new.

**The 5 Smiths v.
NFLPA:**
- Agents could
share informa-
tion of what
players are
paid. Absent an
agreement to
restrain price,
the exchange of
price informa-
tion is benign
and facilitates
efficient eco-
nomic activity.

	could hear the case. Here the court drew heavily from the fact that the league had allowed previous cases dealing with some elements of the reserve clause to be arbitrated. (2) The decision drew its essence from the agreement since there is no express provision in the agreement, some PA reps viewed the system as letting a player become a free agent through playing out their option, and the award arguably didn't change the reserve system only interpreted certain elements of it. **_MLBPA v. Garvey:_** • SCOTUS upholds an extremely questionable arbiter decision under principle of deference **_US v. Cleveland Indians Baseball:_** • Wages in the collusion settlement should be taxed according to the tax rate of the year they were paid (SS tax of 6.2%)			
VII) Right of Publicity and Fantasy Games **Number of Cases: 38**	**_Haelan Labs v. Topps Chewing Gum:_** • Court recognizes an assignable right to the publicity value of one's name and picture **_Orioles v. MLBPA:_** • An employer owns a copyright in a work if the work satisfied the generally	**_Gridiron.com v. NFLPA:_** • A website that signed 150 NFL players individually was forced by the courts to negotiate with the NFLPA directly instead of individual players because it used the property of more than 5 NFL players	**_NBA v. Motorola:_** • Real-time statistics from live basketball games are not copyrightable, thus can be disseminated by non-league entities without license as "hot news"	**_MSG v. NHL:_** • New Media Committee concluded that the best approach for the NHL would be to migrate each team's site into a common technology platform, serviced by a single content management system (CMS) • Court found that the NHL

applicable requirements for copyrightability, the work was prepared by an employee, the work was prepared within the scope of the employee's employment, and the parties have not expressly agreed otherwise in a signed, written instrument

- By virtue of being videotaped, the players' performances are fixed in tangible form, and any rights of publicity in their performances that are equivalent to the rights contained in the copyright of the telecast are preempted

Topps v. MLBPA:

- MLBPA is more analogous to a wholesale distributor of the rights, and does not appear to function at the same level in the market as Topps
- Arrangement between MLBPA and players is one that does not clearly restrict competition, and may in fact enhance competition for players' publicity rights for use on a group basis

Fleer Corp v. Topps Chewing Gum:
Upholding Topps' exclusive player's license against antitrust attacks.

Uhlaender v. Henricksen: A game

Jerry Jones Controversy:

- Jerry Jones signed contracts with rivals of NFL sponsors for the licensing of "Texas Stadium" but not the "Dallas Cowboys"
- Jones and NFL settled on terms that allowed Jones to continue his deals between Texas Stadium and its licensees

has established that there were several pro-competitive effects of the new media strategy

Carson v. Here's Johnny Portable Toilets:

- Commercial exploitation of an athlete's identity infringes upon the player's publicity rights

Morris Communications v. PGA Tour:

- PGA is entitled to prevent others from on-selling the "real-time" golf scores from the golf tournaments that the PGA governs

Zacchini v. Scripps–Howard:

- Court described the right of publicity as focusing on the right of the individual to reap the reward of his endeavors and having little to do with protecting feelings or reputation

§ 43(a) of Lanham Act: unlawful for any person who, or in connection with any goods or services . . . which is likely to cause confusion, mistake, or to deceive as to affiliation.

Ventura v. Titan Sports: Absent a waiver, Ventura had a publicity right entitling him to compensation for use and sale of his name, likeness, or performance on video.

Ali v. Playgirl: A drawing of a boxer

manufacturer couldn't appropriate a players name/statistics for its game.

Palmer v. Schonhorn Enterprises: Found violation of right to publicity when parties sold board games featuring athletes biographical information and statistics.

Gionfriddo v. MLB:
- Advertisements violate right of publicity when P's identity is used, without consent, to promote an unrelated product. The more unrelated the less protection

Cardtoons v. MLBPA:
- Court holds that a set of trading cards which contains caricatures of some MLB players is a parody and does NOT violate publicity rights

CBC v. MLBAM:
- Information used in CBC's fantasy baseball games is all readily available in the public domain
- Non-economic justifications for the right of publicity were unpersuasive as compared with the interest in freedom of expression
- Players Association did not have exclusive right, title and interest in the use of such information, and it therefore breached a material obligation that it undertook in the contract

with words "the greatest" violates Ali's rights

Crazylegs case: Crazylegs as a shaving cream name violated rights of football player who's nickname was "Crazylegs".

Doe v. TCI Cablevision: Cartoon character's use of Tony Twist's name violated his right of publicity

Hooker v. Columbia Picture Industries: Where the use of a P's name doesn't sufficiently identify the P, there can be no relief

Vanna White case: A robot dressed like Vanna next to a Wheel of Fortune set violated CA state law but not federal statutory law

Motschenbacher v. R.J. Reynolds Tobacco Co.: Using a driver's car clearly violated right to publicity because the distinctive features of the car were peculiar to the D and implicated identity

Eastwood v. Superior Court of Los Angeles County: Use of Eastwood's name, photograph and likeness constituted commercial purpose because "the first step toward selling a product or service is to attract the customers' attention."

Hoffman v. Capitol Cities/ABC, Inc: Balanced commercial nature of ad with expressive content (and its 1st Amendment protection). Altered photo of Dustin Hoffman protected as expressive art

	Steinbrenner–Adidas Controversy: • Steinbrenner agreed to a partnership between the New York Yankees and Adidas, which was not consented to by MLB and its central merchandising system		***Waits v. Frito–Lay:*** An unauthorized use of a celebrities voice is a false association claim likely to confuse customers as to plaintiff's sponsor/approval. As a result, this is grounds for a Lanham Act Claim under § 43(a) Standard: Likelihood consumers will believe the celebrity endorsed the product. ***Allen v. Men's World Outlet:*** Applied Lanham Act and ruled in favor of Allen because there was a high likelihood of confusion/consumer belief he endorsed. ***Wendt v. Host Int'l:*** Cheers robots were a Lanham Act violation against the actors because of the high likelihood of confusion. ***Landham v. Lewis Galoob Toys:*** Applied the balancing factors for the Lanham test and concluded that the Predator toys did not violate the actors rights. ***ETW Corp v. Jireh:*** The likelihood of confusion test should only be used in cases where the public interest in avoiding confusion outweighs the public interest in free expression (Tiger Woods Augusta Pictures Case) ***New York Magazine v. Metropolitan Transit Auth.:*** Magazine can use Guliani's likeness to advertise where it is connected to a story about the mayor (under free speech). ***Bolger v. Youngs Drug Products:*** SCOTUS holding Commercial Speech

				is speech related solely to the economic interests of the speaker and its audience ***Central Hudson Gas & Elec. Corp.:*** Advertisements violate right to publicity when P's identity is used, without consent, to promote an unrelated product. ***Comedy III Productions v. Gary Saderup:*** Is celebrity likeness something form which it is derived or is the depiction the entire substance of the work ***Seale v. Gramercy Pictures:*** Is appropriated right related to the work or used to attract attention ***KNG Enterprises v. Mathews:*** If it is tangible and of a nature that would be protected by copyright, federal copyright dominates
VIII) Franchise Relocation and Stadium Naming Rights Agreements **Number of Cases: 33**	***Piazza and Tirendi v. MLB (1993):*** Court held MLB's antitrust exemption is limited to the reserve system and as a result the leagues restraint on the ability of the Giants to move to Tampa violates antitrust law. ***MLB v. Butterworth (2001):*** When baseball announced it wanted to contract 2 teams, the FL attorney general investigated a potential antitrust violation. The court said *Piazza* was wrong and baseball was immunized from antitrust liability for contracting a team. As a result the league didn't need to comply with the investigative demands of	***Raiders I (1984):*** NFL constitution rule 4.3 says ¾ of owners must approve a move. When the owners didn't allow the Raiders to go to LA, Davis sued. Court rules 1. That the teams were competitive to warrant rule of reason analysis 2. jury could have reasonably concluded benefits to the league were outweighed by the rule's competitive harms, and 3. upheld a verdict that the rule violated antitrust law. ***Raiders II (1986):*** League sued Raiders for compensation for "value of goodwill the league had build in LA as a potential expansion site." The court ruled in favor of the	***NBA v. San Diego Clippers Basketball Club (1987):*** After Raiders I, the Clippers moved to LA. The NBA wanted declaratory judgment that it could stop the movement and be compensated for taking away a prime city for expansion. Court for rejected the motion for summary judgment and remanded for trial. ***HMC Management v. New Orleans Basketball Club (1979):*** When Jazz moved to Utah, group sued for breach of lease seeking specific performance. Court held monetary damages are appropriate to compensate for breach of a lease from franchise relo-	***San Francisco Seals v. NHL:*** Court held that the league was 1 entity competition against other leagues, so the league's refusal to allow SF to move wasn't an antitrust violation. ***Continental T.V. v. GTE:*** Dealing with restraints to keep TV sellers of a brand from infringing on each other's territory. Court said sometimes restraints like this may be needed in the interest of competition on a broader level. ***Seattle Totems v. NHL:*** Antitrust suit to force expansion in hockey was summarily dismissed

the AG.

MLB v. Crist: New FL AG appeals, appeals court says <u>Butterworth</u> was correctly decided and that baseball's antitrust exemption applies to "the business of baseball."

Minnesota Twins Partnership v. State of Minnesota: After the league threatened to move the twins and not allow a new team go to Minn if a new stadium wasn't build, the state AG attempted to investigate. The court ignored Piazza and said baseball was immunized by the antitrust exemption.

Metropolitan Sports Facilities Commission v. Minnesota Twins Partnership: The group that runs the Metrodome succeeding in suing for specific performance demanding the Twins play out their lease and preventing baseball from interfering (brought after baseball threatened to contract the Twins).

Expos Drama: As a result of the fact that Loria went from a small owner to owning 94% of the Expos and baseball's proposed 3 team swap, the other Expos owners filed RICO suits in FL. The case was arbitrated in Montreal and that was that.

Selig v. US: Court ruled that 10.8 million (95%) of what Selig played for the team was properly attributable to the 150 players that came with the team.

Butterworth v. National League of Pro Baseball

league and demanded Davis compensate the NFL.

City of Oakland v. Oakland Raiders I: Court held that if a city could build a stadium, then it must be proper public purpose to own/operate a football team and as a result the team could condemn the Raiders to resell them using its eminent domain power.

City of Oakland v. Raiders II: Football is a national business and relocation effects the entire league. As a result, the regulation of this activity is reserved for the federal government only. This means the cities condemnation was not allowed (state level had no regulatory power).

Mayor/City Council of Baltimore v. Baltimore Colts (1985): The team avoided Baltimore's use of eminent domain by packing up/moving to IN in the middle of the night.

Charpentier v. L.A. Rams Football Co (1999): When a former Rams season ticket holder sued claiming breach of K because the club moved to St. Louis (asserting he purchased tickets in 1994 believing he could renew them the following year) the court held that a renewal clause in a season ticket K does not imply a promise not to relocate the franchise.

New York City v. New York Jets Football Club (1977): When the Jets wanted to play

cation.

Levin v. NBA (1974): NBA Board of Governors didn't approve Levin buying the Celtics. Levin sued claiming an antitrust violation. Court said excluding Levin from membership in the league didn't have anti-competitive effects so the league was not in violation of antitrust laws. Owners can choose who their partners are. Antitrust protects competition, not individual competitors.

Seattle Supersonics Relocation Saga: Key legal issue was whether or not the city could obtain specific performance of the lease, forcing the Sonics to remain in Seattle through the 2009–2010 NBA season, or whether monetary damages were sufficient to remedy the club's breach of the lease. Shortly after the city settled with the new owners for $75 million, Schultz dropped his lawsuit, finally allowing the team to move to Oklahoma City.

Clubs (Fla. 1994): *Agrees with Piazza that exemption applies only to reserve clause, not transfer or creation of franchises.*

Morsani v. MLB (Fla. App 1995): Follows *Butterworth* and *Piazza* and rules that baseball could not claim an exemption from state or federal antitrust laws re: blocking efforts of Florida group to buy Minnesota Twins and bring them to St. Petersburg FL.

McCoy v. MLB (WDWash 1995): Explicitly disagrees with *Butterworth* and *Piazza.* Used exemption of "the business of baseball" as the principal grounds for rejecting class action antitrust suit filed against baseball owners on behalf of Mariners fans' who were left with no games to watch when the players went out on strike in 1994.

Curt Flood Act of 1998:
- States that the antitrust laws do not cover the acts, practices, agreements of persons in the business of organized professional MLB directly relating to or affective employer of MLB players.
- Makes clear that new antitrust coverage does not extend, however, to conduct that does not directly relate to or affect employment of MLB players to play at major league level.
- Examples of non-covered ac-

games at the meadowlands instead of Shea during the MLB season, the court stayed an injunction, forcing them to play out their lease in Shea. The court said money damages couldn't compensate for games not being played there. NOTE: LEASE INCLUDED A CLAUSE AUTHORIZING INJUNCTIVE RELIEF.

Mid–South Grizzlies v. NFL: NFL denied an application from a group of WFL teams to create a team in Memphis. The Grizzlies claimed violation of the Sherman Act saying the decision injured competition. Court found for the league saying rejection was pro-competitive regarding inter-league competition and external anti-competitive effects were minimal since Grizzlies didn't show potential for significant competition in its market.

VKK Corp v. NFL: Pats Owner sued the NFL saying its restrictions on relocation forced him to sell the Patriots because he couldn't move them. He lost because of a contractual waiver waiving the right to sue.

St. Louis Convention v. NFL: St. Louis sued saying the NFL charging the Rams 30 million to move greatly increased the subsidy needed to lure the Rams from LA. They lost because of a lack of evidence of any conspiracy.

Seahawks Dispute: King County threatened to sue the Seahawks if

	tivities: employment to play at minor league level, amateur draft, decisions relating to franchise expansion, location, or relocation, sales of IP, relations between/among MLB and MiLB teams. ***Lifteau v. Metropolitan Sports Facilities Commission:*** Commissioner Selig told Congress that he believed that professional sports leagues and Major League Baseball should vigilantly enforce strong polices prohibiting clubs from abandoning local communities which have supported them.	they moved with time left on their lease. Seahawks claimed city violated the lease by letting the Kingdome suck so much it didn't meet earthquake standards. They settled and the team was sold. ***Laird v. US:*** Of $8.45 million paid for the NFL team in Atlanta, $3.05 million was attributable to the player contracts. ***North American Soccer League v. NFL:*** NFL's rule preventing member-owners from having ownership interests in other professional sports clubs violated Section 1 of the Sherman Act. ***City of Cleveland—Cleveland Browns dispute:*** In breach of lease dispute, Browns' defense was that the city was not in privity with the Browns, and was not intended to be a third-party beneficiary of the lease between the Browns and the management company, who owned the stadium.		
IX) Current Issues in Sports and Articles **Number of Cases: 9**	***BALCO Scandal in Baseball:*** • Idea that it's all about the money and home runs benefited the game • MLBPA abdicated its role • Integrity of the game? ***MLB draft and player eligibility:*** • Role of buscones • Slotting system and role in signing young players ***What to do about baseball academies:***	***NFL: Veteran Premium Problem*** • NFL's salary cap, rookie salary pool and reverse-rank draft have helped to create competitive balance • But there are inequities; average player doesn't stay in league long enough to qualify for free agency (players with at least 4 seasons of experience are entitled to be unrestricted free agents)	***Tim Donaghy betting scandal:*** Is he the biggest challenge Stern has with regard to the game's integrity?	***English-speaking requirement on LPGA tour:*** • Can the non English speaking players sue on grounds that requirement violates Equal Protection, as court held in Ludtke?

- Creation of worldwide draft
- Add a fluency requirement?
- Prevent salary skimming

Ryan Howard and not-so-young superstars:
- Players called up to majors after 25th birthday are not eligible for free agency until at least 31 years old

Andrew Oliver case:
- Oliver, currently a college baseball player, had legal representation as a high schooler, violating NCAA rule
- Oliver suing NCAA on basis that prevention of high school players from having agent is illegal

- NFL salary cap: computed as a percentage of total—projected benefits; salary cap is a hard cap
- NFL can apply various tags to players: transition tag, franchise tag, restricted tag

Raiders v. Lane Kiffin:
- Kiffin terminated by Al Davis for losing; is having a losing record just cause for termination

APPENDIX C

SAMPLE FINAL EXAM AND ANSWERS

■ ■ ■

Question I

I. You are acting as General Counsel to MLB Commissioner Bud Selig. In so doing, you have been asked to provide a "confidential/privileged" bullet-point memo to him (including a Table of Contents and an Executive Summary, which should not exceed two (2) pages in length), responding to the following questions:

   A. In the legal history/evolution of the three (3) "major leagues" (i.e., MLB, NFL and NBA), what are the three (3) most "legally significant" court or arbitration decisions (individually, "precedent", and collectively, "precedents") in each sport re: shaping the current "rules of the game" within which each sport must now operate?

   1. Please also advise Commissioner Selig re: (a.) what "non-sports law" "precedents," if any, were most relevant to the reasoning in each of the three (3) "sports-law" "precedents"; and (b.) what "legal advantages," if any, MLB enjoyed at the time of each decision, based on MLB's "antitrust exemption," as it existed at that time.

   B. As to the three (3) selected "precedents," please also advise Commissioner Selig which one (1) "precedent" in MLB's "legal history" he should "overrule," if given permission to do so by the U.S. Supreme Court, pursuant to the Commissioner's ultimate authority to act in "the best interests of the game."

   1. Please answer that same question, i.e. which one (1) "precedent" should be overruled, as if it had been asked by the NFL and NBA Commissioners, in providing Commissioner Selig with a "privileged" context in which he can make his final decision.

Your final memo should not exceed ten (10) pages in length, including your Table of Contents and Executive Summary.

Question II

II. You are acting as General Counsel to the Executive Director of the NBA's Player Association (the "NBPA"), Billy Hunter, as he prepares

195

to renegotiate the current Collective Bargaining Agreement (CBA). In particular, he will be renegotiating the most significant "player sensitive" provisions of the NBA Uniform Player Contract (the "NBA UPC"). In so doing, he has asked you to prepare a "confidential/privileged" bullet-point memo (including a Table of Contents and Executive Summary, which should not exceed two (2) pages in length), responding to the following questions:

A. Please analyze the following provisions of the NBA UPC, focusing on the extent to which the provisions reflect the interests of the player and the league, and compare them to the comparable provisions in the NFL and MLB UPC:[1]:

Paragraph 5—"Conduct";

Paragraph 9—"Unique Skills";

Paragraph 12—"Other Athletic Activities";

Paragraph 13—"Promotional Activities";

Paragraph 14—"Group License";

Paragraph 16—"Termination";

Paragraph 17—"Disputes"; and

Paragraph 19—"Release".

1. Based on the foregoing analysis and our Class discussions/assignments re: "black-lining" the MLB and NFL UPCs, please "black-line" edit four (4) of the above-referenced provisions of the NBA UPC, to make them more "player friendly." In so doing, please advise the Executive Director why you are recommending each of your proposed edits, in anticipation of the upcoming renegotiation of the NBA UPC with the NBA Commissioner. Please also support each of your proposed edits with reference to the most relevant precedents and other Syllabus materials discussed during our classes dealing with the MLB, NFL, and NBA UPCs and CBAs.

a. In particular, you should take into account the fact that the NBPA's "superstar" members are most interested in protecting and expanding upon their individual "publicity rights" for use in broad-ranging product endorsements (including in video games, "website rights," and "fantasy games" that feature the "superstar" in question, etc.). At the same time, the "superstars" are more than willing to trade off re: the current "age eligibility rules," so as to prevent anyone who has not completed two (2) years of college or reached the age of 20 from entering the NBA Draft.

---

1. The "form" of the NFL, MLB, and NBA UPCs should be the "form" distributed and discussed during Class.

B. Please also explain to the Executive Director, with similar citations as support:

    1. The NBA Commissioner's likely responses to each of your proposed edits; and

    2. Your Client's best "replies" thereto.

        a. In so doing, please conduct a "hypothetical negotiation" between the Executive Director and the NBA Commissioner, and render a "final opinion" re: which "final edits" the Executive Director should accept, and why.

        b. Also opine re: if those "final edits" are rejected, whether the Executive Director should recommend that the NBPA "strike" or "decertify."

        c. In closing, please advise what the legal consequences would be if the NBPA pursued either of those "nuclear" strategies.

Your final memo should not exceed ten (10) pages in length.

Sample Answer 1

To: MLB Commissioner Bud Selig
From: MLB General Counsel
Re: Legal History/Evolution of the Three Major Sports Leagues

Dear Commissioner Selig,

I have concluded my analysis of legal history/evolution of the three major sports leagues (MLB, NFL, NBA). The following is a privileged and confidential summary and explanation of my conclusions regarding the issues you have asked me to examine.

Table of Contents:

I. Executive Summary:

- The three most legally significant decisions that have shaped the current rules of MLB are **Finley v. Kuhn** (commissioner's authority), **Flood v. Kuhn** (antitrust exemption), and the **Messersmith/McNally Arbitration** (free agency).

  - The decision that should be overturned in the best interests of the game is **Toolson v. New York Yankees** (antitrust exemption).

- In the NFL, the three most legally significant decisions are **Mackey v. NFL** (non-statutory labor exemption), **Clarett v. NFL** (collectively bargained rules), and the **Personal Conduct Policy** (commissioner's authority in player discipline).

  - The decision that should be overturned in the best interests of the game is **Brown v. Pro–Football** (protection of terms implemented post-impasse).

- In the NBA, the three most legally significant decisions are **Haywood v. NBA** (no antitrust exemption), **Wood v. NBA** (non-statutory labor exemption), and **Central New York Basketball v. Barnett** (contractual interpretation).

  - The decision that should be overturned in the best interests of the game is the **Latrell Sprewell Arbitration** (commissioner's authority in player discipline).

II. Major League Baseball:

- The court's decision in **Finley v. Kuhn** was a turning point in the transition from an earlier era of virtually boundless commissioner authority under the "best interests of baseball" clause (Article I, § 2 of the Major League Constitution) to the modern era in which commissioner authority is often subjected to arbitral scrutiny or limited by the collective bargaining agreement. *Finley,* which recognized the commissioner's unenumerated powers (by holding that the list of powers contained in Article I, § 3 was not exclusive), seems to be "the straw that broke the camel's back." *Finley* was reminiscent of the Landis era, where the commissioner was declared to be an all-powerful pater familias (*Milwaukee Association v. Landis*) and clubs waived recourse to the courts (See Menitove paper). Baseball's exemption from antitrust laws underscored the myth of this era of a benevolent, omnipotent commissioner who at once looked out for the welfare of all constituencies in the game. Following *Finley,* the courts began to infringe upon the authority of the commissioner, using the literal language of the Major League Agreement to limit the scope of the commissioner's powers (*Atlanta Braves/Ted Turner v. Kuhn, Chicago*

National League Ball Club v. Vincent). Arbitrators also started to erode the authority of the commissioner in the area of player discipline, as seen in the Willie Wilson and Steve Howe cases. In 1994, as the Major League Agreement was being read in conjunction with the CBA, a new Article I, § 5 limited the commissioner's "best interests" power to only matters outside of the CBA.

- ***Flood v. Kuhn*** was a landmark decision for baseball because it not only protected the reserve system, but also preserved the anomaly that is MLB's antitrust exemption. The decision in fact granted a double immunity to MLB, exempting it from federal antitrust liability as well as state antitrust liability, under the dormant Commerce Clause doctrine (significant for cases that refused to apply state laws in this area, such as *Partee, Hebert, Matuszak*, and *State of Wisconsin v. Milwaukee Braves*). In abdicating its role in the active enforcement of the antitrust laws (by deferring to Congress), the court followed a long line of cases refusing to apply antitrust law to baseball (See *American League Baseball Club of Chicago v. Chase, Federal Baseball v. National League, Toolson v. New York Yankees*). *Chase* and *Federal Baseball* did not find baseball to be interstate commerce, thus the Sherman Act was inapplicable, while *Toolson* upheld the antitrust exemption based on stare decisis. Two ramifications of *Flood* in the present era are the 1998 Curt Flood Act, which granted major league players exemption from antitrust law, and the legal battles over the scope of baseball's antitrust exemption in dealings with third parties (compare *Salerno* and *Portland Baseball Club* [exemption applies] with *Twin City Sports Service, Henderson Broadcasting*, and *Fleer v. Topps* [exemption does not apply]) and franchise relocations (compare *Piazza, Butterworth v. NL*, and *Morsani* [exemption limited to reserve clause] with *MLB v. Butterworth, Crist, Minnesota Twins Partnership*, and *McCoy* [exemption covers the business of baseball]).

- While the threat of *Flood* was still present, Marvin Miller was able to pressure owners into allowing impartial grievance arbitration in the 1970 Basic Agreement. This soon had drastic consequences, as in the **Messersmith/McNally Arbitration**, neutral arbitrator Seitz interpreted Article 10(a) of the UPC as a one-time option and not a perpetual option on player services, giving baseball players free agency after serving out the renewal year of their initial contracts. Finding that the renewal provision did not explicitly incorporate the option clause, the arbitration panel's decision tracked the NBA's interpretation of the option clause as seen in *Central New York Basketball v. Barnett* and *Lemat Corp v. Barry* (although differed from the NFL in *Dutton*). The arbitration decision was upheld in *Kansas City Royals v. MLBPA*, and was part of a larger trend of judicial deference to arbitrators, even in outrageous circumstances (See *Garvey*, which was shaped by the non-sports *Steelworkers Trilogy*). The immediate impact of the decision was the collusion years under Commissioner Ueberroth, while the long-term impact has been the vibrant free agency that we have today.

- The commissioner should overturn **Toolson v. New York Yankees** because of the unwillingness of the court, thirty years later, to reexamine the basic factual circumstances that led to a decision (*Federal Baseball*) that was questionable even at the time it was made. After recognizing the anomalistic nature of baseball's antitrust exemption among other professional sports leagues, not only was the court unwilling to rectify the unjust advantage baseball had, but it was also unwilling to examine the underlying circumstances (whether baseball was interstate commerce) that governed that determination. Rather than "update" *Federal Baseball* to reflect the modernization of baseball that had occurred by 1953, the court enshrined for all eternity the conception of baseball that existed in 1922. Of course, it would not be in the commissioner's best *self*-interest to overturn baseball's antitrust exemption, but it would be in the best interests of the sport for owners and players to be equally liable under the law for anticompetitive practices.

III. National Football League:

- The court's decision in **Mackey v. NFL** was significant because it articulated a clear three-part test to determine if the non-statutory labor exemption should apply to a league policy, and thus whether labor law deserved preeminence over antitrust law. The NFL has to be concerned about the application of antitrust law, because unlike MLB, the court has held that the NFL is not exempt from federal antitrust law (*Radovich v. NFL*). Although the *Mackey* court recognized that the non-statutory labor exemption applied to non-labor groups to protect collective bargaining (which would be important in later cases such as *Powell, Brown, Zimmerman,* and *Clarett*), the court ultimately found that the exemption did not apply and used a rule of reason analysis (See *National Society of Professional Engineers*) to declare the Rozelle Rule an invalid restraint on trade. The court's analysis of the non-statutory labor exemption was undoubtedly influenced by non-sports law precedents which defined the contours of the exemption (See *Pennington, Connell Construction*) and established a preference for resolving issues through arm's-length collective bargaining rather than through the courts (See *Jewel Tea*). The impact of the *Mackey* decision led to Plan B free agency restrictions, which led to union decertification and successful lawsuits against the NFL (See *McNeil, Jackson, White*). The post–1993 regime is a result of these decisions, but problems persist for some free agents (See Katz article on veteran premium problem).

- The NFL draft rules and the ability of the NFLPA to represent prospective players was upheld in the significant case of **Clarett v. NFL**, where the court applied the *Jewel Tea* balancing test instead of the *Mackey* three-prong test in determining that the collective bargaining relationship between the NFL and NFLPA precluded Clarett from negotiating terms of employment with NFL clubs. The court determined that the NFL eligibility rules were mandatory subjects of collective bargaining and thus any grievances would more appropriately be resolved by the NLRB than by the courts (following the logic of *Wood v. NBA*). In preventing Clarett from entering the NFL draft, the court seemed to contradict its earlier decision in *Smith*, which held the draft to be an anticompetitive practice under the rule of reason. However, these decisions can be reconciled because the court never reached the antitrust question in *Clarett* due to the application of the non-statutory labor exemption (following the non-sports law precedent of *U.S. v. Hutcheson*). The NFL has been somewhat fortunate even when antitrust law has applied, as courts have applied the rule of reason (See *Smith*, *Mackey*) instead of the more restrictive per se ban (See *Haywood*, *Linseman*, *Boris*).

- Commissioner Roger Goodell's imposition of the **Personal Conduct Policy** in the NFL has already had a significant impact on the "rules of the game," and represents the culmination of a long line of cases upholding broad NFL commissioner authority in the area of player discipline (Compare Randy Crowder/Don Reese and *Clayton Holmes* cases to Willie Wilson and Steve Howe cases in MLB). The relatively few challenges to the NFL commissioner's "best interests" authority may be a product of his textual authority, the combination of external/internal pressure, and his personality (See Daniels/Brooks paper). Additionally, Goodell did not make the mistake of imposing the PCP unilaterally, as Commissioner Rozelle had done (*Mackey*). Even arbitrators were unwilling to do in football what they were willing to do in baseball, as Dutton failed to win free agency while Messersmith/McNally did. Because of the PCP, commissioner authority in player discipline may never have been greater (See Vick, Pacman, Tank Johnson cases), but that power may begin to erode over time (See StarCaps case). One area where commissioner power has eroded is in franchise relocation, where despite successful verdicts (See *Raiders II*, *VKK Corp.*, *St. Louis Convention*, *Mid-South Grizzlies*), individual franchise owners still seem to move at will (See *Raiders I*, Irsay's Colts). Six owners have moved their teams to smaller-market sites, something other owners have accepted only reluctantly (See Weiler article).

- Despite being against his self-interest (but in the true "best interests of the game"), the commissioner should overturn **Brown v. Pro–Football**, because of the inherent unfairness it creates within the collective bargaining process. Rather than recognizing that that the non-statutory labor exemption should apply during the term of a valid collectively bargained agreement, and possibly post-impasse under the terms previously agreed upon (See *Powell*), the court went one step too far in allowing the NFL to unilaterally impose the terms of its last pre-impasse proposal. Granted the terms that can be imposed are circumscribed by the terms of the NFL's "last best good-faith offer," but the fundamental purpose of the exemption is to allow agreements that may be antitrust violations to stand only because they were fairly bargained for between management and labor. Rather than conduct fair negotiations, the decision seems to allow the NFL to act unreasonably in driving towards impasse, and then following impasse, implement those unreasonable terms unilaterally. If such practices are allowed under labor law, then the NFL should have to defend its actions under antitrust law, so that there is an accommodation between the two bodies of law, with labor law governing in some cases (*Jewel Tea*) and antitrust law taking precedence in others (*Pennington*).

IV. National Basketball Association:

- The court in **_Haywood v. NBA_** significantly found that the NBA, unlike MLB, was not exempt from federal antitrust laws, and thus the NBA's player eligibility bylaw comprised an illegal per se group boycott under the Sherman Act. The court echoed the reasoning in another seminal case dealing with NBA rules, *Robertson v. NBA*, which struck down the UPC, college draft, and reserve system as per se group boycotts. In both cases, the court found it fundamentally unfair to protect an NBA rule when there was no real arm's-length bargaining between management and the players. The current ramifications of *Haywood* include a new NBA player eligibility rule. While as in *Haywood* the rule likely would not survive the rule of reason test., the rule is likely to be protected by the non-statutory labor exemption (See Applegate article), as the NBA eligibility rule is in the CBA (as opposed to the NFL eligibility rule). Despite the outcome in cases like *Wood*, some scholars argue convincingly that age eligibility should not be covered by the non-statutory labor exemption because it primarily affects workers outside of the bargaining unit (See McCann/Rosen article). There is conflicting case law on league entry restraints, which turn on the restraint's "reasonableness" (Compare *Boris v. USFL*, *Linseman v. WHL*, *Blalock v. LPGA* [restraints overly restrictive], with *Neeld v. NHL*, *Deesen v. PGA* [restraints reasonable]).

- In **_Wood v. NBA_**, the court brought the non-statutory labor exemption to basketball, and used the *Mackey* test to uphold NBA rules that arose out of the collective bargaining process. The court, in viewing the exemption as a shield over potential NBA antitrust violations (like in *Clarett*), held that NBA players can seek the greatest deal for the greatest number by using collective instead of individual bargaining power. A current effect of *Wood* is the actual rookie salary scale that has developed in the NBA. Some argue that the fixed scale, regardless of player performance, prevents younger players such as LeBron James from earning their true market value (See Taylor article). However, any antitrust challenge to the rookie scale would be unsuccessful, as the *Wood* court made clear that it will protect collectively bargained arrangements that may benefit the collective interest over individual player interests. The non-statutory labor exemption was extended even further in *Williams v. NBA*, in which the exemption was used to protect the CBA post-impasse (as in *Powell*), as well as the league's implementation of new terms post-impasse (as in *Brown*). Matching the NFL model was justified by the court, which feared destruction of collective bargaining.

- In **Central New York Basketball v. Barnett**, the court changed the application of contract law to basketball in two significant ways. First, the court determined that the option clause in a player contract was not part of the renewed contract and thus could be exercised only once (See *Lemat Corp. v. Barry*), meaning that clubs did not have a perpetual right of ownership over the players, as in the NFL (See *Dutton*) or MLB (until the *Messersmith/McNally* Arbitration). Second, the court in *Barnett* recognized that players have unique skills and abilities, thus monetary damages were not adequate compensation for their breach of contract. This decision placed basketball on similar footing to baseball in terms of contractual enforcement, as it echoed the reasoning of *Philadelphia Ball Club v. Lajoie*. Though MLB did have a case arise a decade later that seemed at odds with *Lajoie* (*Chase*), by 1960 the courts had adopted the *Barnett* position that the player's representation that he had unique skill and ability satisfied the requirement for an injunction. *Barnett*'s two interpretations also contributed to the courts' tolerance of players signing contracts that were entirely outside of the scope of their present contracts (See *Barry*, *Cunningham*, *Bergey*).

- The commissioner should overturn the decision of the arbitrator in the **Latrell Sprewell Arbitration**, as the intervention of a third party in an internal league disciplinary matter is beyond the competence of an arbitrator or court. These types of matters should be resolved by the commissioner himself, pursuant to the collective bargaining agreement. In general, it appears that courts and arbitrators treat the commissioner's authority in the NBA as weaker than in other two major sports, partly because of the presence of Board of Governors above the commissioner. In *Riko Enterprises v. Seattle SuperSonics*, the court limited the authority of the commissioner in favor of the Board of Governors when it came to regulating owners and teams. Similarly, in *Levin v. NBA*, the court deferred to the Board of Governors in being able to control its own membership. Furthermore, the "best interests" power of the commissioner under Article 35, to punish conduct detrimental to the game, remains subject to review by a neutral arbitrator in all matters except those related to gambling (See *Molinas v. NBA*). Even in egregious cases (Ron Artest melee), the commissioner has had his disciplinary actions second-guessed by arbitrators.

V. Conclusion:

- In all three major sports leagues, decisions that defined the scope of the commissioner's authority were legally significant in shaping the current rules of the game.

- The MLB, with its unique antitrust exemption, has been significantly defined by legal decisions that solidified and applied that exemption to areas such as the reserve clause, third-party contracts, and franchise relocation.

- The NFL, without an antitrust exemption in labor matters, has been significantly defined by the scope of the non-statutory labor exemption, and its particular application to labor negotiations and NFL eligibility rules.

- The NBA, also without an antitrust exemption in labor matters, has been significantly defined by both the non-statutory labor exemption and by contractual interpretations, with specific application in the areas of free agency and age eligibility requirements.

To: NBPA Executive Director Billy Hunter
From: NBPA General Counsel
Re: Renegotiation of the NBA UPC

Dear Executive Director Hunter,

I have concluded my analysis of the proposed edits to the NBA UPC, the likely NBA response, and our subsequent reply. The following is a privileged and confidential summary and explanation of my conclusions regarding the issues you have asked me to examine.

Table of Contents:

I. Executive Summary:

- In the next round of collective bargaining, modifications to **Paragraphs 5, 13, 14, and 16** of the NBA UPC are necessary to adequately protect player publicity rights and to limit the unchecked authority of the team/league in player conduct and contract termination matters.

- If the NBA is unwilling to negotiate on these provisions, then the NBPA should first strike, then decertify if necessary, in order to create financial incentive for a compromise position.

II. Black-lined UPC Provisions:

Paragraph 5—"Conduct":

(b) The Player agrees: (i) to give his best services, ~~as well as his loyalty~~, to the Team . . . (iii) to conduct himself on and off the court according to *reasonable* ~~the highest~~ standards of honesty, citizenship, and sportsmanship; ~~and (iv) not to do anything that is materially detrimental or materially prejudicial to the best interests of the Team or the League~~.

(e) . . . the Commissioner's finding and decision shall be ~~final, binding, conclusive, and unappealable~~ *appealable to a neutral arbitrator consistent with the Grievance and Arbitration Procedure set forth in Article XXXI of the CBA*.

(f) . . . enter into negotiations for or relating to his services *during the period for which he is already under contract* as a basketball player or coach, nor shall he negotiate for or contract for such services *during the period for which he is already under contract*, except with the prior written consent of such team. *Nothing in this subparagraph shall be construed to constrain the Player in his ability to negotiate for or contract for services beginning after the expiration of his current contract*. Breach of this subparagraph, in addition to the remedies available to the Team, shall be punishable by fine and/or suspension to be imposed by the Commissioner, *but appealable to a neutral arbitrator consistent with the Grievance and Arbitration Procedure set forth in Article XXXI of the CBA*.

- In subparagraph (b), there is no reason for a player to commit his "loyalty" to the team, an ambiguous phrase that can conceivably allow a team to punish a player for disagreeing with a mere play call. "Reasonable standards" is fairer and more appropriate than "highest standards," given that there is no mutual obligation on the team to act with the "highest standards." Given the interests of superstar players in enhancing their publicity rights, we do not want to broadly commit the players to not do anything "materially detrimental" to the best interests of the team, as they may wish to endorse a product that the team may dislike. Subparagraphs (c) and (d) are acceptable as they stand, because the CBA protects players by granting the right of appeal to a neutral arbitrator if the value of the fine/suspension to the player exceeds $25,000 (See Article XXXI). Subparagraph (e) draws its essence from *Molinas v. NBA*, but we do not want the commissioner to have unilateral authority over the players in any area, so even gambling-related activities should be appealable to a neutral arbitrator (See right of hearing in gambling-related cases in NFL UPC Paragraph 15). Regarding subparagraph (f), we believe that there is solid precedent allowing a player to solicit employment beyond the expiration of his current contract (See *Barry, Cunningham, Bergey*). Punishment related to breach of contract should also be appealable to a neutral arbitrator. If the commissioner has acted justly, he will be upheld, so we view this just as a check on excessive discipline imposed unilaterally by the commissioner (See wide-ranging grievance procedure in MLB UPC Paragraph 9(b)).

Paragraph 13—"Promotional Activities":

(a) ... at such reasonable times as *are mutually agreeable between the Player and* the Team, the NBA, or the League-related entity ~~may designate~~. No matter by whom taken, such pictures may be used in any manner desired by either the Team, the NBA, or the League-related entity for publicity or promotional purposes, *provided that Player gives written consent to such usage, with consent not to be unreasonably withheld.* The rights in any such pictures taken by the Team, the NBA, or the League-related entity shall belong to the Team, the NBA, or the League-related entity, as their interests may appear, *provided that Player shall have the license to use such pictures for any of his own promotional purposes.*

(b) *(entire subparagraph deleted)*

(d) ... the Player agrees to participate, upon request, in ~~all~~ other reasonable promotional activities of the Team, the NBA, and any League-related entity. ... Team agrees to pay the Player *no less than $2,500, with the actual level of compensation to be determined by negotiation between Player and Team prior to Player participation in any such events.* ~~$2,500 or, if the Team agrees, such higher amount that is consistent with the Team's past practice and not otherwise unreasonable.~~

- In subparagraph (a), the player should have input into determining his availability for promotional work. Given that the content is based around the player, he should have the right to withhold consent to any promotional activity he believes will be detrimental to his image (See *Ventura v. Titan Sports*). Since the team is paying for the expenses related to the promotional campaigns, it is only fair that they retain the rights to the content (See *Orioles v. MLBPA*), but since the player is being used in the promotions, he should have the right to use his likeness to further his own individual promotional efforts (See *Zacchini v. Scripps–Howard Broadcasting*). Subparagraph (b) needs to be stricken from the UPC, because both our superstar players and our less famous players need to be able to solicit promotional work on their own accord, without dependence on team consent. Among other professional sports leagues, the NBA gives teams the broadest authority to prohibit player endorsements, so striking this provision will bring the NBA more closely in line with the MLB, NFL, and NHL (See Shilts article). Under *Portland Trailblazers v. Valentine/Paxson* the team cannot prohibit an endorsement that doesn't mention the team, but the player should also have the right to earn financial compensation on his own accord from the use of his name and likeness (See *Zacchini*). In subparagraph (d), the player should not have to participate in "all" of the team's reasonable promotional activities. If the player is a superstar player, then he should have the ability to demand more than $2,500 per appearance. The $2,500 minimum protects less famous players from receiving even less in individual negotiations.

Paragraph 14—"Group License":

(a) The Player hereby grants ... the ~~exclusive~~ rights to use the Player's Player Attributes ...

(b) ... such Player Attributes may be captured in game action footage or photographs, *pursuant to prior written consent from the Player and the right of the Player to use such content in his own promotional activities.* NBA Properties (and its related entities) shall be entitled to use the Player's Player attributes individually *(defined as in conjunction with fewer than 5 other Players)* pursuant to the preceding sentence and shall not be required to use the Player's Player Attributes in a group or as one of multiple players, *pursuant to prior written consent from the Player and the right of the Player to use such content in his own promotional activities* ...

- Subparagraph (a) is overbroad because while we want to grant NBA Properties Player Attribute rights in order to promote players, these rights shouldn't be exclusive, so that players can promote their image independently as well. In subparagraph (b), the player should have the ability to withhold consent from the use of his Player Attributes in a manner that he deems contrary to his interest, since it is his attributes that are being used (See *Titan Sports*). Similarly, the player should have the ability to use his Player Attributes in his own self-promotion efforts. When the player is being used in a campaign of fewer than six NBA players, the NBA UPC should be brought in line with the Group Licensing Program in the NFL (See right of individual consent when featuring fewer than six players in NFL UPC Paragraph 4(b)). In these cases, the player surely should have the right to withhold consent.

Paragraph 16—"Termination":

(a)(i) at any time, fail, refuse, or neglect to conform his personal conduct to *reasonable* standards of good citizenship, good moral character ~~(defined here to mean not engaging in acts of moral turpitude, whether or not such acts would constitute a crime)~~, and good sportsmanship, to keep himself in *reasonable* ~~first-class~~ physical condition *to play professional basketball*, or to obey the Team's training rules

(a)(iii) at any time, fail, in the ~~sole~~ opinion of the Team's management, to exhibit sufficient skill or competitive ability to qualify to continue as a member of the Team, *to be reviewed by a neutral arbitrator consistent with the Grievance and Arbitration Procedure set forth in Article XXXI of the CBA* ...

(h) The Player may terminate this contract by buying out the contract in full. Contract buyout shall be defined as the Player paying to the Team the full salary remaining on his contract.

- Subparagraph (a)(i) needs "reasonable standards" language inserted, so that the player is protected from ambiguous "moral crimes" that give wide discretion to the team in termination (See Shilts article). In order to avoid having the commissioner wield broad, unchecked authority like Commissioner Goodell in the NFL via the PCP, the language regarding "moral turpitude" must be deleted from the UPC. In subparagraph (a)(iii), rather than give the team sole discretion over whether a player, a neutral arbitrator should determine if the player is truly unfit to continue in the NBA or whether the team has some ulterior motive in terminating the player's contract. We need to add a subparagraph (h), giving the player the right to terminate his contract, adding some mutuality to an otherwise asymmetric termination power. Courts in cases such as *Robertson, Haywood, Chase,* and *Neely* have affirmed a player's right to play for a chosen team and have limited a team's ability to restrict player movement. A buyout provision, which provides the club with full compensation for the value of the player's services, is sufficient to provide the club with the full benefit of its bargain while enabling the player to retain his basic rights as an employee.

III. NBA Commissioner's Response:

- In response to the proposed **Paragraph 5**, the commissioner will argue that teams need to be able to protect their financial interests and good will, so they need language that will deter players from conduct that would be detrimental to these team interests. The commissioner will also point out that since gambling goes to the integrity and public confidence in the sport, he needs unilateral authority to act quickly and decisively as seen in *Molinas* and the Tim Donaghy scandal. Regarding subparagraph (f), the commissioner will stress that it would destroy the league if players were actively setting up future contracts with different teams while they were currently under contract to play for a specific team (See LeBron James–2010 speculation without the proposed modifications). With such a clause explicitly within the UPC, it would be impossible to control tampering by players and team employees. Finally, the commissioner would emphasize the undesirability of arbitrators meddling into internal league matters, and point out the harsh criticism of recent decisions made by third-party arbitrators involving Latrell Sprewell and Ron Artest.

- In response to the proposed **Paragraph 13**, the commissioner will argue that it would be unreasonable to ask for the written consent of each player for everything used in the wide-scale promotion of the product of basketball. Additionally, under *Orioles v. MLBPA*, the team and league own the rights to the tangible media involving the players, as copyright considerations trump player publicity rights in this area, so they are under no obligation to seek player permission or grant individual licenses to players. Furthermore, the team needs some control over the players' publicity rights because the player is a representative of the team in all facets of his life, so the team needs the authority to prevent the player from having a detrimental impact on the team brand or on other players associated with the team. This control is essential in order to promote a certain overall image of the team and to sell lucrative team-wide corporate sponsorships. The commissioner will also argue that the teams should not have to pay superstars more for their promotional appearances on behalf of the team. The same is being asked of every player on the team (showing up to events does not require any special skills that superstars may have), and any difference in player performance level is compensated for in players' different levels of base compensation.

- In response to the proposed **Paragraph 14**, the commissioner will argue that NBA Properties needs the exclusive rights to players' Player Attributes, whether depicted as an individual or in a group, in order to build deliberate marketing campaigns around specific groups of players. Additionally, having multiple rights-holders will create confusion in the marketplace and lessen the value of each player's Player Attributes. The commissioner may also argue that not pooling Player Attributes exclusively into one entity may lead to further erosion of player publicity rights via uncontrolled expansion into the public domain (See *CBC v. MLBAM*). Furthermore, it will hurt the majority of NBA players if superstar players "opt-out" of the Group Licensing Program, such that Player Attributes cannot truly be sold collectively to video game and fantasy sport entities. (See *Gridiron.com v. NFLPA*, *Topps v. MLBPA*, *Fleer v. Topps* regarding the effectiveness of Group Licensing programs).

- In response to the proposed **Paragraph 16**, the commissioner will emphasize that moral turpitude has devastating effects on team image and corporate sponsorships (See Portland "Jailblazers" of the early 2000s, current Cincinnati Bengals), so the team needs the right to terminate a player contract based on immoral conduct (See Michael Vick). Furthermore, the team absolutely must have the right to terminate a player contract based on its sole discretion, as the internal strategic deliberations and the overall performance of the team should not be opened up to messy third-party arbitration. The commissioner will also argue against giving players the right to terminate contracts, as it would ruin the careful planning and stability of teams if players were able to become free agents at any point in the season, and their unique value to the team cannot be compensated for by monetary damages (See *Lajoie, Barnett*).

- Finally, the commissioner will accept the added year prior to NBA eligibility, as he believes this will advance the NBA interest in providing the highest level of basketball to consumers.

IV. NBPA's Reply to NBA Commissioner's Response:

- Regarding **Paragraph 5**, we should emphasize the importance of protecting the free speech and First Amendment rights of the players (See Synder article on Curt Flood's struggle). While players understand and are willing to be contractually bound to their duties to the club, there is no need for them to pledge their "loyalty" or "good citizenship," as these are vague terms and may in fact conflict with players' constitutional rights (See Mahmoud Abdul–Rauf controversy, *Dambrot v. Central Michigan University*). Since the commissioner has been wrong in past gambling cases (See Connie Hawkins and John "Hot Rod" Williams cases), we should remain adamant that there be a neutral arbitrator to check commissioner authority in this area. Overall, we should concede the other points to the commissioner, as long as the overbroad "materially detrimental to the best interests of the team" clause is deleted and there is an appeals mechanism available for gambling-related incidents. Regarding the tampering provision, we should agree on forbidding intra-league tampering, as long as players are able to negotiate future contracts in other professional leagues (NBA–FIBA cannot collude).

- Regarding **Paragraph 13**, we should argue that the current consent obligations are asymmetrical. Overall, we should concede on the flat appearance fee and on obtaining team consent for sponsorships in conflicting categories with team or league sponsors, if players are allowed to solicit sponsorships without team consent in non-conflicting categories. This compromise helps superstar players who may be able to secure lucrative individual sponsorships (See Shilts article), while also giving the team some authority in its players' promotional activities.

- Regarding **Paragraph 14**, we should argue that the players need the ability to use their own Player Attributes, which are unique to them and inseparable from their individual publicity rights (See *Haelan Laboratories v. Topps, Zacchini v. Scripps–Howard Broadcasting, Ventura v. Titan Sports*). Furthermore, we find the use of *CBC v. MLBAM* unpersuasive, given that the MLB Group Licensing Program did not effectively protect player publicity rights. Overall, we should grant NBA Properties category exclusivity in terms of being the only Group Licensee of Player Attributes, as long as each player receives a full license to use his Player Attributes in his own promotional efforts and has the right to consent to his use in "individual" (fewer than 6 players) campaigns.

- Regarding **Paragraph 16**, we should argue for a "reasonable" standard in conduct deemed worthy of termination, as team owners and management are not held to any standards in their off-court dealings (See Mark Cuban). We are not persuaded by the NBA's arguments on player termination rights, as teams terminate contracts throughout the season, and courts have held that injunctive relief is not always applicable in contractual disputes, whether over players or teams (See *Chase, HMC Management v. New Orleans Basketball Club*). Overall, we should accept the "morals clause," as long as compliance with it is determined by a neutral arbitrator and not just the team/commissioner. We can also accept termination at the sole discretion of the team, as long as players have the symmetrical ability to terminate the contract at their sole discretion under the buyout provision.

- We should concede the added year prior to NBA eligibility, as long as the NBA agrees to the compromise terms we have outlined above.

- If the NBA were to reject our compromise edits, then we should first strike, then decertify if necessary, both of which would be preferable to conceding to the NBA. A strike will put substantial additional pressure on the NBA to continue negotiating because of the financial consequences to the league. While the players will lose their salaries during the strike and may also be subject to backlash from the public, the players could potentially benefit from an aggressive public relations campaign which conveys to the public that their demands are reasonable. Decertification would likely be a less effective method of accomplishing our goals. While decertification would allow players to bring antitrust suits regarding terms of the UPC (union decertification eliminates the non-statutory labor exemption which protects the terms of the UPC from antitrust claims—*McNeil v. NFL*), the NBA would then be free to unilaterally implement its proposed edits as a bargaining impasse would have been reached (See *Williams* in the NBA, and *Powell, Brown* in the NFL). Furthermore, decertification will allow the players to continue playing in NBA games, which would certainly be in their short-term interest, but not in their long-term interest, as continuing to play would mean that the NBA would suffer no financial consequences and thus would have little incentive to return to negotiations. Finally, from a tactical perspective, decertification necessarily removes the power of the players to strike, whereas a strike leaves open the possibility of decertification at a later date should circumstances change and decertification becomes more attractive.

V. Conclusion:

- Since the current NBA UPC does not adequately protect player publicity rights, and gives the team/league too much unilateral authority in the areas of player conduct and contract termination, the NBPA should pursue its "nuclear options" if the NBA is unwilling to compromise on Paragraphs 5, 13, 14, and 16 of the UPC.

Sample Answer 2

Sports and the Law, Fall 2008
Prof. Carfagna

MEMORANDUM (Privileged/Confidential)

To: Commissioner Bud Selig
From: MLB General Counsel
Date: December 8, 2008
Re: Most Significant Sports Law Decisions

Table of Contents

I.   Executive Summary

Three decisions loom particularly large in shaping the legal "rules of the game" under which Major League Baseball operates. First, *Milwaukee Am. Assn'n v. Landis* (1931) vindicated Commissioner Landis' claim of extreme latitude in protecting the "best interest of the game," establishing a critical precedent for MLB commissioner's authority for years to come. Second, *Flood v. Kuhn* (1972) affirmed baseball's longstanding antitrust exemption, ensuring that the Court's clearly anachronistic decisions in *Federal Baseball* (1922) and *Toolson* (1953) continued to shape MLB's legal status. Finally, Arbitrator Seitz's decision in the Messersmith / McNally case (1976) invalidated what had been the most significant ramification of that exemption—the perpetually renewable reserve clause—ushering in a dramatically new era for the sport.

The modern NFL has been shaped by the use of the non-statutory labor exemption and its uniquely strong disciplinary policy. The NFL first made the exemption argument in *Mackey v. NFL* (1976); though the league lost, the case created the legal framework for future cases (and foreshadowed the NFL's predominant legal strategy going forward). Indeed, the Court's willingness to apply the exemption in *Brown v. Pro Football, Inc.* (1996) marked a second legal turning point for the league, ushering in an era in which courts have been quite willing to grant the NFL the exemption. Finally, in *Holmes v. NFL* (1996), a court affirmed that, under the NFL CBA, the Commissioner's player disciplinary decisions are immune from review, making the NFL Player Conduct Policy a uniquely powerful tool well-suited for the modern sports world.

The NBA's legal history has been dominated by the lack of an antitrust exemption and a legacy of player conduct problems, rendering three cases particularly significant. First, *Haywood v. NBA* (1970) established that the NBA is subject to the Sherman Act and struck down the NBA's age requirement, leading to 30 years of high school players going pro. Second, *Robertson v. NBA* (1975) contributed to the breakdown of NBA–ABA merger plans and ushered NBA into the free agency era, as well as setting the stage for the applicability of the non-statutory labor exemption to be the key legal factor in future NBA-related litigation. Finally, Arbitrator Ferrick's overruling of Commissioner Stern in the Sprewell case greatly undercut Stern's power to discipline players in the future, providing sharp contrast to PCP-power of the NFL's Goodell.

As requested, after reviewing these nine decisions, I recommend overturning three decisions with the "best interests of the game" in mind: *Flood v. Kuhn* (to correct the anachronistic ruling and put MLB on the same legal footing as the NBA and NFL), *Brown v. Pro Football Inc.* (to stem the tide of the over-application of the non-statutory labor exemption), and the Sprewell arbitration decision (to give the NBA commissioner the power necessary to regulate his league in the modern sports era). A full analysis of these recommendations follows.

II.   Most Significant MLB Decisions

A.   *Milwaukee Am. Ass'n v. Landis* (N.D. Ill. 1931)

In the aftermath of the 1919 Black Sox scandal, in order to convince Judge Landis to become MLB's first Commissioner, MLB's owners signed the "Major League Agreement" (MLA), which gave Landis the unilateral power to investigate and take any actions he saw fit in response to any incident he suspected not to be in the "best interest" of baseball. The first challenge to this authority came when Landis refused to approve the St. Louis Browns' optioning of Fred Bennett to a minor league team. When the Browns' owner sued, the court in *Milwaukee Am. Ass'n v. Landis* (1931) sided with Landis, finding that the MLA "disclosed[d] a clear intent upon the part of the parties to endow the commissioner with all the attributes of a benevolent but absolute despot." *Landis* starkly contrasts a 1919 case prior to the MLA, *AL Baseball Club of NY v. Johnson* (overturning AL President Johnson's suspension of Carl Mays), emphasizing the crucial ramifications of the "best interests" clause and judicial recourse waiver. Though the language bestowing "best interests" power was alternately narrowed and broadened in the ensuing years (and the judicial recourse waiver revoked from 1944–1964), the ability of commissioners to invoke the "best interests" clause remains crucial. Commissioners have used the power to justify altering league rules (*see Turner v. Kuhn; Finley v. Kuhn, Chicago NL Ball Club v. Vincent*), disciplining players for gambling (*see Rose v. Giamatti*), and disciplining players for drug use (*see* Royals' players and Howe sanctions). Though courts have occasionally overruled commissioners' decisions (often dubiously), the broad "best interests" rubric made possible by *Landis* even today remains the touchstone upon which Commissioner Selig relies.

B.   *Flood v. Kuhn* (1972)

When Curt Flood challenged MLB's longstanding reserve system as a violation of antitrust law in 1970, his suit threatened to bring down the legal framework the sport had long relied upon. Instead, the Court's decision in *Flood v. Kuhn* (1972) affirmed the Court's anachronistic decisions in *Federal Baseball Club v. National League* (1922) and *Toolson v. New York Yankees, Inc.* (1953). Based on dubious legal reasoning that exalted *stare decisis* while ignoring the realities of modern baseball, the Court declined to remedy the inequities faced by Flood and other "well-paid slaves" (it would take several more legal challenges for players to win free agency). Just as significantly, it preserved baseball's general antitrust exemption, which still serves to empower MLB owners. Though the Curt Flood Act of 1998 ended the exemption with respect to players, the legacy of *Flood* still provides antitrust exemption for MLB with respect to minor league baseball and to territorial and franchising issues (*see* Twins cases; *Butterworth II; Crist*), giving MLB owners unique leeway and power to hold cities hostage.

C. Messersmith and McNally Arbitration (1976)

If *Landis* and *Flood* marked the high points of commissioner and owner authority, the Messersmith and McNally grievance represents the opposite. After playing the 1975 without a contract, the two players filed grievances (under the independent arbitrator scheme established by the 1973 CBA) claiming that § 10(c) of the UPC authorized only a single unilateral contract renewal, and not perpetual renewal. Arbitrator Peter Seitz agreed with the players, claiming jurisdiction because that the renewal clause "does not deal with the reserve system." The 8th Circuit then upheld the arbitrator's jurisdiction in *Kansas City Royals v. MLBPA* (1977), relying on *Steelworkers Trilogy* (1960). Thus, though MLB's antitrust exemption remained intact, the case stripped the owners of the most powerful tool the exemption had protected—and ushered MLB into the era of free agency. The effects were enormous, as player salaries skyrocketed (creating the incentive for owners to collude, resulting in the *collusion cases*) and, in turn, inherent economic inequities between teams increasingly threatened baseball's competitive balance (necessitating to the eventual creation of the luxury tax and revenue sharing).

III. Most Significant NFL Decisions

A. *Mackey v. National Football League* (8th Cir. 1976)

Though the NFL was held subject to the Sherman Act in 1957 (*Radovich v. NFL*), NFL owners continued to benefit from an empowering set of league rules—most notably the Rozelle Rule which, by requiring "fair and equitable" compensation for the signing of veteran free agents, all but prevented player movement. When John Mackey challenged the Rule in 1976, the NFL sought immunity under the "non-statutory labor exemption," as developed by the Supreme Court in *Allen Bradley Co.*, and *Jewel Tea* (Based on § 6 of the Clayton Act). In response, in *Mackey v. NFL* (1976) the Eighth Circuit elucidated a three-prong test for the application of that exemption (restraint must (1) primarily affect parties; (2) be mandatory subject of collective bargaining; (3) be product of arms-length negotiations). Over the ensuing decades, multiple courts would use this framework to analyze the applicability of the non-statutory exemption, in NFL cases as well as NBA and non-sports cases. The case's outcome was critical to the legal development of the NFL, too: after finding the Rozelle Rule failed the third prong of the test (and thus was not due the non-statutory exemption), the court applied Rule of Reason analysis (*see Nat'l Society of Prof. Engineers*) and found it to be an unreasonable restraint on trade, and thus struck down the Rule. This opened the door to a much more "active" form of free agency in the NFL, the ultimate contours of which were established by a bevy of litigation over the next two decades. Further, the non-statutory labor exemption became the "go-to" defense for the NFL, and its applicability (often based on the *Mackey* test) was frequently outcome determinative.

B. *Brown v. Pro Football, Inc.* (1996)

The applicability of the non-statutory labor exemption was again raised in *Brown v. Pro Football, Inc.* (1996), a case that resulted from the owners' unilateral imposition, after a bargaining impasse, of a standard $1,000 week salary for practice roster players. The Supreme Court ruled with the NFL, this time, finding that the final offer had been "reasonably comprehended" in the good-faith bargaining process prior to impasse, and thus the non-statutory exemption was appropriate. To an extent, *Brown* was the football equivalent of *Flood*: a case in which the Court, apparently blind to the individual inequity of the situation, extended special favorable treatment to a sports league. Indeed, Brown foreshadowed the Court's willingness to extend the non-statutory exemption to the NFL under questionable circumstances (*see e.g. Clarett v. NFL*). Thus, the decision tilted the balance of bargaining power to owners and suggests that the NFLPA's most effective tactic will not be to seek judicial recourse in future disputes, but rather to decertify as a union as it did in 1989 after *Powell v. NFL*.

C. *Holmes v. National Football League* (N.D.Tex.1996)

When Clayton Holmes challenged his suspension for drug use and NFL Commissioner Paul Tagliabue upheld the penalty, Holmes sought relief in federal court, claiming a violation of his due process rights. In *Holmes v. NFL* (1996), the court sided with the Tagliabue, ruling that the he was only bound by the terms of CBA that the NFLPA had voluntarily signed (mandating that the Commissioner serves as the arbitrator for all such drug appeals). The decision solidified the effect of the 1979 Randy Crowder / Don Reese Arbitration ruling that, under the CBA, the commissioner could withdraw disciplinary measures from the grievance process. Thus, unlike in the NBA and MLB, player disciplinary procedures undertaken by the NFL commissioner in response to "conduct detrimental to the integrity of, or public confidence in" the game is immune from judicial or arbitral review. As Mike Menitove has argued, this power is perhaps the most important one a commissioner can have in the modern sports world. Indeed, the effect of *Holmes* has been to enable Tagliabue and successor Roger Goodell to use the Player Conduct Policy (PCP) section of the NFL UPC as a means with which to regulate player conduct, both on-field and off-field, with an iron—and effective—fist (*see* Ricky Williams, Pacman Jones).

IV.   Most Significant NBA Decisions

A.   *Haywood v. NBA* (1971)

In 1970, ABA star Spencer Haywood—only three years removed from his high school graduation—sought to join the NBA, challenging the NBA's "four-year rule" as an illegal restraint on trade. In *Haywood v. NBA* (1971), the Supreme Court sided with Haywood, holding that anti-trust law applied to the NBA, and that the NBA's age eligibility rule was an impermissible group boycott and therefore a *per se* violation of the Sherman Act. *Haywood* thus opened the door for the legions of high school players who would eventually flood the NBA in the 1990s onward. It also meant that when a league imposes an age eligibility requirement, it is crucial the requirement be agreed to through the collective bargaining process (in order to be eligible for the non-statutory labor exemption), as the NBA eventually did in order to enact its current one-year policy in 2006 (and as the Supreme Court said the NFL had in upholding that league's three-year rule in *Clarett*). More broadly, *Haywood*'s holding that the NBA is subject to antitrust scrutiny forced the NBA down a long-term legal path that far more closely resembled that of the NFL then that of MLB, beginning with the antitrust challenge launched soon thereafter by Oscar Robertson. Longer term, *Haywood* forced the NBA to pursue a strategy of claiming a non-statutory labor exemption that immunized it from antitrust persecution, as it did (successfully) in the trilogy of *Wood v. NBA*, *NBA v. Williams*, and *Caldwell v. ABA*.

B.   *Robertson v. NBA* (S.D.N.Y. 1975)

In 1970, amid reports of merger talks between the NBA and ABA, NBAPA president Oscar Robertson launched an antitrust suit against the NBA, alleging a litany of violations—unreasonable restraint of trade in the merger itself, as well as in the college draft, the reserve clause of the UPC, and the restrictions on free agent movement. Against the backdrop of *Haywood* and relying on *Allen Bradley*, *Jewel Tea* and *Pennington*, a federal judge in *Robertson v. NBA* (S.D.N.Y. 1975) refused to grant any sort of labor exemption, holding that the exemption was intended to exempt only labor union activities, and not the activities of employers, as well as that the issues were not mandatory subjects of collective bargaining. The court's refusal to dismiss the claim contributed to the break down of merger talks and ultimately forced the NBA to settle with the players via a CBA: the NBA agreed to grant free agency and compensate players $5M. As expected, free agency changed the course of the league, leading to increased player movement and skyrocketing salaries and, eventually, the modern multi-level free agency and salary cap regime. With the applicability of the non-statutory labor exemption becoming the outcome determinative factor in NBA restraint of trade litigation (as a result of *Robertson* and the ensuing "NBA trilogy"), these ensuing developments were all enacted through the collective bargaining process, rather than unilaterally imposed by the owners as in the pre-*Robertson* era.

C. Sprewell Arbitration (1999)

After Latrell Sprewell choked of Warriors coach P.J. Carlesimo in 1998, the team quickly terminated the remainder of Sprewell's $32M contract and NBA Commissioner David Stern suspended Sprewell for 82 games. Under the NBA CBA, the disciplinary action was subject to "arbitrary and capricious" review by a neutral arbitrator (the penalty imposed exceeded $25,000). Arbitrator John Feerick sided with Sprewell (finding Stern's penalty to have been too harsh and thus "arbitrary and capricious") and reduced the suspension to 68 games; Feerick also held that the Warriors could not terminate the contract, as this constituted double punishment. This arbitral intervention had the effect of weakening Stern going forward (especially compared with the NFL's Goodell, whose player discipline decision are unreviewable). Not surprisingly, then, the NBA continues to struggle with player conduct issues. More broadly, the Sprewell arbitration established the precedent of an arbitrator usurping the commissioner's best interests of the game powers, raising difficult questions as to who is best suited to make such decisions.

V. Decisions to Overrule

A. MLB: *Flood v. Kuhn*

Justice Blackmun's listing of dozens of legendary baseball players was emblematic of the fatal flaw of his decision for the Court in *Flood v. Kuhn:* it followed emotion rather than sound legal reasoning. In choosing to affirm the anachronistic decisions of *Federal Baseball* and *Toolson*, the Court ignored various realities, including the enormous changes in the state of the game between 1922 and 1972, the relevant precedents of *Radovich, Shubert, Int'l Boxing Club,* and *Haywood*, and the futility of inquiries into Congressional intent. Instead, the Court hid behind *stare decisis* and the unsupported assertion that MLB had relied on the exemption and could not cope with a change. Nor did the non-statutory labor exemption provide any support for the decision; the reserve clause clearly was not the result of "bona-fide arm's length bargaining." Thus, the result was among the worst decisions in Court history, a decision which turned a blind eye to the injustices suffered by Curt Flood and other "well-paid slaves" of his era. Though MLB players eventually won free agency through alternate means, *Flood* continues to unjustly immunize owners in from antitrust scrutiny of franchising and relocation decisions. Without question, then, overturning this legal anachronism is in the best interests of the game.

B. NFL: *Brown v. Pro Football, Inc.*

As Justice Stevens wrote in his dissent in *Brown v. Pro Football, Inc.,* the non-statutory labor exemption "has its source in the strong labor policy favoring the association of employees" (quoting *Connell Constr. Co.*). Yet, the Supreme Court's decision in *Brown* did just the opposite by allowing owners to collude to depress wages. Indeed, by extending the non-statutory labor exemption to post-impasse situations, *Brown* unjustly tilted the balance of bargaining in favor of NFL owners, giving them a powerful trump card in the form of the ability to unilaterally impose terms at impasse. Thus, rather than encouraging the robust bargaining that the Court intended the non-statutory exemption to promote, *Brown* incentivizes owners to stop negotiating, leaving the NFLPA with little choice but to decertify as a union in response—steps that will worsen, not ameliorate, bargaining impasses. More broadly, overruling *Brown* would help stem the Court's over-willingness to apply the non-statutory exemption to NFL-related disputes (*see e.g Clarett*). Thus, it is strongly in the best interests of the game to reverse *Brown*; without the non-statutory labor exemption, Rule of Reason analysis would conclude that the uniform salary rule had a decidedly anticompetitive effect (outweighing its precompetitive benefits). Allowing the *Brown* decision to stand unfairly hamstrings future NFL players and perverts the Court's careful crafting of the non-statutory labor exemption in *Jewel Tea, Allen Bradley,* and other decisions.

C. NBA: Sprewell Arbitration

Professional sports should not be bereft of judicial oversight: *Ludtke v. Kuhn* is a perfect example of a court appropriately ensuring that constitutional rights are protected. But it is not in the best interests of leagues for arbitrators and courts to intervene in player discipline decisions which lie far from their institutional expertise (as they have, e.g., in Howe, Willie Wilson/Vida Blue, Rocker, Ban Johnson). Arbitrator Feerick's decision in the Sprewell case is the latest prime example of such arbitral over-reaching, and reversing the decision would powerfully signal that such interventions are not appropriate. Further, Feerick's decision that the decision was "arbitrary and capricious" is legally dubious in its own rights, an example of overreaching use of a subjective standard. Finally, subjecting the Commissioner's disciplinary decision to review significantly undermines the NBA's governance ability; as Mike Menitove has argued, a model of commissioner's authority that insulates disciplinary rulings from review is critical in the modern era of sports, in which player misconduct is perhaps the greatest challenge to the health of professional leagues. Overturning Sprewell would correct these legal ills and strengthen the NBA's regulatory ability, and thus unquestionably is in the best interests of the game.

MEMORANDUM (Privileged/Confidential)

To: Billy Hunter, Executive Director NBA Player Association ("NBPA")
From: General Counsel to Mr. Hunter

Date: December 8, 2008
Re: Upcoming Renegotiation of NBA CBA and UPC

Table of Contents

I.   Executive Summary

As requested, I have reviewed the current NBA Collective Bargaining Agreement and Uniform Player Contract. In light of the concerns you expressed, I recommend proposing changes to the following four clauses which most significantly affect player rights and welfare:

- **"Conduct" (§ 5):** In addition to softening the language describing player conduct requirements in several instances in this clause, I recommend striking sub-clause (f), since the current language is unrealistic and virtually unenforceable in the modern-day NBA.

- **"Promotion Activities" (§ 13)**: I recommend seeking language that gives NBA players more leeway to refuse unreasonable promotional appearances and gain approval for endorsement opportunities via the introduction of arbitral appeals, as well as requiring teams to compensate players for off-court photo opportunities.

- **"Group License" (§ 14)**: I recommend adopting a group licensing scheme similar to that of the NFL which would result in revenue sharing among the NBA, NBAPA, and individual players. In addition, certain publicity rights should be reserved exclusively to individual players, including (most importantly) the use of player names and attributes in any online fantasy sports or other interactive online products.

- **"Disputes" (§ 17)**: The NBPA might propose a revamping of the current Grievance system, under which an independent arbitrator would review all disputes arising from discipline for on-court conduct ("arbitrary and capricious" standard) and from the UPC ("just cause" standard). In return, the NBA Commissioner would be given a "nuclear option" to withdraw any dispute from the grievance system (based on MLB Article XI(A)(1)(b)).

While I expect Commissioner Stern to be amenable to the proposed changes to § 5 and § 13 and ask for only minor concessions in return, I anticipate that he will resist the proposed changes to § 14 and § 17. Given the enormous financial stakes of the Group Licensing program, the NBPA should be prepared to offer a sizeable concession in return—agreeing to a "two years post-high school" age eligibility rule should be a significant bargaining chip. There is likely no trade-off the NBPA could offer, however, that would convince Stern to accept the proposed changes to § 17, given the extreme degree to wish arbitral review undercuts commissioner authority. Since the NBA Grievance process is already subject to significant oversight, I recommend dropping this proposal rather than fighting to impasse. In the event an impasse does occur, the NBA will likely unilaterally impose the current language (a move a court will likely uphold). While the NBPA should seek to avoid a strike, the "nuclear option" of union decertification would be an appropriate tactic if necessary to gain the league's consent to the proposed edits to § 14.

II. Proposed Edits to "Conduct" (§ 5)

A. Suggested "Black-line Edits"

- (a) "The Player agrees to observe and comply with all <u>reasonable</u> Team rules. . ."

- (b) Alter section (ii) to read "to be neatly and fully attired <u>when taking part in official league activities (including off-court promotional activities)</u>"; alter section (iii) to require "<u>reasonable</u> standards of honesty, citizenship, and sportsmanship"

- (f) Entirely strike this section. Replace it with: "Players and coaches are permitted to discuss future contract with any team of their choosing, so long as that employment is not intended to begin before the conclusion of the term of the player's current contract. In such cases, both players and teams will be subject to discipline by the Commissioner."

B. Explanation of Recommended Edits

The proposed change to § 5(a) is intended to protect players from unreasonable team rules. Though the NBPA should, of course, encourage its players to maintain high standards of conduct, it must also protect its members from being subjected to arbitrary and capricious rules. The proposed changes to § 5(b) are motivated by similar concerns and grounded in a more realistic conception of player behavior: the expectation that players will be held to higher standards of honesty, citizenship and sportsmanship than the average citizen is unreasonable. For instance, under this clause, a player could potentially be punished for failing to fulfilling his civic duty of voting. Similarly, the clothing requirements are unreasonable and unnecessary—and possibly even a violation of players' due process liberty rights (*see Ludtke*).

The proposed to change to § 5(f) is also motivated by a realistic recognition of player conduct in the modern era: player and coach friendships span beyond team rosters, making it impossible to prevent players from informally talking to one and other. Thus, conversations that would be impermissible under current clause's language almost certainly occur on a regular basis, making the rare instances in which the rule is enforced arbitrary anomalies (e.g. Kevin McHale–Joe Smith tampering). Further, courts have repeatedly held that there is nothing legally impermissible about the negotiation of a future contract (*see Washington Capitals v. Barry* (1969); *Munchak Corp. v. Cunningham* (1972); *Bengals v. Bergey* (1974)). Given the recent trend of European teams offering NBA players enormous financial incentives to jump leagues, players would certainly benefit from the ability to talk more freely about switching teams.

C. Anticipated Response of Commissioner Stern

Commissioner Stern likely will be reluctant to agree to the softening of language governing player conduct, given his emphatic emphasis on player conduct in recent years. He would dispute, for instance, that any due process rights are due to players once they have signed the UPC (which was agreed to as part of the CBA), even if the contractual provisions result in harsh consequences. *See Holmes v. NFL* (1996). He will likely also be reluctant to effectively abolish the league's tampering rule by striking § 5(f) and will argue that doing so will lead to players breaking their contracts in order to jump to other teams or leagues, leading to chaos.

D. Recommended Response to Stern & Final Recommendations

Because the issues at stake in this clause are critical to player liberties, I recommend the NBPA forge ahead and negotiate for the changes. The NBPA should be prepared, though, to offer the concession of increased penalties under the CBA when players *do* violate the Conduct clause; this is a reasonable trade-off for the requested language "softening." In response to Stern's concerns regarding § 5(f), the NBPA should note that this change would <u>not</u> make it permissible for players to terminate a contract in order to play for another team (whether NBA or foreign) during the term of their existing contract; such action is specifically prohibited by § 9 of the UPC ("Unique Skills"). Given the explicit language of that clause and the precedents of *Central New York Basketball Inc. v. Barnett* (1961), *Boston Celtics v. Shaw* (1990), and *Philadelphia Ball Club v. Lajoie* (1902), the originally-contracting team would almost certainly be granted an injunction that would block the player from playing for any other team or league during the duration of his original contract term. This should assuage Stern's worries.

III.   Proposed Edits to "Promotional Activities" (§ 13)

A.   Suggested "Black-line Edits"

- (a) "The Player agrees to allow the Team, the NBA, or a League-related entity to take pictures of the Player...<u>during any times in which the player is fulfilling his contractual on-court duties (all time spent at arenas and/or practice facilities preparing for and/or playing in games and/or practice, whether or not the player is physically "on the court"). Players will also participate in off-court photo opportunities at such reasonable times as the Team, the NBA, or a League-related entity may designate, but in such instances, players shall be compensated under the "promotional activities provisions of § 13(d).</u>"

- (b) Player will not make public appearances / sponsor commercial products "without the written consent of the Team, which shall not be withheld <u>except when such appearances or endorsements would be materially detrimental or prejudicial to the best interests of the Team or the League. Any such Team or League objections will be subject to review by an independent arbitrator.</u>"

- (d) [Add to end of currently existing clause] "<u>If a player believes the request is *not* reasonable, he may appeal the decision to an independent arbitrator.</u>"

B.   Explanation of Recommended Edits

The recommended edits to § 13(a) are designed to limit the extent to which NBA teams (or other league entities) can mandate that players take part in off-court activities against their will. The proposed revision to the section does not impact the league's ability to photograph players in their on-court capacities, but it would require additional payment for any non-playing related photo opportunities players are required to participate in. This edit, in other words, recognizes that the difference between off-court photo and promotional activities are merely semantic, and that players should be equivalently compensated for the two types of activities.

The recommended edits to § 13(b) clarify in what situations a team or the NBA may prohibit players from accepting sponsorship offers. The current "reasonable" language is quite ambiguous, potentially giving teams leeway to restrict players' financial opportunities out of ill-will, rather than valid concerns. Under the new language, a higher bar is set for refusing a players' request, especially given the ability to appeal the decision to an independent arbitrator. This change is undoubtedly of significant interest and benefit to players: it advances the larger goal of expanding control over individual "publicity rights." Finally, the recommended addition to § 13(d) similarly expands player rights by offering the option of appealing to an arbitrator.

C. Anticipated Response of Commissioner Stern

While Commissioner Stern may initially argue with some of the language clarifications and the requirement to pay players for off-court photo sessions, his most significant objection will be to the language giving players the ability to appeal to an independent arbitrator any refusals of permission for sponsorship opportunities. Stern will be well aware that subjecting league decisions to independent arbitral oversight has historically undercut the disciplinary authority of the NBA (*see e.g.* Sprewell Arbitration; *Rikko Enterprises v. Supersonics*) and other pro sports leagues (*see e.g.* Rocker, Walker, Howe, and Blue/Wilson Arbitrations). Thus, Stern will understandably be reluctant to agree to any increased arbitral oversight here.

D. Recommended Response to Stern & Final Recommendations

Though you should respond that the cited instances in which independent arbitral review has undercut commissioner authority involved player misconduct rather than business decisions, a compromise is in order on this point: if Stern is willing to agree to the clarified language and payment for off-court photos, you should agree to make Stern the ultimate arbitrator of any player appeals stemming from this clause. Though Stern will undoubtedly be biased in favor of team and league interests, the possibility of appeal (and the accompanying negative publicity) should serve as a moderating influence upon league requests and denials of player requests.

IV. <u>Proposed Edits to "Group License" (§ 14)</u>

A. Suggested "Black-line Edits"

● *The following language would entirely replace the existing § 13(a)*: (a) "The <u>player assigns to the</u> **NBPA** <u>the exclusive rights to use the Player's Player Attributes [as defined in 14(b)]</u> for **group licensing purposes**, <u>defined as any licensing program utilizing a total of</u> **five** <u>or more NBA player' player attributes. The NBPA will share the revenues from any such group licensing programs as follows: 25% to the NBA; 25% reserved for NBPA internal operations; 50% to be distributed equally among NBPA members. The Player retains the exclusive</u>

right to grant the use of his player attributes when they are not utilized concurrently with more than three other NBA players.''

- (b) [*To be added to the end of the present clause*]. ''League Promotions shall **not include**, however, the use of player names or attributes for the purpose of **fantasy games and other similar online interactive content**, even if those content and/or content are run and operated solely by the NBA and NBA properties. The use and licensing of player attributes for such purposes shall be exclusively reserved to **individual players** (and not considered to constitute group licensing).''

B. Explanation of Recommended Edits

The recommended edits to § 14(a) is based in large part on similar language in § 4 of the NFL Uniform Player Contract. The revision serves two main purposes. First, it defines group licensing rights more narrowly and mandates the sharing of the resulting revenue between the NBA, NBPA, and the players themselves. (The ability to grant such exclusive licenses and thus profit financially, it should be noted, was affirmed in *Fleer v. Topps* (1981) and *Topps Chewing Gum v. MLBPA* (1986).) This group licensing revenue-sharing scheme compensates all parties involved. At the same time, however, the reservation of individual licensing rights to players allows ''superstar'' players to retain the majority of the financial value of their unique skill and fame. To an extent, then, this represents a prioritization of the interest of some union members at the expense of those of others, which was held to be permissible in *Wood v. NBA* (1987).

The recommended edits to § 14(b) maintain the NBA's ability to use player names and attributes to promote the league and sport itself, while reserving to players the ability to reap financial gains from the burgeoning world of interactive online sports games. Leagues have attempted to build fantasy games into their websites (*see CBC v. MLBAM* (2007), in which MLBAM created its own fantasy sports game); this clause ensures players are compensated for such uses, as they would be if an external vendor created the game. Further, the clause's clear reservation of individual rights should help avoid a ruling similar to *CBC* (finding that players are not owed compensation), as well as ensuring that any online games seek individual licensing rather than relying on group licensing (as occurred in *Gridiron.com v. NFLPA* (2000)).

C. Anticipated Response of Commissioner Stern

Commissioner Stern will almost certainly resist the proposed changes to this section. Group licensing rights are a valuable source of revenue for the NBA, especially in light of the sport's growing popularity in Asia and the burgeoning opportunities for online licensing. Stern will, therefore, seek to extract valuable concessions on the part of the NBPA as a trade-off, as well as seeking to increase the NBA's take under the proposed revenue-sharing arrangement.

D. Recommended Response to Stern & Final Recommendations

Given that the changes to this clause are the players' top priority, I recommend that NBPA take the steps necessary to convince Commissioner Stern to accept the proposed changes, including making concessions related to the NBA's age rule. Of course, these demands may well lead to a bargaining impasse, the response to which is discussed in Part VI of this memo.

V. Proposed Edits to "Disputes" (§ 17)

A. Suggested "Black-line Edits"

Currently, this clause refers to the procedure set forth Article XXXI of the CBA, so the following suggestions would override contrary provisions in the CBA:

- (a) "Discipline for on-court behavior will be subjected to 'arbitrary and capricious review' by an independent arbitrator."

- (b) "Any other dispute arising under this Contract (except for a dispute arising under paragraph 9) will be resolved in accordance with a Grievance Procedure such that an independent arbitrator shall apply a **just cause** standard of review."

- (c) "For the commissioner to withdraw a dispute arising under this Contract from the Grievance Process, he must declare a 'best interests of the game emergency.' Such a declaration and withdrawal automatically reopens the CBA."

B. Explanation of Recommended Edits

Given the weight and deference that courts have placed upon collective bargaining and contract provisions mandating arbitration as a means to resolve disputes (*see e.g, Holmes v. NFL; Steelworkers Trilogy; MLBA v. Garvey*), this clause is critically important to players' rights and status. Undeniably, NBA players would enjoy far greater rights under a legal regime in which all contract disputes are subject to independent review (*compare e.g.,* Sprewell Arbitration; Howe Arbitration *with* Crowder/Reese Arbitration; *Holmes v. NFL*), especially given that the NBA Commissioner is officially a partisan representative of the owners (in contrast to the NFL, as discussed by Mike Menitove). Thus, proposed clause (a) subjects discipline arising from on-court issues to independent review; currently, under XXXI(8) of the CBA, Commissioner Stern has final say over appeals of such disputes. Next, proposed clause (b) shifts the standard for all other disputes arising from the UPC (including those implicating the "integrity of, or the maintenance of public confidence in" the NBA) from the current highly deferential "arbitrary and capricious" standard to the more favorable "just cause" standard. Finally, proposed clause (c)—modeled on Article XI(A)(1)(b) of the MLB CBA—would offer Commissioner Stern a nuclear option if he ever felt a dispute were so critical to the "best interests" of the NBA to achieve a certain outcome that it would be worth reopening to the CBA.

C. Anticipated Response of Commissioner Stern

Commissioner Stern will certainly be highly resistant to these changes, which would reshape the legal regime under which the NBA operates. After having his suspension of Latrell Sprewell reduced in 1999, Stern is well-aware that independent review of his decisions deeply undercuts his authority as commissioner. Indeed, he will argue that the arbitrator's decision to overrule him even under the more deferential "arbitrary and capricious standard" applied in Sprewell is evidence that players are already amply protected and that there is, therefore, no need for a shift to the less deferential "just cause" standard. Finally, though the "nuclear option" is facially a significant grant of power, Stern will point out that Bud Selig has promised in writing never to invoke that power, presumably since reopening the CBA is too high a price to pay.

D. Recommended Response to Stern & Final Recommendations

Though increased arbitral oversight of disputes arising from the UPC would greatly benefit NBA players, it is quite unlikely that the NBPA could offer any concession that would convince Commissioner Stern to agree to these revisions. Given that Stern's "best interests" authority is already subject to a greater degree of review than that of his NFL and MLB peers, I recommend dropping these proposals rather than fighting to a likely impasse over them.

VI. Recommendation if Bargaining Impasse is Reached

As discussed, I expect the NBPA and NBA to reach consensus on the proposed revisions to §§ 5 and 13, and I recommend that the NBPA not pursue the proposed revision to § 17. This leaves the proposed revision to § 14 ("Group License") as the most likely to lead to impasse if Stern is unwilling to accept the NBPA's age-eligibility rule concession. In the case of impasse, the NBA can be expected to unilaterally impose the current terms of § 14. Though the NBPA could challenge this move as an unreasonable restraint on trade (Sherman Act), a court will likely side with the NBA. Following the framework of *Powell v. NFL* (1987) and *Brown v. NFL* (1996), a court would likely find that a collective bargaining relationship still existed between the parties, that the imposed terms primarily affect the parties to the CBA, that the imposed terms are a subject of mandatory collective bargaining under *Jewel Tea*, and the imposed terms would be "reasonably comprehended" in the owners' final good faith offer. Based on these findings, the court would then apply the non-statutory labor exemption, immunizing the NBA's actions. The NBPA's best option at impasse, then, would be to end the "bargaining relationship" by decertifying as a union, as the NFLPA did in 1989 after *Powell*. Given the financial implications for the NBPA's members of revising § 14, I conclude that such drastic action is justified. That said, the NBPA should attempt to avoid a strike, as the resulting lost income and negative publicity would likely cost players more than a revised Licensing provision would benefit them.

Sample Answer 3

Memo to Commissioner Bud Selig Re: Most Legally Significant Precedents in MLB, NBA and NFL and Recommendations for Overruling Landmark Precedents

Table of Contents

in the Legal Process and Undermining Each Game's Best Interests

a. Sprewell Arbitration

b. Brown v. Pro Football, Inc.

c. National and American League Baseball Clubs v. MLBPA (Messersmith)

Memorandum (Privileged/Confidential)

To: MLB Commissioner Bud Selig

From: General Counsel to the MLB Commissioner

Re: Most Legally Significant Precedents in MLB, NBA and NFL and Recommendations for Overruling Landmark Precedents

Mr. Selig,

As requested, I have prepared a final analysis regarding the most legally significant precedents in the history of each league, and my recommendations for overruling three landmark precedents.

I. Executive Summary:

In MLB, Finley v. Kuhn re-established the broad reach of the broad reach of the commissioner's best interest power, upholding the commissioner's ability to make critical decisions without court interference. Flood v. Kuhn upheld baseball's antitrust exemption, immunizing baseball from widespread antitrust challenge. Finally, Messersmith and McNally opened the gates to free agency, setting in motion the widespread player movement which characterizes today's game.

In the NBA, Haywood v. NBA ruled that i) basketball is subject to antitrust law and ii) that the NBA's 4–year eligibility rule violated § 1 of the Sherman Act. Wood v. NBA upheld the NBA's draft and salary cap while specifically defining the strictures of the player-union relationship in the collecting bargaining context. Finally, NBA v. Williams, following Powell v. NFL, upheld multi-employer bargaining post expiration of the CBA.

In the NFL, Smith v. Pro Football declared the NFL draft unlawful under § 1 of the Sherman Act and attempted to define the complex relationship between NFL clubs and the league as a whole. Mackey v. NFL (Part 2) defined the application of the non-statutory labor exemption and formed the future basis for numerous future precedents. Finally, Raiders I opened the floodgates to franchise relocation by forcing the NFL to articulate objective criteria for allowing teams to move between cities.

Three landmark precedents should be overruled in the best interests of the game. These are the Sprewell Arbitration, which represented a usurpation of the commissioner's power to rule on important matters of player discipline; Clarett v. NFL, which opposed Haywood and incorrectly applied the non-statutory exemption; and Messersmith and McNally, which struck down baseball's reserve system through an unlawful use of power by an arbitrator.

II. The Most Significant Precedents in MLB History Defined the Commissioner's Broad–Reaching Best Interest Power, Upheld Baseball's Antitrust Exemption and Set Free Agency in Motion

a. Finley v. Kuhn

Finley v. Kuhn (1978) re-established the far-reaching power of the MLB commissioner in the game's modern age. Article I, § 1 of the Baseball Agreement provides the commissioner with the power to "investigate... any act, transaction or practice alleged to not be in the [game's] best interests."[2] While seemingly firmly established after the Black Sox scandal of 1919, and after Milwaukee Ass'n v. Landis (1931), where the court allowed the commissioner to veto an owner's secret transactions, this power was gradually eroded. This occurred through the replacement of the commissioner as league arbitrator, and with the Messersmith decision (1975). Therefore, when Kuhn blocked A's owner Charles Finley's sale of three veteran stars, expressing concern about the debilitation of the A's, the stage was set for an important test of the commissioner's power. The court's ruling, based on the court's refusal to interfere with the commissioner's good faith decision, was a validation of the commissioner's broad sway over the game. Furthermore, the ruling was one of a string of cases which validated the commissioner's power in matters of player discipline (see Willie Wilson arbitration, (1983)) and owner discipline (see Atlanta Braves/Ted Turner v. Bowie Kuhn (1976)).

b. Flood v. Kuhn

Flood v. Kuhn (1972) was significant because fifty years after Federal Baseball (1922) and twenty years after Toolson (1953), the Supreme Court again refused to strike down baseball's antitrust exemption.[3] The court did so despite a myriad of sports precedents (U.S. v. International Boxing Club (1955), Haywood v. NBA (1972), Radovich v. NFL (1957)) and non-sports precedents (U.S. v. Shubert (1955)) which denied application of the antitrust exemption. Blackmun's justification was that Congress' inaction, combined with a significant reliance interest, was sufficient to leave in place the anomalous exemption.[4] Curt Flood had brought suit against the MLB under federal and state antitrust law, arguing that he was not a piece of property "to be bought and sold irrespective of [his] wishes." This was an argument which previous courts had vindicated (see Chicago Ball Club v. Chase, declaring baseball's reserve system to be a "peonage system"). However, Blackmun's holding meant that Flood and his fellow

---

2. Article I, § 5 limits this best interests power to matters outside the collective bargaining agreement.

3. Blackmun's holding was sufficiently conflicted, however, as to enable subsequent courts to argue that baseball's exemption was limited to the reserve clause, therefore exposing the "business of baseball" to antitrust scrutiny (see Piazza and Tirendi v. MLB and Morsani v. MLB).

4. Salerno v. American League and Portland Baseball Club v. Kuhn also left the antitrust exemption in place as applied to umpires and the minor leagues, respectively.

players had to wait until Messersmith, and finally until the Curt Flood Act, to fully enjoy the rights of free employees who could choose their employer.

c. National and American League Baseball Clubs v. MLBPA (Messersmith)

Messersmith and McNally (1975) struck the first fatal blow to the reserve system. As is argued below, this occurred through the backdoor, as two players challenged the reserve system despite a specific provision in the 1983 CBA stating that the reserve system was not included. Arbitrator Seitz's ruling (upheld in KC Royals v. MLBPA) did what the Supreme Court could not do, enabling players to become free agents by exercising the UPC option clause. This opened the gates to free agency, fundamentally shaping today's modern game. Perhaps as an important footnote, Messersmith resulted in large part because of a new system which enabled players to have grievances heard before a third-party arbitrator, a critical loss of power by the commissioner.

III. **The Most Significant Precedents in the History of the NBA Struck Down the Draft Eligibility Rule, Established the Limits of the Player–Union Relationship, and Upheld Multi–Employer Bargaining Post CBA Expiration**

i. Haywood v. NBA

Haywood v. NBA (1971) and the subsequent district court trial, Denver Rockets v. All–Pro Management, were significant because i) they ruled that basketball does not enjoy antitrust exemption and ii) that the NBA's 4–year eligibility rule violated antitrust law. Spencer Haywood challenged the NBA's eligibility rule mandating a period of 4 years after high school and before draft entry. While subsequent courts have applied a rule of reason analysis to draft and eligibility rules (see Smith v. Pro Football (1978) and Clarett v. NFL (2004)), the court in Haywood applied a *per se* analysis, holding that there was a substantial probability that the rule was a group boycott under § 1 of the Sherman Act. In so doing, the court denied the antitrust exemption to pro basketball, struck down the 4–year eligibility rule, and implicitly stated that there were limits to a sports league's power to define its members. Whereas in previous cases courts had held that the NBA had the power to restrict its members (see Molinas v. NBA, where the court held that the league had the power to impose a rule banning a player who had gambled, and Levin v. NBA, where the court held that league owners had the power to restrict their membership), Haywood stated that such restrictions on membership cannot be anti-competitive.

Were MLB's eligibility rules to be similarly challenged on the basis of antitrust, such claims would likely be dismissed as a result of the antitrust exemption. However, as proposed in the recent Tazawa affair concerning amateur Japanese players, the Curt Flood Act may preclude the exemption if the players seeking eligibility were deemed to be "major league players."

ii. Wood v. NBA

Wood v. NBA was significant both because it upheld the NBA's draft and salary cap and because it specifically defined the limits of the player/union relationship in the context of collective bargaining. Ruling on Leon Wood's challenge to the maximum $75,000 salary for players whose teams exceeded the salary cap, Judge Winter emphasized the fundamental principle that "federal labor policy allows employees to seek the best deal for the greatest number by the exercise of collective rather than individual bargaining power." Winter was arguing that by agreeing to union representation, players could avail themselves of collective benefits but in turn had to preclude themselves of benefits which could be achieved alone. This foreshadowed Clarett v. NFL almost two decades later (see below). Winter's decision also upheld the salary cap, which has had a major impact in both the NBA ("soft" cap) and NFL ("hard" cap) in promoting competitive balance but also skewing club incentives.[5]

iii. NBA v. Williams

NBA v. Williams (1995) upheld the ability of NBA teams to bargain as a multi-employer unit post CBA expiration, preserving their ability to "band together as a single entity" and to establish the uniformity of rules required for the proper functioning of sport. Following Powell v. NFL, the case was critical because it upheld the clubs' use of group negotiating leverage in the collective bargaining process, validating tactics of economic force such as lockouts.

IV. The Most Significant Precedents in the History of the NFL Declared the Draft Unlawful, Defined the Prongs of the Non–Statutory Labor Exemption, and Opened the Gates to Franchise Relocation

a. Smith v. Pro Football

Smith v. Pro Football (1978) declared the NFL draft to be an illegal restraint of trade, violating § 1 of the Sherman Act. The court's holding was significant because it struck down a fundamental pillar of the league and the other major sports leagues, the player draft, which the court held was anti-competitive in both purpose and effect. While the court in Robertson v. NBA applied a per se analysis to strike down the NBA draft, the Smith court instead delved into the unique nature of professional sports leagues under the rule of reason, foreshadowing the single entity analysis in Raiders I.

i. Mackey v. NFL (Part 2)

Mackey v. NFL (1976) was critical because it defined the prongs of the non-statutory exemption in striking down the Rozelle Rule, its test becoming the basis for tests of the exemption in the NHL (McCourt v. California Sports, Clarett), NFL (Zimmerman v. NFL) and NBA. Following non-sports precedents such as Allen Bradley Co. v. IBEW (refusing to apply the

---

5. David E. Katz, "The Veteran Premium Problem and the Effects of the NFL Collective Bargaining Agreement on the League's Reserves."

exemption to a selectively prejudicial agreement), <u>Meat Cutters v. Jewel Tea</u> (applying the exemption to a working hours restriction), and <u>UMWA v. Pennington</u> (refusing to apply the exemption to a provision benefiting one set of employers), <u>Mackey</u> sought to unite the important precedents in a single test. The resultant <u>Mackey</u> 3–point test states that a term or agreement may be protected under the non-statutory exemption where it i) affects only parties to the collective bargaining relationship; ii) concerns a mandatory subject of collective bargaining; and iii) is the product of bona fide arms' length bargaining.

ii.   Raiders I

<u>Raiders I</u> (1984) opened the floodgates to franchise relocation challenges. At issue in the case was Rule 4.3 of the NFL Constitution, which required the approval of 75% of owners for a club to move into another's home territory. The court held that Rule 4.3 was an unreasonable trade restraint because there were less restrictive alternatives to the rule, and that a rule which would withstand antitrust scrutiny only if it were based on objective factors. <u>Raiders I</u> therefore removed the power of the commissioner and the clubs to prohibit relocation without just cause. It also precipitated a flood of suits attacking relocation rules, including <u>VKK Corp v. NFL</u>, <u>St. Louis Convention & Visitors Comm'n v. NFL</u>, and <u>NBA v. San Diego Clippers</u>.

V.   Three Landmark Precedents Should be Overruled Because They Detrimentally Impacted Vital Aspects of their Respective Leagues, Weakening the Collective Confidence in the Legal Process and Undermining the Game's Best Interests

a.   Sprewell Arbitration

The Sprewell arbitration (1998) was a landmark precedent which was wrongly decided because it imposed an arbitrator's will into an important matter which was traditionally the commissioner's jurisdiction. At the time of the decision, the NBA commissioner's best interests power had not been tested to the extent that it had been in the MLB (see <u>Yankees v. Johnson</u>, <u>Chicago Club v. Fay Vincent</u>) and the NFL (see <u>Holmes v.NFL</u>, <u>NFL Management Council v. NFLPA (Crowder/Reese)</u>). Therefore, the Sprewell arbitration was an important litmus test. The arbitrator's decision was flawed, and should therefore be overruled, because the arbitrator placed his view what a just punishment should be above the commissioner's. Furthermore, he incorrectly imposed his will to limit a club's power to determine its team members, where the player had violated an express provision of his contract.

b.   Clarett v. NFL

<u>Clarett</u> upheld the NFL's rule on age eligibility and re-emphasized the limits of the player-union relationship defined in <u>Wood</u>. However, because it opposed a line of cases striking down eligibility rules and misinterpreted the non-statutory exemption, it should therefore be overruled. The holding

in Clarett, which cited a string of precedents including Wood, Williams and Caldwell v. ABA, was based upon the federal labor policy governing the player's representation by the union, notably that the player ceded to the union the right to bargain for the player's rights through collective action. However, because Clarett and the NFL were "complete strangers" to the bargaining relationship, and because the eligibility rules were never the product of arms' length negotiation[6], they should not have received the protection of the non-statutory exemption. Further, courts have refused to apply the non-statutory exemption where it selectively prejudices a specific group (see Connell Construction v. Plumbers), and in this case early-entry candidates were selectively prejudiced. Finally, Clarett opposed the line of cases stemming from Haywood which held that courts will enjoin league-mandated eligibility restraints if they are anti-competitive. For all of these reasons, it should be overruled.

c. Messersmith and McNally

Messersmith and McNally (19775) dealt the fatal blow to baseball's reserve clause, forever changing the relationship between players and owners. But it did so through an application of power which the arbitrator did not have. In Article XV of the 1973 Basic Agreement, the union and owners agreed that "this agreement does not deal with the reserve system." Further removing any doubt, MLBPA chief Marvin Miller had stated that "[the MLBPA] will acquiesce in the continuance of the enforcement of the rules as house rules and we will not grieve over house rules." Therefore, Seitz did not have the power to interpret § 10(a) as it extended to the reserve system. The fact that he did so is all the more egregious because his decision fundamentally changed the course of the game, and you should overrule this incorrect decision. For over 50 years baseball's antitrust exemption had been tested and upheld in a myriad of landmark cases (see Flood; American League Club of Chicago v. Chase; Philadelphia Ball Club v. Lajoie; Toronto Blue Jays v. Danny Ainge; Salerno v. American League; Portland Baseball Club v. Kuhn). Suddenly a lone arbitrator determined that he had the power to reverse it. The ruling should be reversed because it was wrongly decided and has had a major detrimental impact on today's game. Due to free agency, salaries have been bid to astronomical levels and players switch teams with regularity. As Bowie Kuhn stated, "It is just inconceivable that after nearly 100 years of developing this system for the overall good of the game, it should [have been] obliterated in this way."

Memo to NBPA Executive Director Billy Hunter Re: NBA UPC and CBA Renegotiation

Table of Contents

---

6. The CBA in existence at the time of Clarett's suit did not contain the eligibility rules. While the NFL Constitution and Bylaws continued the rules before 2003, in 2003 the bylaw containing the rules was amended. While the CBA required the NFL to notify and bargain over any bylaw amendment that "could significantly affect the terms and conditions" of player employment, this amendment to the rules was never bargained over.

II. **Recommended Changes to UPC:** The NBPA should seek the following UPC changes in the best interests of the union and the league (listed in declining order of priority):

 a. **(§ 14) Group License:** remove NBA Properties' monopoly on player rights; exclude fantasy games; require individual licensing contracts for star players.

 b. **(§ 13) Promotional Activities:** grant players an interest in the pictures created by league; remove requirement of team consent for standard promotional activities.

 c. **(§ 9) Unique Skills:** Permit player to negotiate with other clubs in last year of his contract; provide for arbitration to determine whether damages are adequate in cases of breach; enable player to bring counterclaims.

 d. **(§ 5) Conduct:** Explicitly limit commissioner's sole discretion; provide for dispute resolution through balanced 3–member panel.

 e. **(§ 17) Disputes:** change CBA Article XXXI to reduce commissioner's excessive control over the grievance process; remove exemption of paragraph 9 from Article XXXI procedure.

 f. **(§ 16) Termination:** remove (a)(i), which is overly vague and oversteps commissioner's jurisdiction; provide for termination by player.

 g. **(§ 19) Release:** enable players to bring claims arising from injuries, whether physical, emotional or psychological, suffered during the course of employment.

 h. **(§ 12) Other Athletic Activities:** Permit player to participate without club consent in activities reasonably intended to improve basketball ability.

III. **Recommended Action if Final Proposal Rejected by Commissioner**

IV. **NBPA "Black–Line" UPC Edits, Commissioner Responses, and Final Proposal**

Memorandum (Privileged/Confidential)

To: Billy Hunter, NBPA Executive Director
From: General Counsel to the Executive Director
Re: NBA UPC and CBA Renegotiation

Mr. Hunter,

I have prepared a final analysis of the NBA UPC, in anticipation of the upcoming CBA renegotiation, with the purpose of making the UPC more favorable to all of our union members.

I. Executive Summary

The proposed changes focus on effecting the players' intention to expand upon their endorsement rights; limiting NBA Properties' current monopoly on player attributes; granting the players an interest in pictures and media created by the league; providing players increased rights in the context of contract negotiation and breach; and limiting the commissioner's sole discretion to punish player conduct and his excessive control over the grievance process. The final proposed edits (see black-line edits) account for the Commissioner's likely responses and represent a fair resolution of player concerns. If these proposed edits are not accepted, the NBPA would be best advised to seek decertification.

II.   Analysis of NBA UPC and Recommended Revisions (in declining order of priority)

§ 14.   Group License: This section is substantially changed to remove NBA Properties' monopoly on player rights and effect the players' stated intention to expand upon their publicity rights. Because "Player Attributes" are not currently defined in the UPC, they are explicitly defined in the black-line edits. In addition, clause (a), which gives NBA Properties an exclusive right to use Player Attributes, is likely void under CBC v. MLBAM to the extent that it includes the player's name and statistics and under NBA v. Motorola to the extent that it includes real-time statistics. To account for these precedents and to provide the players greater rights, the NBA Properties license is made non-exclusive and specifically excludes player information and statistics. If NBA Properties files suit to block the non-exclusive change, the NBPA will likely prevail under Topps v. MLBPA.

In addition, players are provided the right to withhold use of their Attributes for promotion of products of which they do not approve, particularly unrelated products (see Gionfriddo v. MLB). Players are also explicitly given the right to license images and likenesses either individually or through the NBPA for video games, websites, and fantasy games, and to preclude use of those same characteristics by third-parties without license. NBA Properties is precluded from using film footage in any "commercially marketable game or interactive use," as in § 4(a) of the NFL UPC.

Finally, with the aim of specifically benefiting "superstar players," a clause is inserted specifying that if any specific player solely generates more than 5% of gross revenue attributed to the "Group License" in the previous year, NBA Properties will be required to enter into an individual licensing contract with such player for his Player Attributes.

The NBA commissioner will likely object to many of these suggested changes, most notably making the group license non-exclusive, excluding names and statistics, and requiring individual licensing deals with star players.

§ 13.   Promotional Activities: This section is changed to i) grant the Player an interest in the pictures and other media created by the league and ii) remove the requirement that players seek consent from Teams for standard activities. The court in Haelan Laboratories v. Topps Chewing Gum held that there exists an independent and assignable common law right to the publicity value of one's name and picture. (a) of this section abrogates this right in two ways, by i) enabling the Team or NBA to use pictures in any manner desired and ii) by giving the Player no right in the pictures. This section is therefore changed to require the Player's consent for the club's use of the pictures, and also providing the Player an equal share in the pictures. While the reasoning in Baltimore Orioles v. MLBPA might lead a court to declare the pictures works for hire which preempt the Player's state law publicity right, this default presumption can be explicitly changed in a written instrument, which is done so here. Further, if the Teams do not grant the players a share in the rights, they are potentially liable under Ventura v. Titan Sports. This section is also changed to require player consent for the use of player likenesses and drawings, which fall under the right of publicity as in Ali v. Playgirl, and do not contain enough of a parody element to fall under Cardtoons v. MLBPA. Finally, (b) is changed to prevent Players from having to solicit consent from Teams for standard appearances and sponsorships.

While the Commissioner and the Clubs are expected to object to several of these changes, the weight of case precedent favors the players.

§ 9. Unique Skills: This section should be substantially modified to ensure that i) the Player can seek arbitration to determine whether contract breach can adequately be compensated by damages and ii) that a player has the right to negotiate in good faith with other teams in the last year of his contract. Cases such as Chicago Club v. Chase, which opposed Philadelphia v. Lajoie, held that courts will not enforce agreements which are inequitable and whose purpose is to create a monopoly for player services. This contract is inequitable because it states that all players have "extraordinary and unique skill" which cannot be compensated by damages, bars negotiation with other teams, and prevents players from bringing counterclaims. In removing these anti-competitive effects, players are given the right to seek arbitration for a determination of whether irreparable harm has been suffered (see Syracuse Nationals v. Barnett), similar to the analysis employed in the Sonics breach of contract case to determine whether damages to the city could be quantified. In addition, the provision stating that the player waives his right to jury trial or to bring counterclaims is removed. One particular counterclaim contemplated here is that of unclean hands, successfully applied in the Flowers case.

Following cases such as Washington Capitals v. Barry and Bengals v. Bergey, which refused to proscribe a player's negotiating a new contract during the term of his current contract, this section is substantially changed to enable the player to negotiate a contract in his final year. It is inequitable to allow teams to prepare for multiple years to sign specific players on other teams (see the Knicks preparation for Lebron James' 2010 free agency) without permitting players to make preparations themselves.

§ 5. Conduct: The desired changes focus on explicitly limiting the commissioner's sole discretion regarding discipline of player conduct, introducing a 3–member panel for grievance arbitration, and modifying vague sections which expose players to wide potential liability. (b) is changed to remove the clause "neatly and fully attired in public" because it is overly vague, subjecting players to penalty for dress considered acceptable in many contexts. Actions which are "materially detrimental or prejudicial" are explicitly listed in the proposed edits. (c) is modified to introduce a good faith materiality standard. (d) is removed subject to modification of Article 35, which provides excessive power to the commissioner, notably through 35(d), which allows the commissioner to "indefinitely" suspend any player who makes any statement that "does not conform to the standards of morality."[7] This is excessive commissioner power which could subject a player to unjustified punishment. (e) and (f) are modified to provide appeal of the commissioner's decision to a 3–member panel, consisting of one member appointed by the NBPA, one member appointed by the team owners, and one independent member.

The commissioner can be expected to strenuously object to limitation of his power relating to punishment for gambling, particularly given the Tim Donaghy scandal.

§ 17. Disputes: This section is changed to remove the exemption of disputes arising under paragraph 9 ("Unique Skills") from the Article XXXI procedure, because such disputes should also be subject to arbitral review. In addition, Article XXXI of the CBA should be changed to reduce the commissioner's excessive control over the grievance process. Such changes shall include modification of 5(c) to specify a "rule of reason" standard; and removal of Section 8 and designation of such disputes to be covered under the normal Arbitrator Procedure. Finally, this section is changed to read that if the CBA has expired, disputes need not be resolved in accordance with the standard CBA Grievance Procedure, opening up UPC provisions to antitrust challenge through the courts.

§ 16. Termination: This section is changed to remove clause (a)(i), which is overly vague. Absent specific enumeration of what constitutes "good citizenship" or "good moral character," a Player is subject to termination for all and any manner of subjective actions, which oversteps the bounds of the commissioner's best interests power. Further, this section is changed to provide a provision for termination by the player, similar to clause 7(a) of the MLB UPC.

§ 19. Release: This section is substantially changed to enable players to bring claims arising from injuries, whether physical, emotional or psychological, suffered during the course of employment as NBA players, similar to those currently pursued by Chris Nowinski and former NFL players such as Ted Johnson. NBA players should have the right to seek similar redress for injuries caused by unsafe playing conditions (i.e, major knee

---

7. "Excerpt from NBA Constitution (Misconduct)," NBPA Player's Association, CBA Exhibits, http://www.nbpa.com/cba_exhibits/exhibitA-excerpt.php.

injuries resulting from unsafe playing floors), unruly fans (see objects thrown by fans in the Pacers–Pistons brawl) or other players.

§ 12. Other Athletic Activities: This section should be moderately changed to prevent teams from enjoining reasonable activities engaged in by players either i) in furtherance of improving their basketball playing ability or ii) in furtherance of their training for a different sport for which they have been drafted. The list of prohibited activities might also be shortened, to mirror the more limited list in MLB UPC § 5(b).

"Trading Off" Between NBA Superstars and Early–Entry Candidates: While concessions are provided for superstar players, the NBPA should not be engaged in "trading off" of rights of early entrants in favor of superstar concessions. Such action might raise a claim of unfair representation, a claim which was successfully brought this year by NFL retirees against the NFLPA, which failed to properly market said retirees' images. The NBPA should therefore strongly advocate on behalf of early-entry candidates in collective bargaining, perhaps by seeking a return to the rule enabling eligibility post high school.

III. Recommended Action if Final Proposed Edits Rejected

If the final proposed edits are rejected, the best strategic move for the NBPA would be to decertify, following the strategy employed in McNeil v. NFL. This would preclude the application of the non-statutory exemption to collective bargaining provisions such as the age eligibility rules, limits on free agency, and maximum player salaries. At the same time, the players could continue to earn their salaries as players.

The option to strike is a less attractive one because it places the players in a disadvantaged situation while not providing any mitigating legal benefit. In fact, following Powell v. NFL and NBA v. Williams, the NBA would be able to impose the status quo agreement post CBA expiration, and under Brown, be able to potentially unilaterally impose provisions post-impasse. In addition, a strike would i) result in lost player salaries; ii) the potential use of replacement players as in the 1987 NFL strike; iii) a possibly protracted battle; and iv) and the public turning against the players.

IV. Proposed Black–Line UPC Edits, Likely Responses, and Final Recommendations

Note: Sections of the below provisions which are unchanged are not shown.

Suggested NBPA Edits	Likely Commissioner Edits	Final Proposed Edits
§ 5. Conduct: (b) The Player agrees (i) to give his best services, as well as his loyalty, to the Team, and to play basketball only for the Team and its assignees during the full playing season; (ii) to conduct himself on and off the court according to the highest standards of honesty, citizenship and sportsmanship, and iii) to not publicly disparage the league, clubs or other players; not knowingly associate with gamblers; not use or provide	**§ 5. Conduct:** (b) The Player agrees (i) to give his best services, as well as his loyalty, to the Team, and to play basketball only for the Team and its assignees during the full playing season and outside of the season only according to § 12; (ii) to refrain from wearing attire which portrays a negative public image of the player, including but not limited to apparel related to gangs, apparel advocating criminal or offensive behavior, apparel por-	**§ 5. Conduct:** (b) The Player agrees (i) to give his best services, as well as his loyalty, to the Team, and to play basketball only for the Team and its assignees during the full playing season and outside of the season only according to § 12; (ii) to refrain from wearing apparel related to gangs, apparel advocating criminal or offensive behavior, apparel portraying offensive or illicit slogans; iii) to conduct himself on and off the court according

other players with illegal or NBA-banned drugs; and not engage in crime.

(c) For any violation of Team rules, any breach of any provision of this Contract, or for any conduct impairing the faithful and thorough discharge of the duties incumbent upon the Player, all of which are subject to a good faith materiality standard, the Team may reasonably impose fines upon and/or suspensions on the Player in accordance with the terms of the CBA.
(d) Removed subject to modification of 35 of NBA Constitution.

(e) ...The Commissioner shall have the power to suspend the Player indefinitely or to expel him as a player for any member of the NBA. The Commissioner's finding shall be appealable to a 3-member panel composed of one PA member, one member selected by the commissioner, and one independent member. The Commissioner shall not have the power to overrule such panel's final decision in the game's best interests.
(f) ... Breach of this subparagraph, in addition to the remedies available to the Team, shall be punishable by fine and/or suspension to be imposed by the Commissioner, subject to appeal to a 3-member panel as designated in (e).

§ **9. Unique Skills:** Upon the Team's seeking equitable relief to prevent contract breach by Player, the Player shall have the right to seek arbitration for a determination of whether such breach would

traying offensive or illicit slogans, and other clothing to be solely determined by the Commissioner; iii) to conduct himself on and off the court according to the highest standards of honesty, citizenship and sportsmanship, and iv) to not publicly disparage the league, clubs or other players; not knowingly associate with gamblers; not use or provide other players with illegal or NBA-banned drugs; and not engage in crime, or not engage in any other behavior found objectionable by the Team or the League.
(c) For any violation of Team rules, any breach of any provision of this Contract, or for any conduct impairing the faithful and thorough discharge of the duties incumbent upon the Player, all of which are subject to a good faith materiality standard, the Team may reasonably impose fines upon and/or suspensions on the Player in accordance with the terms of the CBA.
(d) The Player agrees to be bound by Article 35 of the NBA Constitution, which is subject to good faith negotiation in the drafting of the new CBA. The Player acknowledges that the Commissioner is empowered to impose fines upon and/or suspend the Player for causes and in the manner provided in such Article.

(e) ...The Commissioner shall have the power to suspend the Player indefinitely or to expel him as a player for any member of the NBA.

(f) ... Breach of this subparagraph, in addition to the remedies available to the Team, shall be punishable by fine and/or suspension to be imposed by the Commissioner, subject to appeal to a 3-member panel composed of two members appointed by the Commissioner and one member appointed by the NBPA.

§ **9. Unique Skills:** The Player represents and agrees that he has extraordinary and unique skill and ability as a basketball player, and that the services to be rendered by him hereunder cannot be replaced

to the highest standards of honesty, citizenship and sportsmanship, and iv) to not publicly disparage the league, clubs or other players; not knowingly associate with gamblers; not use or provide other players with illegal or NBA-banned drugs; and not engage in crime.

(c) For any violation of Team rules, any breach of any provision of this Contract, or for any conduct impairing the faithful and thorough discharge of the duties incumbent upon the Player, all of which are subject to a good faith materiality standard, the Team may reasonably impose fines upon and/or suspensions on the Player in accordance with the terms of the CBA.
(d) The Player agrees to be bound by Article 35 of the NBA Constitution, which is subject to good faith negotiation in the drafting of the new CBA. The Player acknowledges that the Commissioner is empowered to impose fines upon and/or suspend the Player for causes and in the manner provided in such Article, provided that such fines and/or suspensions are consistent with the terms of the CBA. The Commissioner's finding shall be appealable to a 3-member panel composed of one PA member, one member selected by the commissioner, and one independent member.
(e) ...The Commissioner shall have the power to suspend the Player indefinitely or to expel him as a player for any member of the NBA. The Commissioner's decision shall be appealable only to the Commissioner.

(f) ... Breach of this subparagraph, in addition to the remedies available to the Team, shall be punishable by fine and/or suspension to be imposed by the Commissioner, subject to appeal to a 3-member panel composed of one PA member, one member selected by the commissioner, and one independent member.

§ **9. Unique Skills:** The Player represents and agrees that he has extraordinary and unique skill and ability as a basketball player. Upon the Team's seeking equitable relief to prevent contract cause irreparable harm. Player shall not be precluded from trial by jury or for bringing counter-claims related to the equitable relief sought by the Team. In the final year of his contract, the Player may negotiate and sign a contract for the purpose of playing for another Team upon termination of his current contract, provided that such activity does not impact his required obligations or detrimentally detract from the Player's on-court performance.

or the loss thereof adequately compensated for in money damages. Upon the Team's seeking equitable relief to prevent contract breach by Player, the Player shall have the right to seek arbitration for a determination of whether such breach would cause irreparable harm. However, such finding shall not preclude equitable relief if the arbitrator finds that the Team cannot presently be adequately compensated through damages. The Team shall also not be precluded from equitable relief during the period in which arbitration proceedings are occurring.

breach by Player, the Player shall have the right to seek arbitration for a determination of whether such breach would cause irreparable harm. The Team shall not be precluded from equitable relief during the period in which arbitration proceedings are occurring.

§ 13. Promotional Activities: (a) The Player agrees to allow the Team, the NBA, or a League-related entity to take pictures of the Player, alone or together with others, for still photographs, motion pictures or television, at such reasonable times as the Team, the NBA or other League-related entity may designate. The Player shall, however, retain the right to withhold consent to the use of such pictures if such pictures either portray the player in an undesired manner, subject to a good faith standard. The Player shall also have the right to withhold consent of use of player images and likenesses. Both the Player and the Team, the NBA or the League-related entity, shall own an equal right to such pictures, images and likenesses individually. Players need not seek consent from the Team for standard public appearances, to permit their pictures to be taken, or for radio, Internet or television programs.

§ 13. Promotional Activities: (a) The Player agrees to allow the Team, the NBA, or a League-related entity to take pictures of the Player, alone or together with others, for still photographs, motion pictures or television, at such reasonable times as the Team, the NBA or other League-related entity may designate. The Player shall, however, retain the right to withhold consent to the use of such pictures if such pictures either portray the player in an undesired manner, subject to a good faith standard. The Player shall also have the right to withhold consent of use of player images and likenesses. Players need not seek consent from the Team for standard public appearances, to permit their pictures to be taken, or for radio, Internet or television programs.

§ 13. Promotional Activities: (a) The Player agrees to allow the Team, the NBA, or a League-related entity to take pictures of the Player, alone or together with others, for still photographs, motion pictures or television, at such reasonable times as the Team, the NBA or other League-related entity may designate. The Player shall, however, retain the right to withhold consent to the use of such pictures if such pictures either portray the player in an undesired manner, subject to a good faith standard. The Player shall also have the right to withhold consent of use of player images and likenesses. Players need not seek consent from the Team for standard public appearances, to permit their pictures to be taken, or for radio, Internet or television programs.

§ 14. Group License: Player Attributes are hereby defined as the name, nickname, statistics, image, picture or video broadcasted image of the Player in the course of the Player's participation in Team or league activities, including games, practices, Team-related activities, or other activity outside of Team activities, subject to Player consent. The Player hereby grants to NBA Properties, Inc the non-exclusive rights to use such Attributes as will be set forth in a new Agreement between NBA Properties and the NBPA (the "Group License"). This license shall not permit NBA Properties to preclude third-party use of Player Attributes to the extent such use is consistent with the use of names and player statistics as in CBC v. MLBAM or real-time statistics as in NBA v. Motorola. The Player shall also retain the right to reasonably withhold consent for use of Player Attributes in a manner found objectionable. If Player's inclusion in a particular program is

§ 14. Group License: Player Attributes are hereby defined as the name, nickname, statistics, image, picture or video broadcasted image of the Player in the course of the Player's participation in Team or league activities, including games, practices, Team-related activities, or other activity outside of Team activities. The Player hereby grants to NBA Properties, Inc the exclusive right to use such Attributes as will be set forth in a new Agreement between NBA Properties and the NBPA (the "Group License"). The Player shall retain the right to reasonably withhold consent for use of Player Attributes in a manner found objectionable. If Player's inclusion in a particular program is precluded by an individual exclusive endorsement agreement, NBA Properties will exclude Player from that particular program.

§ 14. Group License: Player Attributes are hereby defined as the name, nickname, statistics, image, picture or video broadcasted image of the Player in the course of the Player's participation in Team or league activities, including games, practices, Team-related activities, or other activity outside of Team activities. The Player hereby grants to NBA Properties, Inc the non-exclusive right to use such Attributes as will be set forth in a new Agreement between NBA Properties and the NBPA (the "Group License"). This license shall not permit NBA Properties to preclude third-party use of Player Attributes to the extent such use is consistent with the use of names and player statistics as in CBC v. MLBAM or real-time statistics as in NBA v. Motorola. The Player shall retain the right to reasonably withhold consent for use of Player Attributes in a manner found objectionable. If Player's inclusion in a particular program is precluded by an individual

precluded by an individual exclusive endorsement agreement, NBA Properties will exclude Player from that particular program. The NBPA and the Players solely retain the right to license Player images and likenesses for video games, fantasy websites and fantasy games. NBA Properties is therefore precluded from using Player Attributes in any commercially marketable game or interactive use. Notwithstanding the Group License above, if any individual Player generates more than 5% of gross revenue under the Group License for a given year, NBA Properties shall enter into an individual contract with such Player for use of that Player's Attributes for the following season if such an individual contract has not yet been entered into.		exclusive endorsement agreement, NBA Properties will exclude Player from that particular program. The NBPA and the Players solely retain the right to license Player images and likenesses for video games, fantasy websites and fantasy games. NBA Properties is therefore precluded from using Player Attributes in any commercially marketable game or interactive use.

*

INDEX

References are to Pages

---

†